CULTURAL ENCOUNTERS

Remapping Cultural History

General Editor: Jo Labanyi, Institute of Romance Studies, University of London and University of Southampton.

Published in association with the Institute of Romance Studies, School of Advanced Study, University of London.

The theoretical paradigms dominant in much of cultural history published in English tend to be derived from northern European or North American models. This series will propose alternative mappings by focusing partly or wholly on those parts of the world that speak, or have spoken, French, Italian, Spanish or Portuguese. Both monographs and collective volumes will be published. Preference will be given to volumes that cross national boundaries, that explore areas of culture that have previously received little attention, or that make a significant contribution to rethinking the ways in which cultural history is theorized and narrated.

Cultural Encounters: European Travel Writing in the 1930s
Edited by Charles Burdett and Derek Duncan

CULTURAL ENCOUNTERS
European Travel Writing in the 1930s

edited by

CHARLES BURDETT AND DEREK DUNCAN

Berghahn Books
New York • Oxford

First published in 2002 by **Berghahn Books**

www.berghahnbooks.com

© 2002 Charles Burdett and Derek Duncan

All rights reserved.
No part of this publication may be reproduced in any form or by any means without the written permission of Berghahn Books.

Library of Congress Cataloging-in-Publication Data

Cultural encounters : European travel writing in the 1930s / edited by Charles Burdett and Derek Duncan.
   p. cm. -- (Remapping cultural history ; v. 1)
Includes bibliographical references.
ISBN 1–57181–810–3 (alk. paper) -- ISBN 1–57181–501–5 (pbk. : alk. paper)
  1. Travellers' writings, European--History--20th century. 2. Europeans--Travel--History--20th century. 3. Nineteen thirties I. Burdett, Charles, 1966– II. Duncan, Derek. III. Series.

G465 .C85 2002
910.4--dc21
                                            2002066603

British Library Cataloguing in Publication Data
A catalogue record for this book is available from the British Library.

Printed in the United States on acid-free paper

ISBN 1–57181–810–3 hardback, 1–57181–501–5 paperback

Contents

List of Illustrations   vii
List of Contributors   viii

Introduction
    Cultural Encounters: European Travel-Writing in the 1930s
    Charles Burdett and Derek Duncan   1

Part 1: Introducing Travel
1   Journey with Maps: Travel Theory, Geography and the
      Syntax of Space.   11
      Andrew Thacker
2   Sa(l)vaging Exoticism: New Approaches to 1930s Travel
      Literature in French.   29
      Charles Forsdick

Part 2: Journeys in Europe
3   Travel and Autobiography: Giovanni Comisso's Memories of
      the War.   49
      Derek Duncan
4   Bringing Home the Truth about the Revolution: Spanish
      Travellers to the Soviet Union in the 1930s.   65
      Mayte Gómez
5   The Politics of the Everyday and the Eternity of Ruins: Two
      Women Photographers in Republican Spain
      (Margaret Michaelis 1933–37, Kati Horna 1937–38).   85
      Jo Labanyi

Part 3: Liminal Spaces
6   Signs of Roman Rule: Italian Tourists and Travellers in
      Greece and Egypt.   107
      Charles Burdett
7   Tradition and Modernism in Gustav Rene Hocke's Travel Books,
      1937–39.   121
      Helmut Peitsch
8   Dramatic Encounters: Federico García Lorca's Trip to Cuba (1930).   131
      Sarah Wright
9   Gide in Egypt 1939.   143
      Naomi Segal

Part 4: Colonial Encounters

10 Making the Case for Cross-Cultural Exchange: Robert Byron's
    The Road to Oxiana.   159
    Howard J. Booth

11 Investigating Indochina: Travel Journalism and France's
    Civilizing Mission.   173
    Nicola Cooper

12 Aristocrats, Geographers, Reporters ... : Travelling through
    'Italian Africa' in the 1930s.   187
    Loredana Polezzi

Index   205

List of Illustrations

Figure 1.1	Map from Graham Greene, *Journey Without Maps*, 1953 edition.	13
Figure 1.2	Map from Graham Greene, *Journey Without Maps*, 1936 edition.	14
Figure 1.3	Map from Graham Greene, *Journey Without Maps*, 1978 edition.	15
Figure 5.1	Kati Horna, 'Shop window', Valencia, October 1937.	86
Figure 5.2	Kati Horna, 'On guard after the air raid', Barcelona, March 1938.	92
Figure 5.3	Margaret Michaelis-Sachs, 'Untitled', Barcelona, March 1933–4. Used here on the cover of J. Grijalbo's and F. Fàbregas's book *La Municipalitazió de la propietat urbana* (1937), published by the Socialist trade union UGT.	93
Figure 5.4	Margaret Michaelis-Sachs, 'Kitchen, 24 Calle San Rafael', Barcelona c. 1933–4.	94
Figure 5.5	Margaret Michaelis-Sachs, 'Untitled (woman in doorway)', Barcelona c. 1934.	95
Figure 5.6	Margaret Michaelis-Sachs, 'Untitled', Barcelona c. 1932.	96
Figure 5.7	Margaret Michaelis-Sachs, 'Comisariat de Propaganda postcard (woman with line of children in Barcelona Stadium)', Barcelona 1936–7.	96
Figure 5.8	Kati Horna, 'Refugee Centre in the Alcázar de Cervantes (Alcázar de San Juan)', undated.	97
Figure 5.9	Kati Horna, 'Centre for pregnant women from Madrid in Vélez Rubio', August 1937.	98
Figure 5.10	Kati Horna, 'Field hospital at Grañeu', March–April 1937.	99

List of Contributors

Howard J. Booth is Lecturer in English Literature at the University of Manchester. He is the author of a number of articles on nineteenth- and twentieth-century literature and is co-editor of *Modernism and Empire* (MUP, 2000).

Charles Burdett is Senior Lecturer in Italian at the University of Bristol. He is the author of *Vincenzo Cardarelli and his Contemporaries: Fascist Politics and Literary Culture* (OUP, 1999) and co-editor of *European Memories of the Second World War* (Berghahn, 1999).

Nicola Cooper is Lecturer in French at the University of Bristol. She has published widely in the field of post-colonial studies and is the author of *France in Indochina: Colonial Encounters* (Berg, 2001).

Derek Duncan is Senior Lecturer in Italian at the University of Bristol. He has published widely on twentieth-century Italian literature and film with particular reference to issues of gender and sexuality.

Charles Forsdick is Professor of French at the University of Liverpool. He is the author of *Victor Segalen and the Aesthetics of Diversity* (OUP, 2000) and co-editor of *Reading Diversity* (Glasgow, 2000).

Mayte Gomez is Lecturer in the Spanish Department of Lancaster University. She publishes on Spanish cultural and intellectual history. She is preparing a book on the cultural politics of the Communist Party of Spain between 1920 and 1939.

Jo Labanyi is Professor of Spanish and Cultural Studies at the University of Southampton, and the Director of the Institute of Romance Studies. She is the author of *Gender and Modernisation in the Spanish Realist Novel* (OUP, 2000). She is co-editor of *Spanish Cultural Studies: An Introduction* (OUP, 1995) and *Constructing Identity in Twentieth-Century Spain: Theoretical Concepts and Cultural Practice* (OUP, forthcoming).

Helmut Peitsch is Professor of German Literature at the University of Potsdam. He has published widely on German literature, culture and politics of the 18th and 20th centuries. He is the editor of the first complete English translation of Heinrich Mann's *The Loyal Subject* (1998) and the co-editor of *European Memories of the Second World War* (Berghahn, 1999).

Loredana Polezzi is Lecturer in Italian at the University of Warwick. She publishes on translation, Italian national identity and travel writing. She is the author of *Translating Travel: Contemporary Italian Travel Writing in English Translation* (Ashgate, 2001).

Naomi Segal is Professor of French at the University of Reading. Her books include: *The Unintended Reader* (CUP, 1986), *Narcissus and Echo* (MUP, 1988), *The Adulteress's Child* (Polity, 1992), *André Gide: Pederasty & Pedagogy* (OUP, 1998). She is co-editor of *Freud In Exile* (Yale UP, 1988), *Scarlet Letters* (Macmillan, 1997), *Coming out of Feminism?* (Blackwell, 1998).

Andrew Thacker is Lecturer in English Literature at the University of Ulster. He has published extensively on cultural issues of the early twentieth century and is the author of *Moving Through Modernity: Space and Geography in Modernism* (MUP, forthcoming).

Sarah Wright is Lecturer in Hispanic Studies at the University of Hull. She publishes on Spanish literature of the twentieth century. She is the author of *The Trickster-Function in the Theatre of García Lorca* (Tameside, 2000).

Introduction

CULTURAL ENCOUNTERS
EUROPEAN TRAVEL-WRITING IN THE 1930S

Charles Burdett and Derek Duncan

The 1930s were one of the most important periods in defining the history of the twentieth century. The decade opened in the wake of the Wall Street Crash, an event that shook U.S. society to its foundations but that was to be felt in all parts of the global economy. It was an event that altered the relationship between national governments and that was to spawn a series of political solutions ranging from the imaginative to the malevolent. In the United States itself, Harding's efforts to relieve mass unemployment and to counter the tremendous slump in production were to prove, for the most part, ineffectual. The radical programme of state intervention that Roosevelt sponsored from his inauguration in 1933, through the agencies and public works programmes of the New Deal, brought relief to large sections of the urban and rural population of the U.S. But not all the schemes that the New Deal envisaged were successfully planned and carried through: the workings of a number of agencies were fiercely criticized by forces on the right and were eventually declared unconstitutional by the Supreme Court. For all his success in inspiring confidence and a renewed sense of purpose in the nation, Roosevelt was never able to banish the spectre of economic crisis that had arisen suddenly at the end of the 1920s. Britain and France both felt the full severity of the Depression. In Britain, the extent of the crisis broke McDonald's Labour government and ushered in a period of cross-party consensus. Without adopting radical solutions to deal with the enormity of the problems faced by industry, the National Government managed to introduce legislation that had some effect in alleviating the rigours of the Depression and to stave off social unrest. France proved less able to contend with the huge pressures that resulted from the downturn in world trade. In the 1930s a series of governments of both the left and right sought to modernize the economy and to reduce the country's crippling levels of unemployment. But one attempt at reform after another floundered amidst heightened social tension and financial crisis.

Despite the unremitting hardship experienced by whole swathes of the population in the U.S., Britain and France, the authority of parliament, though at times challenged or compromised, did not come under serious threat. If anything, the work of the agencies of the New Deal and Roosevelt's frequent addresses to the nation, served to encourage participation in the democratic process. The rise of right-wing nationalism proved the corollary of, and the apparent answer to, the failures of capitalism in other parts of Europe. In Italy, fascism had emerged from the waves of social unrest and reactionary violence that had followed the end of the First World War. In the 1920s the regime had more or less consolidated its position by appropriating the institutions of the state. By the 1930s the bellicose rhetoric of involvement in the collective life of the nation was well established. Mussolini was presented as the saviour of Italy's fortunes and the all-seeing incarnation of power. The fascist answer to the Depression was an economic policy of autarky and the pursuit of massive building projects that stretched from the wholesale remodelling of Rome to the building of the new towns on the freshly drained Pontine marshes. In Germany, the Weimar Republic was to fall victim to the Wall Street Crash. As industrial production plummeted and unemployment soared, then the administrations of first Brüning then von Papen became increasingly vulnerable. Hitler successfully exploited the trauma of the Depression and the weaknesses of German democracy. By early 1933 he had been sworn in as Chancellor and, as the decade progressed, Germany's neighbours watched with growing trepidation the sinister development of Nazism.

The seizure of power by Mussolini and Hitler found its analogue on the left with Stalin's inexorable rise in Communist Russia. Promoting a reorganization of society more wide-ranging and more profound than that envisaged by Lenin or Trotsky, Stalin saw through agricultural collectivization and industrial modernization with an appalling indifference to the cost in human lives. By the time the policy of collectivization was slowed down, famine in the Ukraine had claimed hundreds of thousands of lives. The feverish industrialization of the country, structured by the Five Year Plans, may have been successful in allowing Russia to catch up with the more advanced states of the West, but it involved unimaginable hardship for those who were involved in the building of Russia's new industrial might (Brendon 2000: 209–12). In the latter part of the 1930s, the collective struggle towards a modern, industrial state was accompanied by the terror of Stalin's purges and show trials. No section of Russian society was left untouched by the frenzy of supposedly counter-revolutionary activity and by the climate of intimidation.

The policy of rapid industrialization pursued by many regimes of the interwar years was accompanied by the full force of imperialist aggression. In the autumn of 1931 Japanese troops had begun the invasion of Manchuria. It was the first step in a ruthless expansionist policy that was to lead Japan ultimately towards an alliance with Hitler's Germany and entry into the Second World War. In the Italian press, the invasion of Manchuria was looked on admiringly. In October 1935, Fascist Italy began its assault on the Ethiopia of Haile Selassie. The conquest of the country was intended to avenge earlier imperial setbacks (the crushing defeat at Adowa in 1896), to cancel the memory of the treaty of Versailles (Italy's 'mutilated victory') and to establish the newly 'reborn' nation as a major power. By the spring of 1936, the ferocious double pronged attack on Ethiopia had largely succeeded. Addis Ababa had capitulated (though armed resistance was to continue throughout the Italian occupation) and a particularly brutal form of colonial rule was rapidly established. Italian journalists attempted to justify their country's invasion of Ethiopia by claiming that Italy was simply emulating the earlier imperial activities of Britain and France. The sanctions that the League of Nations had imposed as a result of the invasion were characterized as an unjust impediment to Italy's rise as an imperial power determined to reap the economic benefits of empire.

The disparities in the extent of European countries' overseas possessions were keenly felt not only by members of Mussolini's ruling elite. Yet such disparities pointed to the different colonial history of each country. The Spanish-American War (1898) had reduced Spanish rule beyond Europe to northern Morocco. In the latter part of the 1930s, Nazi Germany like Fascist Italy, was seeking to alter the balance of power that Versailles had established. The British Empire had been placed under strain by the demands of the First World War, yet it remained largely intact. Exploiting a variety of administrative techniques that depended on the nature of the territory under British rule, the Empire was able to withstand challenges to its legitimacy. The Commonwealth was formally established in 1931. With overseas dependencies including Indochina, Algeria, and Tunisia only France could rival Britain as a colonial power. But in the 1930s France witnessed clear indications of the sustained opposition to its rule that would erupt in the immediate post-war period.

The major imperial foray of the 1930s was the assault on Ethiopia, but within months of Mussolini's torch-lit declaration of the reappearance of the Roman Empire (9 May 1936), the focus of European diplomatic attention shifted from North East Africa to Spain. Azaña's efforts to establish the basis of a secular state had met with some success in the early 1930s and in February 1936 the Popular Front was rewarded with electoral success, despite the bitter campaign waged by Catholic and conservative Spain. Yet, the ability of the Popular Front to govern a country riven by social and cultural tensions was rapidly brought into question. By the summer of 1936, what had begun as the conspiracy of a handful of influential generals had developed into a full scale military revolt. The country rapidly divided between regions and cities loyal to the Republican government and others which were willing to support the military insurrection. As Nationalist troops advanced towards the capital, atrocities were committed by both sides. Once Madrid was under siege and Catalonia increasingly isolated, military support from Italy and especially from Germany had begun to sway the Civil War in the favour of the Nationalists. The non-intervention of the democratic powers was to seal the fate of the Republic. In April 1937 Guernica was bombed, by the summer of 1938 the Nationalists were moving on Valencia and by the spring of 1939 Madrid and Catalonia had succumbed.

The development of radically different ideologies across Europe, the imperialist incursions in Asia and Africa, the rising tension between nation-states and the general climate of distrust motivated a number of politically curious travellers. A stream of writers and journalists – including such names as Louis Aragon, Beatrice and Stanley Webb (1937), Corrado Alvaro (1935) – made the long journey from western Europe to see Stalin's Russia. Hitler's Germany was examined with anxiety by Philip Gibbs (1934) and with admiration by A. M. Zecca (1936). Mussolini's Ethiopian campaign was followed by the world's media and produced such works as Evelyn Waugh's *Waugh in Abyssinia* (1936) or Louise Diel's travelogue, translated into English as, *Behold our New Empire* (1939). During the Spanish Civil War news agencies frequently hired distinguished writers to observe the reality of the conflict (Thomas 1961: 235–36).

All these observers aimed specifically to chart the impact of new ideologies in confronting the social and economic realities of the time. All such writing speculated on the validity of imperialism, it represented the conflict (real or potential) of nations, it articulated the strengthening of traditional boundaries. Yet, not all travel was motivated by concern over a political geography that was rapidly changing. The pursuit of leisure and the desire to escape the repressive constraints of home were also powerful factors in charting the itineraries of various travellers. Indeed, the interwar period has been seen as the golden age of travel (Praz (1982); Fussell (1980)), as a time when it was still possible for individuals to explore countries and cultures that were free from an all-encompassing

Western influence: the age of package holidays and mass tourism being still just around the corner. It is certainly true that a series of highly original travelogues were produced in the 1930s: figures as well known as André Gide, Graham Greene, Henri Michaux, Margherita Sarfatti and Federico Garcia Lorca all wrote formally inventive and alluring accounts of journeys to sites beyond Europe. Their writings, and those of a range of other practitioners of the travel book, were clearly susceptible to modernist imperatives.

The 1930s are often seen as the chronological limit of Modernism. The repetitive style of much conventional travel writing seems ill-suited to a period in which art was driven by the desire for formal innovation. Compared to a literature that actively favoured the subjective and the oblique over more transparent forms of communication, it could also appear anachronistic, a residue of the nineteenth century rather than an expression of the contemporary. The art forms that in retrospect were best thought to characterize the early years of the twentieth century, offered a shared challenge to conventional modes of representation. Modernist art was self-consciously difficult in formal terms. Its thematic concerns, however, were very often everyday. The familiar was shown in ways that caught its subject unawares. The act of showing itself was brought to the fore and its power to construct the object underlined. Narrative was no longer guided by a solid plot and secure temporality, as space, both material and psychological, became the more dominant medium. The relationship between modernist art and the society that produced it has been formulated in numerous ways. One of the most resonant for the aims of this book is that it can be seen as the metropolitan art of diaspora, the art produced in the wake of waves of migration and displacement that brought together millions of men and women of different nationalities, religions, and social classes in the great cities of Western Europe and the United States. The formal alterity of modernist art is therefore the consequence of travel and of the unpredictable fusions and fragmentations that occur when cultures are forced into unusual proximity. What had been familiar, and indeed normal, did not stand the test of comparison with the new as the world and those in it found themselves altered. Difference was no longer absolute but relative and hierarchies only temporary and susceptible to reversal. The vagaries of personal experience became the measure of reality.

With respect to place, the experience of modernity was a profoundly contradictory one. While many were forced to travel for political or economic reasons, others chose to travel for pleasure, adventure, instruction, or profit. Travel was both a mass and highly individual phenomenon. It is necessary to make a qualitative distinction between the kind of travel undertaken by the leisured classes and the vast demographic movements caused by poverty and persecution. They were, however, both thoroughly modern phenomena. Even those travellers who fled the West in order to escape what they considered the ruinous excesses of industrialization and modern society generally succeeded because of the prerogatives of their own place in modernity: their wealth and access to transport networks. By the 1930s, tourism on some scale had become a possibility for the middle classes. Organized group travel allowed quite large segments of the Western population to visit exotic locations at limited monetary cost and personal risk. The advent of tourism parcelled the world up into manageable segments that were knowable and worth knowing. To travel in modern space was to engage in a search for the already discovered. Even apparently more intrepid travellers who set off alone usually had quite a firm idea of what they might come across. The tellingly named, guide book, prepared the traveller so that places of interest were discovered in advance, and places to avoid could be sidestepped with circumspection. Not only did people travel more frequently, but visual technologies such as photography and then cinema created a greater familiarity with locations that previously had been barely imaginable. The spoils of empire were displayed through the still flourishing exhibition culture, and the commercial advertizing of imported goods increasingly brought the exotic into the home. Jazz was also popular, and in art, the 'primitive' was transformed into a European idiom. It might, with some justification, be argued that culture of all sorts played a conservative role in domesticating the unknown, removing the edge of its otherness.

It is perhaps more productive to think of the cultural fusions of modernity as points of exchange and negotiation rather than straightforward instances of appropriation. For example, it would be wrong to assume that even those sites most degraded by the advent of mass tourism were exhausted by their description. The point of a lot of travel for the leisured classes was simply to leave home. If the experience of home was one of constraint, the prospect of going abroad intimated freedom and even the possibility of becoming someone else, albeit for a limited time. The actual destination was secondary to the promise it held out for self-invention. For the role of fantasy in the construction of place also implicated the traveller's own sense of identity. At the beginning of the century, the Italian Futurists had made a cult out of speed and modern modes of transport such as the aeroplane, yet many others found that modernity produced a sense of vertiginous alienation rather than awe. For the traveller standing in idle contemplation of Giotto's *Belltower*, or lying marooned on the dark continent, the experience of travel could be one of savage displacement. For journeys were also, and primarily, inner journeys. A stroll round London, Dublin, Trieste, or Paris could lead the European flâneur as far through the unfamiliar byways of the psyche as any tour to the farthest corners of Africa and Asia. The experience of migration, or diaspora, could also be a devastating affair psychologically and economically, not least in the attempt to find a means of inhabiting a new and alien space. Yet what both types of experience seem to share is that they problematized notions of home and of identity. Home just like any other place is both a material and imaginary site. Prison, haven or somewhere in between, it is an economic reality and a phantasmatic construction. For the person who travels, is 'home' the place one happens to be, or is it always a lost place? What is the temporality of home if its moment is already past, or displaced indefinitely to an unlikely future? Similarly, to what extent is a sense of identity bound to that trauma of loss or aspiration, and how free is it to embrace the new? Perhaps the experience of those Italian immigrants who spent their lives travelling across the Atlantic between Italy and both North and South America is more typical than is often realized; their permanent inbetweenness always located somewhere, in a place seared through with the knowledge of their other space, an experience not of separation, but of grafting.

Many of the contributors to this volume refer to the work of Sigmund Freud as a means of understanding the contradictory sensations that the experience of travel evoked as new places were discovered and familiar places made strange by that encounter. In 1936, only two years before he would be forced to flee from Vienna to London, Freud himself wrote a short piece that seems to capture very well the ambivalent feelings that travel could evoke. He recalls a trip he made to the Acropolis with his brother some years before and tries to elucidate the very contradictory feelings he had at the time. For years Freud had longed to visit this great site, yet once he got there his main feeling was one of incredulity. He couldn't believe the Acropolis actually existed. On analysing his response more closely, he realizes that it wasn't the reality of the Acropolis that was in doubt, but the fact that he himself should ever have been privileged enough to gaze on what he considered the birthplace of Western civilization. Freud's real journey was not the geographical one from Vienna to Athens, but his ascent from obscure origins in Central Europe. The Acropolis is not simply a place of interest, a cultural landmark, but the unexpected materialization of Freud's own sense of cultural and social displacement. Its significance extends far beyond its location in the well-worn tourist itinerary through the Ancient World.

Perhaps even to talk of travel writing as a genre is to outlaw such unpredictable confrontations in advance and to fall into the trap of assuming that it can only reveal what we already know. The idea of genre imposes upon travel writing a grid of intelligibility that detects only its moments of leaden sameness rather than its more complex knots of opaque diversity. The essays in this volume are not bound by fixed notions of genre; they deal with the representation of place by travellers. The contributors extend the category of 'travel writing' to include poetry, fiction, diaries, journalism and photography. Some of these representations fit more comfortably into the conventional category of travel writing than others in that their primary intention is to log or recount a specific experience. Others are more impressionistic, or seem to use the experience of travel as source of metaphor, a prism through which to reflect on other displacements. What they share is an engagement with the dilemma of how place might be represented in such a way as to express its imaginary, subjective dimensions as well as its political realities.

Bibliography

Alvaro, C., *I maestri del diluvio. Viaggio nella Russia sovietica*. Milan, 1935.
Brendon, P., *The Dark Valley. A Panorama of the 1930s*. London, 2000.
Diel, L., *Behold Our New Empire*, trans. K. Kirkness, London, 1939.
Freud, S., 'A Disturbance of Memory on the Acropolis' (1936), in *On Metapsychology*, Penguin Freud Library, vol.11, Harmondsworth, 1984.
Fussell, P., *Abroad. British Literary Travelling Between the Wars*. Oxford, 1980.
Gibbs, P., *European Journey*. London, 1934.
Praz, M., *Il mondo che ho visto*. Milan, 1982.
Thomas, H., *The Spanish Civil War*. London, 1961.
Waugh, E., *Waugh in Abyssinia*. London, 1936.
Webb, B. and S., *Soviet Communism: A New Civilization*. London, 1937.
Zecca, A., *Il momento della Germania*. Piacenza, 1936.

PART 1

INTRODUCING TRAVEL

Chapter 1

JOURNEY WITH MAPS
Travel Theory, Geography and the Syntax of Space

Andrew Thacker

Graham Greene's *Journey Without Maps* (1936) draws attention, in its very title, to the ambiguous role played by maps in travel writing. What is the status of pictorial maps that illustrate a written text, seemingly supplementary textual features to the central narrative of the travel book? A preliminary understanding of the marginal status of such maps might invoke Derrida's work upon the significance of such supplementary forms of textuality. A map, such as the one at the start of Greene's book, is supplementary, in Derrida's sense, in that it both *adds* to the text and *substitutes* for the written text (1976: 144–45).[1] Such maps, often occurring in the frontispiece or endpapers of books, imply a marginal status in relation to the written text; but they are also images that act as a kind of guide to the journey taken by the author. It is curious how a map functions as a form of textual representation that alters how we read works of travel writing; if the map is an image of spatial *fixity*, how does it function in relation to a discourse concerned above all with representing *movement*? Maps also open up travel writing to questions drawn from geographical work upon the nature of cartography as a discourse embedded in structures of power. As the prominent critic of ichnography as an objective science, J.B.Harley, states: 'Cartographers manufacture power: they create a spatial panopticon' (1996: 439). Maps should be regarded, like all 'practices of representation', as 'situated, embodied, partial' (Gregory 1994: 7),[2] with different meanings being signified as a result of features such as choice of cartographic projection, type of coloration or employment of scale. Of course, some cartographers may wish to distinguish the productions of GIS (Geographical Information Systems) from the less technical maps accompanying books of travel writing: however, we can regard both kinds of map as simply different styles of representing spatial information. If the map found in a book of travel writing employs a more 'artistic' approach to representation, it is still an image conveying meaning about the spaces travelled through, and can be explored for how these meanings interact with the written text.

We have become very, perhaps overly, familiar with the use of 'mapping' as a metaphor in current theoretical discourse; it seems important to try to return to the map as a set of material signs, to understand what is at issue when travel writing employs actual maps as a component of the narrative. This argument is partly prompted by recalling Fredric Jameson's concept of history as the syntax that ultimately organizes texts, and by the idea that space has, over recent years, come to be seen as another social syntax for understanding writing (1988: viii). Focusing upon the spatial syntax of maps also helps introduce a key distinction from cultural geography and spatial theory, that between space and place, that I wish to explore in relation to Greene's book. One significant theorist of the space/place dichotomy is Michel de Certeau, whose parallel distinction between map and tour forms of discourse offers another helpful tool for understanding the singular spatial syntax of Greene's book. I shall return to these distinctions later.

Greene visited the African state of Liberia in 1934, accompanied by his cousin Barbara Greene, and embarked upon a 350 mile walk through the heavily forested interior, aided by a party of native guides.[3] The choice of Liberia for Greene's journey is of some interest. Liberia was originally created by the American Colonization Society (ACS) in the early nineteenth century as a place for freeborn and emancipated slaves to be transported 'back' to Africa. The motives of the ACS were mixed, as many members supported the transportation on the grounds that freed blacks would cause trouble if they stayed in the States, and that freed blacks could not be trusted. By 1861 over 12,000 had been transported and in 1847 the Liberian state, modelled upon the U.S. constitution, was established. The introduction of ex-slaves into Liberia created conflict with the native inhabitants of the land, for the freed slaves believed themselves superior to the native peoples.[4] In the 1920s and 1930s Liberia came to the attention of the European and U.S. media because of a series of reports by the League of Nations into allegations of slavery, forced labour and massacres of certain tribes in the country. Most of these allegations seemed suspect, fuelled by writers eager to see Liberia taken out of the control of its native government. Britain attempted to rid Liberia of its independent status and put it into the control of a white administration, such as that of the United States. Sir Alfred Sharpe, whose unreliable maps of the country Greene studied prior to his visit, suggested in

Figure 1.1 Map from Graham Greene, *Journey Without Maps*, 1953 edition.

1923 that every branch of administration in Liberia be taken over by 'some civilized power or powers' (Anderson 1952: 289). The English author of a book on slavery in Africa, Lady Kathleen Simon, argued in 1929 that the Liberian government be replaced by an administration of 'strong high-minded white men' (Anderson 1952: 97). Greene's journey into Liberia was, then, without maps, but with a certain perception of the country formed from government and international reports, which he refers to and quotes from in numerous places. In a sense his book is an attempt to find, in the fashion of the journalist or war correspondent, something of the supposed 'truth' of Liberia as a country accused of supporting slavery and 'savagery', and of being unable to administer itself.

The 1953 edition of Greene's book highlights the republic of Liberia by rendering the other bordering countries in darkest blue. [Fig.1.1 1953 edition] The most interesting feature, however, is the border cartouche with its representations of imagined primitive/native/African sculptures or totems. They create a spatial frame of otherness to the Western discourse of the map. As Harley notes of the supposedly merely decorative features of maps, they should not be regarded as 'inconsequential marginalia' but rather 'the emblems in cartouches and decorative title-pages can be regarded as *basic* to the way they convey their cultural meaning' (1996: 434). Note how the map is divided into a geometric grid or graticule, apparently representing markers of latitude and longitude that are not

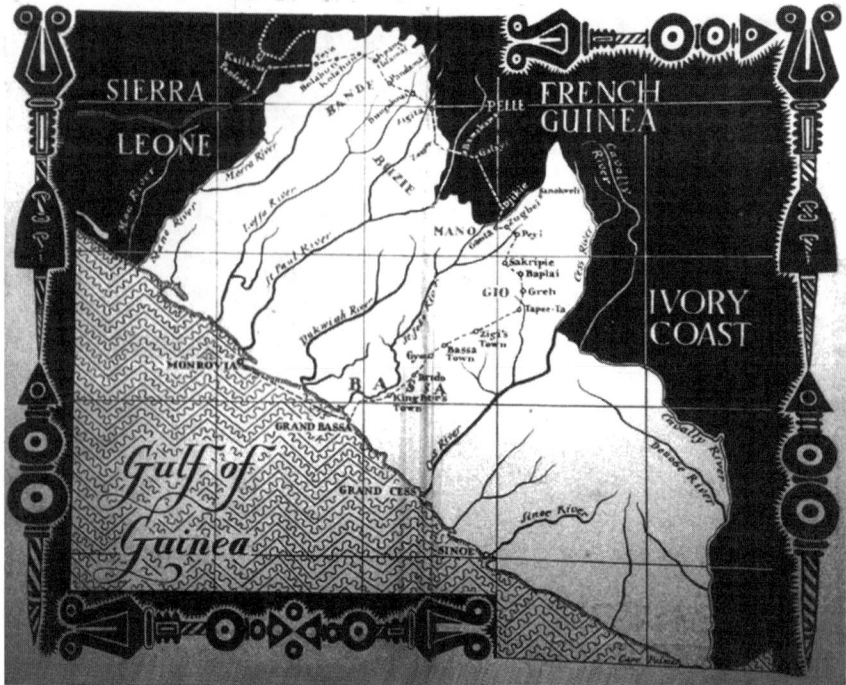

Figure 1.2 Map from Graham Greene, *Journey Without Maps*, 1936 edition.

explicitly indicated. This sense of cartographic order is broken on the right hand side by sharp, teeth-like incisions from the ornamental images: Western reason is bordered by savage African otherness. The blue/white colouring is another stark visual representation of the travel writer's quest for an otherness, and a horror, not found at home.

The sense of mystery conveyed here is intensified in the map attached to the first edition of 1936 [Fig.1.2 1936 edition]. In this map the 'Atlantic Ocean' is rendered as the 'Gulf of Guinea' and the semi-abstract pattern here seems to signify that the sea is itself part of the 'Africanness' of the land mass. The changed nomenclature points to the way that maps are relativist texts, where the fit between signifier and signified is, despite the scientific pretensions of cartography, a strictly arbitrary one. But the most significant textual signifier in this 1936 map is another absent presence. Here, quite extraordinarily, Liberia is not even named upon the map, emphasizing the image of Greene as explorer rather than traveller. It is as if this is still, in some sense, uncharted territory, ripe for conquest by the writer and cartographer: it is a literal 'blank space' on the map. Another way to read the absent toponym is to argue that travel writers must *produce* space as an undiscovered entity before the narrative commences, in order to justify their journey.[5]

Writing of interwar British literary travel writing, Paul Fussell distinguishes between explorer, traveller and tourist by suggesting that the explorer 'seeks the undiscovered' and 'moves towards the risks of the formless and the unknown', whereas the tourist seeks that which has been discovered by business and 'moves towards the security of pure cliché'. The traveller exists between these two poles, 'retaining all he can of the excitement of the unpredictable attaching to exploration, and fusing that with the pleasure of "knowing where one is" belonging to tourism' (Fussell 1980: 39).[6] However, it is a useful distinction to bring to bear upon the use of the frontispiece map in Greene's text. That Liberia is not signified on the 1936 map accentuates the land as 'unknown' and 'formless', waiting for Greene's literary discourse to fill in the 'blank spaces' on the map.[7] Another way to view Fussell's distinction is to refigure it as one between a discourse of place (where the geography is known or 'we know where one is') and a discourse of space (where the geography is not known and is 'formless'). Here I want to use Greene's text to demonstrate an argument found in recent cultural geography that queries the sharpness of this division between place and space, or here the motif of a journey with maps and without them.

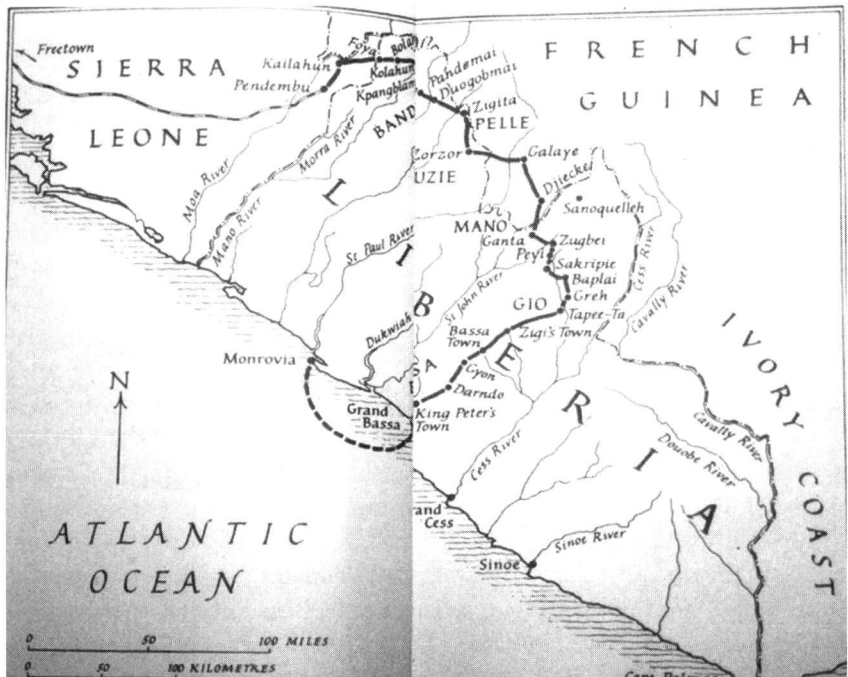

Figure 1.3 Map from Graham Greene, *Journey Without Maps*, 1978 edition.

The 1978 Penguin edition of the book omits the grid, the colouring and the ornamental borders. [Fig.1.3 1978 edition]. It adds an indication of magnetic north, and a scale. Additional details are added: the courses of rivers, or the coastal outline of Sierra Leone. This is a more technical style of map, conveying a rational guide within the image to help orientate the reader more swiftly. It is a map more within the dominant contemporary cartographic *episteme*: it aims to be an objective picture of a particular land mass (Harley 1996). However, certain places mentioned in the text are still absent from the map, and the air of a mysterious journey is still preserved by the very paucity of information on the map – the bareness of design again conveys uncharted territory, whereas the blue elaborate borders conveyed a different kind of otherness. There is still no indication of the type of projection, or graticular information. The place-names on the later map are also significant: they resemble a hand-written map, perhaps allying Greene's journey with that of early explorers – here is still a *terra nullius* upon which the literary explorer can inscribe his mark. The 1953 map uses, on the whole, a more mechanical typography for toponyms. So, if the earlier map is more akin to painting in its employment of visual signifiers of mood, the later map is the more literary, we might say, eschewing texture for the empty parchment of the writer's page, emphasizing the point of Greene's title, that although his journey was without maps the reader is supplied with a cartographic guide, that of the text itself.

Of course, the notion of a journey 'without maps' is a convenient fiction. Greene has maps; they are merely, and pleasurably, inaccurate. A map is not just a piece of paper, but a mental map, a cognitive map to use Kevin Lynch's term taken up by Jameson as a hermeneutic tool for reading postmodernity (Jameson 1991: 415–16; Lynch 1960). Greene's cognitive map is one shared by all travel writers, a map of home and abroad. In this case, of Europe and its other, of contemporary 'civilization' and the primeval quality of Liberia, or of Greene's Freudian image of Liberia as a journey into his unconscious past. In this way Greene's text accords with Dennis Porter's claim that, in some deep sense, all travel books commence at home (1991: 170). *Journey Without Maps* contains an early section on the 'seediness' of Liverpool, where Greene boards the boat for Africa, and the book repeatedly returns to memories of other English and European towns. The fiction of travelling 'without maps' away from home is thus a device emphasizing the authenticity of the journey as exploration; of endeavouring to escape the feeling outlined by numerous writers in the 1930s of the earth as a known place. D.H.Lawrence, for example, complained in 1931 that 'Superficially, the world has become small and known [...].We've done the globe and the globe is done' (1971:

125).[8] Lévi-Strauss echoed this complaint when commenting upon the travels undertaken in the 1930s that became the source of his *Tristes Tropiques:* 'I wished I had lived in the days of real journeys, when it was still possible to see the full splendour of a spectacle that had not yet been blighted, polluted and spoilt' (1976: 50). To travel without maps is to aspire to recapture the idea of the unspoilt voyage into uncharted space, rather than a journey into a familiar and cartographically represented place. It is also to give the literary traveller the right to contest the scientific discourse of cartography with a more artistic or exotic discourse.[9] At one point in his trip Greene comments: 'I shall call the next village we stayed in Darndo. It sounded like Darndo, and it is marked on no map' (1980: 218). Except now, inscribed upon the literary map of Greene's tour.

Greene repeatedly refers to the uncharted nature of his journey through 'rough, unmapped country' (1980: 107). His visit had been notified in advance to the Secretary of the Interior of the country, who had indicated a potential route for the travelling party. Greene, however, rejects this help – 'it would be quite easy for me to avoid it' – on the basis that if 'there was anything to hide in the Republic I wanted to surprise it' (1980: 45). Although Greene's journey was occasioned by reports of slavery and massacres in Liberia, his account does not dwell upon this as a secret he wishes to surprise; the journalistic motive for the journey is soon transformed into a search for other forms of concealment. To be without maps is thus a metaphor for a covert exploration of unknown territory and Greene explains at length the cartographic status of Liberia:

> The Republic is almost entirely covered by forest, and has never been properly mapped, mapped that is to say even to the rough extent of the French colonies which lie on two sides of it. I could find only two large-scale maps for sale. One, issued by the British General Staff, quite openly confesses ignorance; there is a large white space covering the greater part of the Republic, with a few dotted lines indicating the conjectured course of rivers (incorrectly, I usually found) and a fringe of names along the boundary. These names have been curiously chosen: most of them are quite unknown to anyone in the Republic; they must have belonged to obscure villages now abandoned. The other map is issued by the United States War Department. There is a dashing quality about it; it shows a vigorous imagination. Where the English map is content to leave a blank space, the American in large letters fills it with the word "Cannibals". It has no use for dotted lines and confessions of ignorance; it is so inaccurate that it would be useless, perhaps even dangerous, to follow it, though there is something Elizabethan in its imagination (1980: 45–46).[10]

Greene clearly enjoys the archaic and imaginative qualities of these maps. Their blankness offers him the chance to characterize his journey as an epic into the unknown, replete with the frisson of fear indicated by the possibility of cannibals. It is also, significantly, a map that constructs Liberia as an archaic space, as 'something Elizabethan' and hence unlike the 'done globe' of the twentieth century. Greene's need for a reliable map is unsure, for as he notes 'I had never been out of Europe before; I was a complete amateur at travel in Africa' (1980: 47–48), and he admits that he 'could never properly remember the points of the compass' (1980:48). Certainly, his mapless condition intensifies his sense of the freedom offered by the trip: it would, he notes, 'be possible to travel all down West Africa without showing papers from the moment of landing' (1980: 62). With 'no passports, no Customs, no barriers' (1980: 62) Greene feels 'the happy sense of being free; one had only to follow a path far enough and one could cross a continent' (1980: 62), later characterizing this sense of travel as an experience of 'letting myself drift with Africa' (1980: 66).[11] This image of unrestrained drifting is, of course, another convenient traveller's fiction, and assists 'true' travellers to distinguish themselves from the itineraries and plotted routes of tourists. The 1930s saw the establishment of tourism as an industry in many European countries, following the first national board for tourism established in Italy in 1919. In the first statistical survey of the economics of tourism in 1933, F.W.Ogilvie noted that 'the international aspect of the tourist movement is now so widely recognized as important that there is hardly a country in the world which does not devote public money [...] to the development of tourist facilities' (1933: vii).[12] That Liberia can be traversed without maps, passports, papers or other tourists also represents this as a space of otherness to contemporary Europe: it is simply not subject to the same forms of spatial organization.

Drifting without maps, but with a party of Liberian guides, enables Greene to believe he cannot be designated a tourist in any sense, and that he is moving daringly through space, rather than being safely guided through a known place. At the start of his journey Greene follows the route of Sir Alfred Sharpe in 1919 and then engages in 'Long study of the manuscript maps the Dutch prospectors had made of the Western province' (1980: 95), before venturing further east until he reaches regions he feels happier with since they are unmapped by either Sharpe or the Dutch. When he returns to Monrovia at the end of the book, an old man on the boat exclaims to him out of the blue: 'Do you know in Monrovia they have a map of the whole of Liberia? I am going to go and see it. It is in the possession of a family called Anderson. They have had it for years. Everyone who goes to Monrovia goes to see the map. Sinoe is marked on it, and Grand Bassa and Cape Palmas' (1980: 228). Greene passes no comment on the old man's claim, as if the author is either glad or aggrieved not to have seen this map, but also perhaps aware that his book will now replace or supplement this incredulous object.

Another motivation for Greene's trip was the attraction of the 'seediness' he discerns in Liberia's history and which he links to the appeal of 'the seediness of civilization, of the sky-signs in Leicester Square, the tarts in Bond Street, the smell of cooking greens off Tottenham Court Road, the motor salesmen in Great Portland Street' (1980: 19). Urban seediness appeals since it represents 'temporarily, the sense of nostalgia for something lost; it seems to represent a stage further back' (1980: 19). Africa represents a deeper, more intense sense of 'seediness', 'when one is less content to rest at the urban stage' (1980: 19) and possesses a 'quality of darkness [...] of the inexplicable' (1980: 20). This seediness represents for Greene an earlier stage in life and of how one's present has emerged from the past. The context here seems to be very much that of an awareness of 1930s history: 'we [...] are living after a war and a revolution' (1980: 21). Greene's project aims to trace 'one's place in time' (1980: 19) via a journey into 'our' past. This is, therefore, another explanation for eschewing the consolations of cartography: if Liberia were properly mapped it would lose this sense of the 'inexplicable' and of being 'a stage further back' (1980: 19). We can now discern how Greene's anti-cartographic discourse is one that is deeply embedded in a spatial history of Africa constructed by European imperialist views of the continent's seeming achronicity.[13]

The significant presence of absent maps is emphasized in one of Greene's many interesting references to psychoanalysis in the text.[14] Greene's journey has now reached beyond the area where a noticeable western influence is evident. Now he must stay in 'native huts' and become accustomed to rats running around at night. This thought leads Greene to perceive fear itself as a quality his journey must explore:

> I was afraid of moths. It was an inherited fear, I shared my mother's terror of birds, couldn't touch them, couldn't bear the feel of their hearts beating in my palm. I avoided them as I avoided ideas I didn't like, the idea of eternal life and damnation. But in Africa one couldn't avoid them any more than one could avoid the supernatural. The method of psychoanalysis is to bring the patient back to the idea which he is repressing: a long journey backwards without maps, catching a clue here and a clue there, as I caught the names of the villages from this man and that, until one has to face the general idea, the pain or the memory. This is what you have feared, Africa may be imagined as saying, you can't avoid it, there it is creeping round the wall, flying in at the door, rustling the grass, you can't turn your back, you can't forget it, so you may as well take a long look (1980: 96–7).

The idea of a journey backwards into memory and time is attached – cathected in Freud's sense (1984: 151–52) – onto the idea of a spatial journey into Liberia. It is significant that Greene sees Liberia as a synecdoche for Africa as a whole; viewing a specific place as representative of a wider geographical entity. The space of Africa is then displaced onto an image of Greene's psychic topography, representing fear itself. Crucial here is the imperialist discourse of Africa as a place of childhood, of the primitive stage of development of 'man'. Greene's final image in the book is of the 'innocence, the virginity' (1980: 250) of Africa; in the Liberian forest he writes that 'again and again one caught hints of what it was we had developed from' (1980: 93).

It is, at any rate, a rather odd analogy: in psychoanalysis there are no maps, but there is a guide, the analyst, who helps plots the way forward. Freud, of course, imagined the unconscious in topographical terms, as an area of the mind through which the psychoanalyst must navigate (1984: 174). Again we return to the central tension between a journey with and without maps; a voyage through a known place and one through some unknown space. In another remark Greene explicitly links the project of psychoanalysis with earlier explorers: 'Freud has made us conscious as we have never been before of those ancestral threads which still exist in our unconscious minds to lead us back. The need, of course, has always been felt, to go back and begin again. Mungo Park, Livingstone, Stanley, Rimbaud, Conrad represented only another method to Freud's, a costly, less easy method [...] but one is not certain how far the explorers knew the nature of the fascination which worked on them in the dirt, the disease, the barbarity and the familiarity of Africa' (1980: 248).

In Greene's analogy of travel with psychoanalysis we have a significant and revealing way of reading travel writing as a form of metaphorical mapping. Travel writing provides a textual map of some geographical zone; but it is also a map of the psychic journey undergone by the traveller. To 'begin again' is to remap; or, we might say, to supplement one's original psychic topography with a new, and unadorned, map. Greene's travels represent an initial transformation of a discourse of place into a discourse of space. To 'begin again' means to regard the self as a blank space rather than some charted region or place. This is perhaps why Greene is so attracted by the motif of drifting without maps, for the maps must be provided or created by the traveller; the writing is itself the proper map of the journey. As Porter suggests, the most interesting travel books are those that 'combine explorations in the world with self-explorations', texts that create a self through 'a dialogic encounter with others' (1991: 5; 8). In Greene's case the spatial otherness of Liberia is thus an encounter with another, and temporally earlier, part of his own identity. This perhaps explains his apparently puzzling comment near the end of the book that 'what has astonished me about Africa was that it had never been really strange' (1980: 248). Without a map Greene has seemingly stumbled upon himself, tripped over a map of his own psyche. In other words, he has now transformed this space of otherness into a familiar place once again.[15]

Greene's journey is an overdetermined spatial narrative in the sense conceived by Michel de Certeau: 'narrative structures have the status of spatial syntaxes' (1984: 115). For de Certeau, stories 'traverse and organize places; they select and link them together', such that 'Every story is a travel story – a spatial practice' (1984: 115). *Journey Without Maps* narrates two such spatial practices: the trip through Liberia, and the psychoanalytic journey through Greene's unconscious fears and desires. The peculiar spatial syntax of both is described by Greene as one 'without maps'. However, in the act of writing the travel narrative itself, Greene supplies the missing map – the spatial syntax of being mapless is displaced by the literary map of Greene's text, a supplementary spatial syntax reinforced by the cartographic illustration to the volume. Two corresponding distinctions introduced by de Certeau provide further guidance for understanding how space and place might function within travel writing: a demarcation between *space* and *place*, and a related division between *tours* and *maps*. For de Certeau, a place 'implies an indication of stability' and is a location where 'elements are distributed in relationships of coexistence' (1984: 117). Two things cannot occupy the same place, elements can only exist beside one another, each situated in its 'proper' location. De Certeau uses 'proper' in a specific sense meaning the official, legitimated use to which a place or activity belongs. A space, however, is based not upon stability but upon direction, movement and velocity:

> Space is composed of intersections of mobile elements. It is in a sense actuated by the ensemble of movements deployed within it. Space occurs as the effect produced by the operations that orient it, situate it, temporalize it, and make it function in a polyvalent unity of conflictual programs or contractual proximities. (1984: 117)

Space, in this sense, writes de Certeau, 'is a practiced place', it is like the meaning of a word actually being spoken rather than its 'proper' meaning found in a dictionary. De Certeau's example is that of a city street that has been planned by urban authorities in a geometrical fashion. This place is 'transformed into a space by walkers' in much the same way that 'an act of reading is the space produced by the practice of a particular place: a written text, i.e., a place constituted by a system of signs' (1984: 117). Places, argues de Certeau, are always determined by a focus upon fixity, or what he calls 'the *being-there* of something dead', so that an inert body, whether a pebble or a cadaver, serves as the foundation of place. Spaces, however, are determined by *operations* attributable to historical subjects rather than inert bodies: 'a movement always seems to condition the production of a space and to associate it with a history' (1984: 118).

Stories constantly oscillate around these two poles, transforming spaces into places, and places into spaces. De Certeau thus suggests that it might be possible to produce a typology of the ways in which stories either enact an 'identification of places' or an 'actualization of spaces' (1984: 118). De Certeau is careful to suggest that these are not fixed binary terms since places and spaces are constantly being transfigured into one another in the play of spatial stories. What seems to happen in Greene's ambivalent relationship to maps is an instance of such a transformation: actualizing spaces is akin to drifting, or exploration, whereas the physical map functions to identify place. Another example of such a transformation occurs in Greene's description of a village called Duogobmai. Initially, Greene describes the village in terms of a discourse of place: 'Duogobmai came in sight, a line of blackened huts at the top of a long red-clay slope' (1980: 125). The village is identified primarily by its physical features: it 'looked very old and very dirty', the huts are very crowded together and small inside, and replete with numerous rats. It was, notes Greene, 'a really horrible village. The only thing to do in it was to get drunk' (1980: 128). Greene renames this 'shifty and mean' place 'in which I found nothing to admire' (1980: 129), calling it 'The Horrible Village' in a sub-heading, using the same appellation in two photos of Duogobmai in the 1936 edition.[16] But this 'horrible' place becomes transformed, even without the help of Greene's trusty supply of whisky, into a narrative agent that emphasizes one of the central themes of the book, the encounter with fear and the 'primitive'. Lying down in his hammock that night Greene actualizes the village into a space that is part of his own personal journey:

> And suddenly I felt curiously happy and careless and relieved. One couldn't, I was sure, get lower than Duogobmai. I had been afraid of the primitive, had wanted it broken gently, but here it came on us in a breath, as we stumbled up through the dung and the cramped and stinking huts to our lampless sleeping place among the rats. It was the worst one need fear, and it was bearable because it was inescapable (1980: 126–7).

The village is animated space, breathing a primeval fear that Greene welcomes since it confirms his desire to escape from western places fixed upon maps. After a disquisition on rats in England, Paris and Liberia, Greene again turns the visit to Duogobmai into a space indicating a stage in his own journey: 'below the fear and the irritation, one was aware of a curious lightness and freedom; one might drink, that was a temporary weakening; but one was happy all the same; one had crossed the boundary into country really strange; surely one had gone deep this time' (1980: 132). The geographical movement is one, as de Certeau suggests, that produces a space by associating it with a history, here the history of Greene's personal voyage, as well as the long colonial history of European encounters with 'strangeness'.

Interestingly, de Certeau argues that 'identification of place' relies upon a mode of discourse he terms the *map*. This is opposed to the *tour*, an experiential discourse which is associated with the 'actualization of space'. In the discourse of the map there is a precise ordering of where elements or features occur; the hypercomplexity of social space is constrained by a visual discourse which presents a 'tableau' or 'knowledge of an order of places', and which finds its apogee in the conventional map with its 'plane projection totalizing observations'. Tour discourses refuse to present a visual tableau and are, instead, rooted in 'spatializing actions' that 'organize(s) *movements*' (1984: 119). The difference is thus between a discourse that lists where sites are located ('The girl's room is next to the kitchen, opposite the bathroom') and one which describes a location through a set of actions ('You enter the hallway, go along, you turn right, and then go across the room'). This resistance to geographical mapping is displayed early on in his book, when Greene muses upon Africa, not as 'a particular place, but as a shape, a strangeness, a wanting to know [...] and the shape, of course, is roughly that of the human heart' (1980: 37).

For de Certeau most narratives combine both map and tour discourses, although one mode tends to dominate. However, the tour is the primary form of spatial discourse because it is connected with the actions of human subjects through space, which are then fixed and codified into mapped places. The growth of geometric and scientific discourses of modern mapping has, over a period of centuries, gradually suppressed the role of tour itineraries. The map 'colonizes space' and eliminates the movements and practices of subjects that have produced and observed the very spaces initially:

> The map, a totalizing stage on which elements of diverse origin are brought together to form the tableau of a 'state' of geographical knowledge, pushes away into its prehistory or into its posterity, as if into the wings, the operations of which it is the result or the necessary condition. It remains alone on the stage. The tour describers have disappeared [...] maps, constituted as proper places in which to exhibit the products of knowledge, form tables of legible results. Stories about space exhibit on the contrary the operations that allow it, within a constraining and non-'proper' place, to mingle its elements anyway (1984: 121).

Travel writing of Greene's variety thus attempts to resist the colonization of space by the map and to reinscribe the tour as the dominant form of spatial syntax in the narrative. The highly stylized visual maps in the different editions of *Journey Without Maps* also appear designed to recapture the discourse of the tour, rather than resembling de Certeau's view of the static tableau of cartography.

A binary discourse of place/map and space/tour is open to question, however, if we view the two terms not as antonyms, but as implying different attitudes towards social space. A sense of place might, in reality, not be understood as a site of fixity, but as a social and cultural construction in its own right. Doreen Massey, for example, suggests that we understand place not in terms of fixity and dwelling, in the way de Certeau seems to, but as 'formed out of numerous social relationships stretched over space' (1995: 69). Any particular place is formed from specific sets of intersecting social relationships. In Greene's text we can point to the historical discourse of imperial exploration as determining the book's pleasure in Liberia's unmapped state, as well as a desire to escape what is seen as the restrictions of a Europe which, by the 1930s, had seemingly become insufficiently alluring.

Travel writing is perhaps always a form of mapping, of offering an alternative vision to that endorsed by various cartographic regimes. Thus travel writing is a representational space, in Lefebvre's terms, a set of discourses that imagines space in a certain way, often at odds with official representations of space (although they can easily be complicit with them).[17] Travel writing seems at times to be an impossible discourse in terms of space and place. Such writing aspires to the condition of de Certeau's definition of space: it wants to recapture in textual form a journey, a movement or a tour. But writing up one's journey translates movement into fixity, with travel writing always threatening to employ a mapping discourse of some specific place. Narrative disruption and disjunction might well be understood as another resistance to this incorporation of space into place, of the movements of the tour turning into the static map. Foucault's concept of heterotopia helps illuminate this feature. As Foucault defines it, heterotopias describe texts that disorder normal syntax and 'dessicate speech', as well as referring to 'placeless places' that somehow have the character of a profound 'otherness' about them.[18] The otherness of a foreign country is thus something that travel writing must strive to render: to demonstrate spatial practices of otherness. If we cannot see, touch, smell or hear otherness then travel writing must translate these effects into the spatial syntax of the writing itself, and produce the narrative disruptions of the travel text. Thus the actual material spaces of heterotopia are transformed into textual heterotopias that disturb. An example of this heterotopic writing is found in the section headed 'The Way Back' that forms the end of part one of Greene's book. Here, at the frontier of Liberia, the narrative breaks off to sketch a variety of English characters: a pompous English major in London; an old woman in the Cotswolds; a mentally disturbed inhabitant of another English village; and a gypsy gardening in the Ridge Way in Gloucestershire. One sentence in this section conveys the spatial disorientation caused here: 'It was winter now, snow in London, the fierce noon sun on the clearing, yellow fever in Freetown, behind on the way to the Coast the mist was rising from the forest, drifting slowly upwards, like the smoke of burning weeds below the Ridge Way' (1980: 73–74).

Another impossibility for travel writing is that in representing otherness, in capturing an image of a space unlike our own, the natural temptation is to turn this other space into a known place, of familiarity. If the travel writer succeeds in describing otherness in a rich and full portrait, then precisely that which the writer tried to convey – the strange alterity of another space – disappears; spatial alterity becomes the textually mapped. If we feel we know fully the Liberia of Greene's *Journey without Maps*, then the writer has both succeeded and failed; he has made a strange space appear like a known place to us, and hence heterotopia turns homotopic. In a sense the reader can never experience the travelogue without a map, since the text itself is almost always bound to function in that way. Hence the writer tries to preserve the strangeness of other spaces in the spatial form of the text, rather than in the content, the representation of the other region.

Travel writing should, I have argued, be more closely linked to an understanding of historical forms of social space, such as those found in maps, and of debates within cultural geography surrounding space and place. The three maps in the different editions of Greene's book demonstrate, as Richard Phillips suggests, the ability of maps 'to circumscribe geography, by enclosing, defining, coding, orienting, structuring and controlling space' (1997: 14). I have suggested that there is a significant interaction between these maps and the spatial syntax of Greene's narrative, where the cartographic image functions as a place-discourse against which Greene can construct a discourse of spatial movement. Interpreting these maps as forms of representation rather than naturalized images of 'fact' demonstrates how the discourses of space and place are not to be taken for granted, but must be understood as forms of Lefebvrean social space. De Certeau's distinctions between space/tour and place/map provide a useful initial stage in conceptualizing the spatial syntax employed in travel writing, but must not be reified into an absolute binary distinction. The social production of spatiality is, then, a primary syntax forming the contours of travel writing. As Duncan and Gregory argue in a recent book of essays, there is a need when discussing travel writing to stress 'the physicality of representation' and the 'spatiality of travel', given a tendency towards focusing purely upon travel writing as literary representation (1999: 1;5). All geography is earth-*writing*, but a literary geography would be one which emphasizes the socio-spatial forms of texts. To understand travel writing we must not only pay attention to how the text represents a space, region, or country, but also how it is that social space shapes and exercises an influence upon the spatial form of the text. No journey is ever without maps, and the study of the form and function of maps and charts as discourses can help us think more spatially, and hopefully more richly, about travel writing.

Notes

1. Greene's book, as I discuss below, contains slightly different maps in the three editions I have consulted. Thanks to Debbie Lisle for helpful comments on an earlier draft of this piece.
2. For an interesting example of this point in relation to the influential early twentieth century British geographer Halford Mackinder, see Chris GoGwilt 1998.
3. For Barbara Greene's version of the journey see, *Too Late to Turn Back* (London 1990); this was first published as *Land Benighted* (1938).
4. For the history of Liberia see Wiley 1980; Anderson 1952; Beyan 1991.
5. I owe this point to Debbie Lisle. The notion of the production of space derives from Lefebvre 1991. Many other British travel texts from this period contain maps designed to allow the literary explorer to claim first rights/writes over a territory: see, inter alia, Byron 1937; Waugh, 1934; and Greene 1939, which contains an extraordinarily evocative map of Mexico.
6. This is a problematic distinction, as Caren Kaplan has shown, relying upon a quasi-imperialist rhetoric of exploration as conquest masquerading as 'discovery'; see Kaplan 1996: 49–57. Greene himself said that his favourite childhood book, Rider Haggard's *King Solomon's Mines* (1886) had perhaps drawn him to Liberia (quoted in Fussell 1980: 69).
7. 'Blank spaces' is an echo of Conrad's famous image of the map of Africa dreamed over by Marlow in *Heart of Darkness*. In many ways Conrad's text haunts Greene's book, in the manner described by Dennis Porter as a feature exemplifying the 'belatedness' of all travel writing (1991: 12).
8. Fussell argues that the 1930s is the last golden age of travel writing because of the onset of tourism (1980: 41).
9. By the 1930s mapping had embraced the vision of scientific objectivity whole-heartedly. Conrad, for example, described geography as a 'science of facts' (1926: 10).
10. This lacunae in geographical knowledge of Liberia was still true in 1952, when Earle Anderson noted the lack of a satisfactory map, partly due to border disputes and an absence of actual surveys (1952: ix–x).
11. In one sense Greene's desire to 'drift' through Africa is a reaction to what historians have noted as an excessive feature of 1930s Britain, the stress upon planning – from the economy to housing to holidays. A.J.P.Taylor notes that 'Planning was the key word of the thirties', (1975: 375).
12. Buzard notes how in this period 'the unsystematic observations made by novelists, poets, and travel-writers took second place to the rational administration of knowledge about tourism and "the tourist"'(1993: 17). For the development of tourism in the British context see Urry 1990.
13. For a discussion of this form of 'time-lagged colonial moment' see Bhabha 1994, ch.12.
14. The link between psychoanalysis and mapping is indicated in one of Greene's epigrams to the book, a quote from Oliver Wendell Holmes which starts, 'The life of an individual is in many respects like a child's dissected map'. Greene

had undertaken analysis while an adolescent.
15. In one of his autobiographies Greene wrote that 'he proposed to make memory the very subject of my next book [*Journey Without Maps*]' (1999: 45).
16. The 1936 edition of *Journey Without Maps* includes some thirty-one black and white photos of people and places encountered on the trip. The 1950 edition includes sixteen of these, although the most recent Penguin edition contains none. The photos draw upon another discourse, that of 1930s anthropology, to construct this travel text.
17. The terms representational space and representation of space are taken from Lefebvre 1991: 38–46.
18. See Foucault 1970; 1986.

Bibliography

Anderson, R.E., *Liberia: America's African Friend*. Chapel Hill, 1952.
Beyan, A.J., *The American Colonization Society and the Creation of the Liberian State: A Historical Perspective 1822–1900*. Lanham/London, 1991.
Bhabha, H.K., *The Location of Culture*. London/New York, 1994.
Buzard, J., *Off the Beaten Track: European Tourism, Literature, and the Ways to 'Culture' 1800–1918*. Oxford, 1993.
Byron, R., *The Road to Oxiana*. London, 1937.
Conrad, J., 'Geography and Some Explorers' in *Last Essays*. ed. R. Curle. London, 1926.
de Certeau, M., *The Practice of Everyday Life*. trans. S. Randall, Berkeley, 1984.
Derrida, J., *Of Grammatology*. trans. G. Chakravorty Spivak, Baltimore and London, 1976.
Duncan, J., and Gregory, D. eds. *Writes of Passage: Reading Travel Writing*. London and New York, 1999.
Foucault, M., *The Order of Things: An Archaeology of the Human Sciences*. London, 1970.
———, 'Of Other Spaces', *Diacritics* vol. 16, no.1 (1986): 22–7.
Freud, S., 'The Unconscious' (1915), in *On Metapsychology*, Penguin Freud Library, vol.11, Harmondsworth, 1984.
Fussell, P., *Abroad: British Literary Travelling Between the Wars*. New York and Oxford, 1980.
GoGwilt, C., 'The Geopolitical Image: Imperialism, Anarchism, and the Hypothesis of Culture in the Formation of Geopolitics', *Modernism/Modernity* vol. 5, no. 3 (September 1998): 49–70.
Greene, B., *Too Late to Turn Back*. London, 1990; Originally published as *Land Benighted*. 1938.
Greene, G., *The Lawless Roads*. London, 1939.
———, *Journey Without Maps*. 2nd edn London, 1980.
———, *Ways of Escape*. London, 1999.
Gregory, D., *Geographical Imaginations*. Cambridge, MA/Oxford, 1994.
Haggard, H. Rider, *King Solomon's Mines*. London, 1886.
Harley, J.B., 'Deconstructing the Map', in *Human Geography: An Essential Anthology*. eds. J. Agnew, D. N.Livingstone and A. Rogers, Oxford, 1996.
Jameson, F., *The Ideologies of Theory Essays 1971–1986 vol.2: Syntax of History*. London, 1988.
———, *Postmodernism or, the Cultural Logic of Late Capitalism*. London, 1991.
Kaplan, C., *Questions of Travel: Postmodern Discourses of Displacement*. Durham and London, 1996.

Lawrence, D.H., 'New Mexico', in *A Selection from Phoenix*. ed. A.A.H. Inglis. Harmondsworth, 1971.
Lefebvre, H., *The Production of Space*. trans. D. Nicholson-Smith, Oxford, 1991.
Lévi-Strauss, C., *Tristes Tropiques*, trans. J. and D. Weightman, Harmondsworth, 1976.
Lynch, K., *The Image of the City*. Cambridge, Massachusetts, 1960.
Massey, D., 'The Conceptualization of Place', in *A Place in the World? Places, Cultures and Globalization*. eds. D. Massey and P. Jess, Oxford, 1995.
Ogilvie, F.W., *The Tourist Movement: An Economic Study*. London, 1933.
Phillips, R., *Mapping Men and Empire: A Geography of Adventure*. London and New York, 1997.
Porter, D., *Haunted Journeys: Desire and Transgression in European Travel Writing*. Princeton, 1991.
Taylor, A.J.P., *English History 1914–1945*. Harmondsworth, 1975.
Urry, J., *The Tourist Gaze: Leisure and Travel in Contemporary Societies*. London, 1990.
Waugh, E., *Ninety-Two Days*. 1934.
Wiley, B.I., ed. *Slaves No More: Letters from Liberia 1833–1869*. Lexington, 1980.

Chapter 2

SA(L)VAGING EXOTICISM
New Approaches to 1930s Travel Literature in French

Charles Forsdick

> An unstable literary phenomenon which eschews traditional categorisation and rhetorical divisions and, at its extremes, is absorbed into ethnography or popular literature, exoticism is as present at trials of literary superficiality as it is absent from theories of literature and from the manifestos of specific schools. Denouncing exoticism means perpetuating a hazy discourse which confuses the various different meanings actually encompassed by the notion; ignoring the term or using it in a restrictive way in specific studies with few ambitions in terms of providing definitions is to refuse to come to terms with a literary phenomenon which is most likely to become extremely important in the history of European literature (Moura 1998a: 36).

This article was triggered by growing dissatisfaction both with uses of the term 'exoticism' in post-colonial criticism and with the tendency to conflate colonial and post-colonial understandings of the term. The focus is in particular on the French tradition and on the rich semantic field of the term 'exotisme' itself. Exoticism is a complex, controversial and even contradictory term which certainly cannot be reduced to the purely geographical although it is most commonly used to describe an aesthetic by-product of travel. It is, however, the link between the symbolic field of the exotic and the geographical field of travel, specifically in French-language literature of the 1930s, that this paper explores. Between the First and Second World Wars, France witnessed a complete renewal in the field of travel writing. The 1930s in particular have become a privileged moment for considerations of this body of texts, for this decade witnessed rapidly multiplied contact between Europe and elsewhere before the post-war collapse of colonial dependency. This contact resulted not only from new opportunities for travel and new means of transferring information (like the radio), both of which favoured the emergence of fresh genres such as *reportage* and new literary characters such as Tintin; but also – if travel writing is to be understood in a much wider sense as travel literature – from a crisis in European civilization which caused many intellectuals and authors to travel elsewhere. Such expansion and reassessment of the potentials of the journey beyond the geographical boundaries of Europe occurred against the backdrop of a series of threats to the field of travel itself: the failure of the colonial system; growing intimations of the rise of globalization; and a vehement anti-exoticism which meant that a hitherto staple element of travel writing was undergoing radical change.

Since it was coined just over 150 years ago, the term 'exotisme' has been subject to steady semantic shifts between two poles: one signifying an exotic-ness essential to radical otherness, the other describing the process whereby such radical otherness is either experienced by the traveller from outside or translated, transported, and finally represented for consumption at home. It is this final sense of translation, transportation and representation – all three of which depend on the metaphor of travel, since they imply not only distance but also the bridging of distance – on which contemporary critics have focused. The authors of the 1998 Routledge *Key Concepts in Post-Colonial Studies* describe, for instance, the shift in the field of the exotic from signifying relative indigeneity to connoting, in a nineteenth-century context, 'a stimulating or exciting difference, something with which the domestic could be (safely) spiced' (Ashcroft et al 1998: 94). Citing an article by Renata Wasserman on James Fenimore Cooper and José de Alencar, they see exoticism as a process of domestication, of turning what is potentially threatening into 'innocent signifiers of an otherness which was simply exotic, that is, nonsystematic, carrying no meaning other than that imposed by the culture in which they were exhibited' (Wasserman 1984: 132). Responding to this analysis, the authors of these *Key Concepts* conclude: 'Isolated from their own geographical and cultural contexts, they represented whatever was projected onto them by the societies into which they were introduced. Exotics in the metropoles were a significant part of imperial displays of power and the plenitude of empires' (Ashcroft et al 1998: 95). The idea of 'imperial displays of power' is perhaps most manifest in the European tradition of competing colonial exhibitions, and any consideration of 1930s exoticism in the French tradition must take into account the 1931 Paris *Exposition coloniale*, peak not only of French colonial exoticism but also (when seen in relation to the 150th anniversary celebrations of the 1830 French conquest of Algeria the previous year) of French colonial ideology or what the colonial historian Raoul Girardet calls the 'idée coloniale' (Girardet 1972).

The commonly accepted meanings of 'exoticism' in post-colonial criticism are therefore, pertinent for considerations of 1930s France. However, what exploration of this 'key concept' often omits – and what any consideration of 1930s exoticism which fails to go beyond metropolitan displays of empire seems to ignore – is the constant contestation which has marked twentieth-century uses of the term. From the early twentieth-century attempts of Victor Segalen to redefine the concept in his *Essai sur l'exotisme* (Segalen 1986) to more recent efforts in a variety of fields – narratology, anthropology, historiography and post-modern sociology – to forge positive contemporary uses, the notion of 'exoticism' has constantly eschewed reduction. Whereas in contemporary critical currency, the term has almost universally pejorative overtones and is restricted by its coupling to colonial discourse, close analysis reveals a need for more attenuated understandings which, avoiding pan-European generalizations, explore specific cultural traditions and not only encompass reflexivity but also propose a potential challenge to the reductive overtones implied above.

In his study of fin-de-siècle engagements with alterity, Chris Bongie has emphasized a central element of exoticism: its stubborn persistence in the face of the prophesied decline of its symbolic field, in the face of the supposed absorption of difference by sameness, of indigenous specificity by the forces of globalization. Describing this deferral of the collapse of an elsewhere on which exoticism depends, he claims: '"In theory" there are no more horizons, but "in reality" they still exist' (Bongie 1991: 4). Exoticism is thus characterized by a twin yet contradictory movement: decline and recovery, being at once (in terms of the tension implied by my title) savaged and salvaged. James Clifford had already explored this idea in his *Predicament of Culture*, in whose preface he adopts Raymond Williams's concept of a repetitive 'structure of feeling' to describe the cyclical recurrence of 'lost authenticity, of "modernity" ruining some essence or source' (Clifford 1988: 4). For Williams, in *The Country and the City* where the phrase first appears, this 'structure of feeling' describes an emergent pattern of general experience which characterizes a generation of creative artists (Williams 1985).[1] Hence, it is the individuality of each moment that is striking: the decline of the exotic means different things in different places at different times, and in varying contexts quite different values are to be explored and brought into question.

If one were to take a diachronic approach to 1930s travel writing and attempt to situate it in a wider context of twentieth-century exoticism, the privileged status of this corpus of texts is immediately apparent. It was produced in the decade leading up to the watershed of the Second World

War and accordingly predates (whilst simultaneously heralding) the effects of post-war cultural shifts: the rapid modernization of France; the equally rapid decline of Empire; and the growing awareness of the changing nature and implications of travel. This decade represents, therefore, a key period before the rapid changes brought about by the war and by the effects of its aftermath – the principal amongst these being the sudden reconfiguration of relations between Europe and its others, particularly in the light of the severing of direct colonial links and the forging of new patterns of cultural interrelations that either undermined or refuted Western hegemony. 1930s travel writing is to be situated, therefore, before the critical assaults – in particular in the postwar work of Aimé Césaire, Frantz Fanon and Claude Lévi-Strauss – on this hazily defined genre and the exoticism with which it is invariably allied; it is to be situated also before the notion of 'exoticism', so closely linked to Empire, had fallen into several decades of obsolescence.

It is not necessarily this chronological approach, however, that the idea of a 'structure of feeling' invites. To tease out the implications for studies of contemporary travel literature inherent in 1930s uses of the concept of exoticism, a synchronic approach is perhaps a more effective means of exploring the tensions and contradictions becoming particularly acute in this decade. Material presented as representative is inevitably selective, but will reveal how the decline – as a result of rejection or violent critique – of a certain strand of colonial exoticism encapsulated, in embryo, the foundations of a more positive, less reductive understanding of the term. It is such an understanding which has achieved renewed critical currency – particularly in the French tradition – in the later twentieth century. What will emerge from this brief reflection is an awareness of the need, when exploring exoticism and travel writing, to balance its two elements: *littérarité* (its textual nature) and *culturalité* (its links with dominant contemporary ideologies and intellectual movements).[2]

It is not the intention in this article to deny outright the clearly pejorative overtones of exoticism (whose accuracy in certain contexts is irrefutable), but instead to place the notion of a specifically colonial exoticism within a much wider contextual frame. In early 1930s France, some of the most vociferous criticism of exoticism emerged from the colonial propagandists whose work is, in retrospect, most likely to be characterized by the very term they attempted to reject. Roland Lebel, leading apologist for and first would-be theorist of French colonial literature, categorizes exoticism in his *Histoire de la littérature coloniale en France*: 'it is the lure of those beautiful countries where we instinctively locate characters belonging to the dream of Eden, the mirage of islands blessed by the Gods, the aroma of travel and of the unknown' (Lebel 1931: 8), and insists on a distinction between 'the colonial tourist' and 'the colonial author in the true sense' (Lebel 1931: 79), between 'exotisme' and 'colonialisme' (Lebel 1931: 86). Colonial literature is presented as 'a reaction against false exoticism, against clichés, against prejudices and foolish conceits' (Lebel 1931: 82). The tradition of exoticist literature, rooted in the nineteenth century and epitomized perhaps by the work of Loti, was said to lack the qualities of colonial literature: a depth of analysis, a wealth of documentary detail, and an authenticity offered by an author either born in the colonies or at least posted there for most of their career.[3] Whilst the *littérature coloniale* movement attempted to define itself negatively and chronologically against the previous benchmarks of a exoticist tradition perceived to have failed, its exponents and apologists failed to recognize that it served in many ways as an extension of nineteenth-century exoticism and as a recurrence of its representational practices. Colonial propagandists nevertheless found in the 1931 *Exposition* an overemphasis on the picturesque which turned an essentially pedagogical event into what Messimy, President of the Association Sciences-Coloniale, called a 'huge festival' (Ageron 1997: 508).

It was, however, the aim of the principal organizer of the *Exposition*, Field Marshal Lyautey, to avoid such exoticizing overtones of a 'travelling fairground exhibition' and to present a 'source of practical instruction' (Ageron 1997: 497). Yet as Panivong Norindr has claimed in his recent *Phantasmatic Indochina*, the result of the *Exposition* – and in particular the reconstruction as its centre-piece of the temple of Angkor Wat – was to suppress politics, to erase historical forces, and to counter the threat of contemporary insurrection by presenting the French colonies in South East Asia as a kingdom at peace (Norindr 1996: 7). According to Norindr's analysis, Indochinese students and workers holding demonstrations in the grounds of the *Exposition* were removed as their protests revealed not only the false nature of the indigenous characters required for the exhibition's living diorama, but also the ideological implications of the very colonial exoticism on which the event depended: 'Because they contested the representations elaborated at the Exposition, these unruly natives had to be removed from this new colonial Eden. Otherwise they could have exposed the whole exoticizing project of the fair' (Norindr 1996: 33). These indigenous extras were required to be docile, compliant and above all silent. The myth of the Noble Savage they were supposed to perpetuate was threatened, however, by a number of discordant voices among their ranks, challenging visitors' right to photograph them or to address them – like animals or children – with the familiar 'tu' (Ageron 1997: 508).

As the French colonial historian Raoul Girardet has explained, despite the lip service paid to pedagogic intentions by the event's organizers, visitors in 1931 were drawn more by the 'wonder of exoticism' than by any overwhelming desire to discover or understand the colonial other (Girardet 1972: 134). And this attraction to a tamed, alluring, titillating exotic other was seemingly catered for by the *Exposition* itself, during which 'authentic' indigenous performers (brought to France for the duration) were included in an often inauthentic decor whose detail was dictated by aesthetic concerns more than by a desire for ethnographic accuracy. There were camel races, canoe trips and regular opportunities to sample suspiciously generic 'colonial cuisine and exotic beverages'. The marketing of the event depended heavily on an illusion of colonial travel, offering 'a journey round the world in four days' and underlining the potential efficiency of a visit to the exhibition site: 'What is the point of going to Tunisia when you can visit it at the gates of Paris?' (Ageron 1997: 502). An article in a special issue of the periodical *L'Illustration* makes the advantages of this opportunity for vicarious travel explicit. In 'Promenade à travers les cinq continents', Paul-Émile Cadilhac claims:

> I advise those who dread sea crossings to travel the planet by visiting the Exhibition. There is no rolling or pitching on a ship; seasickness is unheard of; you go by train or coach from Madagascar to Oceania and from Martinique to the Dutch East Indies. Distances are abolished, oceans swept away – and these are not the least of the miracles performed by Field Marshal Lyautey. (Cadilhac 1931: 73).

Other texts inspired by the *Exposition* similarly insist on the stage-managed nature of the event, underlining not only its artificiality but also the domesticating mechanisms of the exoticism on which much of it was posited: 'Nearby, terrifying Kanaks, all black skin and swirling raffia, made your blood curdle with their war dances, but then they queued up – and this civilized practice had a cosy and reassuring feel to it' (Ramel-Cals 1931: 9).

Unlike Ousmane Socé's *Mirages de Paris*, an account of a Senegalese protagonist's experiences in 1931 France, texts with such a metropolitan focus cannot perhaps be integrated into a traditional understanding of 1930s travel writing. The *Exposition* and texts which emerged from it nevertheless form an essential context in which such writing can be considered. Moreover, accounts of virtual circumnavigation on the exhibition site continue an earlier tradition of vicarious travel, epitomized by the eleventh chapter of Huysmans's *À Rebours* in which the discovery of London within Paris leads to 'an immense aversion to travel' and to the perplexed prophesy of an end of journeying: 'What is the point of moving when you can travel so magnificently sitting in a chair?' (Huysmans 1978: 247).[4] Des Esseintes's parodic exoticism in this decadent journey is a literary variation on a popular late nineteenth-century theme which Vanessa Schwartz summed up in her *Spectacular Realities* as 'fin-de-siècle panoramania' (Schwartz 1998). Schwartz describes the 1880s and 1890s craze for dioramas and virtual journeys which allowed a whistle stop tour of exotic locales without leaving Paris itself. Read in this wider historical context, the *Exposition coloniale* is to be seen both as a further stage in the erasure of elsewhere foreseen by Huysmans and as an integral part of the 1930s reassessment of the symbolic and actual fields of travel. On the one hand, its staging of colonial cultures represents a conquest and reorganization of space – France is not only the centre of the world, but is also even transformed into a self-contained representation of the world; on the other, it stood as a clear indication of what was implied by the growing mechanization of travel and in particular the rapid growth of transport by air.

The interwar period, and in particular the 1930s, was marked by the first regular flights between France and Africa and by a series of transcontinental car journeys – such as the Citroën *Croisière Jaune* in 1931 – which combined a public fascination with speed with the lure of exoticism.[5] Such rapid acceleration of travel brought with it a blurring of cultural diversity and an erosion of radically different cultures, access to which was often seen in terms of the spread of global sameness. One of the authors in the period to draw almost exclusively on the theme of travel and on a fascination with speed was Paul Morand, whose cosmopolitanism can be read as the antithesis of an earlier exoticism – and accordingly, in Sartre's terms, as 'the death knell of exoticism' (Sartre 1948: 226).[6] Morand's travel writing is a sustained commentary on the effects of the interwar mechanisation of travel whose implications he explores in the aphoristic 1927 text *Le Voyage*: 'Poor old geography: last century, atlases changed every twenty years. These days, we ought to bring them out hourly as special editions' (Morand 1994: 30). In his 1932 text, *Flèche d'Orient*, Morand describes the journey across Europe by air of an expatriate Russian prince. As the text progresses, there emerges not only a new aesthetics of space triggered by the new perspectives allowed by air travel but also a radically different experience – particularly in terms of time – of the space crossed in travel. What can be seen is 'a cross-ruled, partitioned, geometric universe' (Morand 1932: 41) in which speed erases contour and colour to impose a universal greyness. Morand had certainly claimed in a 1924 interview that his purpose was to render outmoded an exoticism dependent on superficial aspects of local colour (Lefèvre 1992: 79). His own textual response appears paradoxical, however, for he often embraces the sensation of speed whilst bemoaning its effects.

As such, Morand's texts can be associated with those of authors such as Saint-Pol-Roux (on whose work modern theorists of speed like Paul Virilio have drawn) who considered, especially in the aphorisms of his 1932 text *Vitesse*, the implications of an ever-accelerating experience of travel: a sense of immobility – 'Car seat = cinema seat' (Saint-Pol-Roux 1973: 25); 'Mechanized speed is no more than motorized motionlessness' (Saint-Pol-Roux 1973: 30) – and a radical alteration of any notion of dimension: 'Human speed reduces the dimensions of the Earth. Speed = blindness' (Saint-Pol-Roux 1973: 53). Morand's response to this apparent redundancy of the experience of travel and to the transformation of the journey into little more than a geometric vector is contained in the 1937 text, *Éloge du repos* (initially entitled: *Apprendre à se reposer*). This text, written shortly after the adoption by the Front Populaire of the universal right to paid holidays, develops Morand's comments in earlier works on the effects of speed, emphasizing its destructive implications: 'Speed eradicates form. What is left of a landscape seen at 500 kilometres an hour? [...] The earth loses its variety; when you are in a plane, there are no longer poplars and chestnuts beneath you; there are simply trees' (Morand 1996: 118). Criticizing any cult of speed and counselling slowness, he claims that the erosion of radical otherness previously located elsewhere can be compensated for by the discovery of a new sense of exoticism within France itself: 'closer to home, there are rivers which are only known by frogs and canoeists; as he rushes past, the motorist is not aware of them, for you need to be on the water to discover another side of France invisible from dry land' (Morand 1996: 106). Morand's apparently positive attitude to the reforms of 1936 must be attenuated, however, by his realization that paid holidays and greater mobility presented yet another threat to the field of cultural differences which permits travel.

For as the reconstructed temple of Angkor Wat stood in 1931 as an icon for the brief interlude of the *Exposition* (during which an illusion of travel was permitted for all), so the image of a working-class couple on a tandem in 1936 – and of bottles of Ambre Solaire or Orangina, both launched in the same year – represented the possibility of actual if more modest travel for all and even the dawning of an age of mass tourism (Weber 1995: 162). The colonial exoticism of the exposition was a threat to the aesthetic or symbolic field of cultural diversity; the democratization of travel became a challenge to its actual, geographical field.[7] From the mid-nineteenth century onwards, anti-tourism had become a common defence used by certain travellers to protect their privileged access to traces of cultural difference.[8] As a human, the tourist is classed as a mediocre spectator whose vision is limited to a superficial, kaleidoscopic exoticism. The traveller's vision is distinguished then from the tourist's gawping, and the field of the exotic remains intact.

In her *Le Flâneur sous la tente*, for instance, Constantin-Weyer perpetuates this tradition when she creates an anti-touristic collusion with her reader: 'The movement of glaciers escapes the notice of the tourist's untrained eye. However, we know that they are far from being inert' (Constantin-Weyer 1935: 159). Such aristocratic attempts at elaborating hierarchies of perception of otherness were eclipsed by a number of texts which foregrounded instead the all-encroaching erasure of cultural diversity and refused any sense of exoticism as a quest for radical difference. This refusal of exoticism is particularly marked in a number of French 1930s novels set in Tahiti, such as Georges Simenon's *Touriste de bananes*, in which a tracking of the decline of a French exoticist myth of several centuries' standing reveals the swallowing of local specificity by a spectre of global entropy.[9] For Simenon, the *homme-nature* – or Westerner in search of a utopian lifestyle in an exotic locale – is an anachronism or a zoological curiosity. The quest of such characters inevitably founders as they discover an exotic culture stage-managed for outsiders in which traces of past 'authenticity' are either imported or acted out. The indigenous characters in *Touriste de bananes*, for instance, are by day taxi drivers and prostitutes; it is only by night that they don the trappings of a supposedly pre-colonial Polynesia to create an artificial version of their island for tourist consumption.

In a series of reports entitled 'L'Afrique vous parle' written for the magazine *Voilà* in 1932, Simenon's exasperation led him to conclude: 'Elle nous dit merde!' (Simenon 1976: 106), and this idea of former colonial or exotic subjects talking back in a manner likely to shock the European listener is integral to the decline or critique of the dominant strand of colonial exoticism described above. Although two of the major French novels of the decade, *Voyage au bout de la nuit* and *La Nausée*, both articulate a disillusionment with travel and a rejection of the traps of exoticism, Simenon's recognition of the emergence of indigenous voices suggests an approach to 1930s exoticism which qualifies any foretelling of its total decline. Céline's journey to the end of the night is a voyage of confirmation and not of discovery; the horror of circumnavigation which characterizes it emerges from the narrator's sense of interminable progress through a series of situations which differ in superficial detail rather than in substance. Even the North American stage of the journey, initially in tune with the technological exoticism which characterized other 1930s accounts by transatlantic travellers, eventually leads beneath the facade of concrete and steel to the seamy underside of the American dream. The contemporary topos of the journey is subverted and, especially in the character of Robinson, the ideal of adventure entirely negated.[10] As such, Céline's portrayal of the end of travel resonates with Simenon's model of a linear and geometrical decline of a culture only residually 'exotic' in the non-pejorative sense of this epithet. However, as my title indicates and as my introductory remarks suggested, travel literature in French of the 1930s marks the decline of a certain understanding of exoticism and not of exoticism per se. In a concluding consideration of a selection of travel accounts, it will be suggested that a more complex notion of intercultural contact begins to emerge which remains permanently conscious of the risks of a domesticating exoticism, whilst nevertheless maintaining a focus on cultural specificity and a belief in the existence of diversity as the raw material on which travel literature depends. This salvaging of exoticism does not so much emerge from individual texts as from the interplay of a number of texts which – to borrow Edward Said's terms in *Culture and Imperialism* – can be brought together in contrapuntal arrangements. Such an understanding reveals the intertwined and overlapping histories of metropolitan and formerly colonized societies and avoids the destructive expiation for empire which the rapid descent into obsolescence of the term exoticism often seems to suggest (Said 1993).

A useful starting point for such an attenuation of previous understandings of 1930s exoticism are the early travel narratives of Henri Michaux, *Ecuador* and *Un Barbare en Asie*. *Ecuador* is an anti-travel text which defines itself generically as the antithesis of previous travel accounts.[11] As such, Michaux marks a break with any previous tradition of travel writing for he describes – in Sartre's terms – 'China without lotus plants and without Loti' (Sartre 1964: 8). *Ecuador* itself is marked by a stubborn refusal of diversity, a discovery of monotony and a loss of any sense of dimension which leads its exasperated narrator to exclaim: 'The earth's exoticism has been rinsed out' (Michaux 1929: 35). Refusing to become a 'dabbler in exoticism' (Michaux 1929: 98), the narrator constantly questions the value of his journey, seeing individuals in those he meets rather than ethnotypes and discovering the 'quotidien' instead of the anticipated 'exotique'. It is in such a reflection on the everyday, however, that a renegotiation of the exotic begins to emerge: 'what is everyday life for one person can confuse to death somebody for whom everyday life is situated elsewhere, that is the foreigner, even if for the local population this everyday life is as banal, as grey and as monotonous as can be' (Michaux 1929: 159–60).

This exploration of the everyday is developed in *Un Barbare en Asie* in which Michaux's focus on 'the man in the street' (Michaux 1933: 12) leads to a series of reflections on radical otherness in which he refuses to render the exotic neutral or inoffensive. However, as the title of the work itself suggests, the text also implies a reversal, an exoticization of the European travelling self which grants the narrator an ambiguous position as outsider. For Michaux, the exotic is perhaps exhausted or redundant as a geographically fixed essence, but exoticism itself is reinterpreted as a potentially reciprocal process of negotiating the experience of the new or unknown. André Gide describes in a 1935 diary entry this foregrounding of selectivity and subjectivity in considerations of contact between radically different cultures: 'What constitutes the charm and lure of the *Elsewhere*, of what we call exoticism, is not so much that nature is more beautiful there as that everything seems to us so new, surprises us and is presented to our gaze with a sort of virginity' (Gide 1951: 1236). It is this kind of new approach to exoticism that is implicit in Michaux's narrator's response to those surprised by his failure to write about his native Belgium:

> How on earth could you not write about a country whose appearance to you was characterized by an abundance of new things and by the joy of being able to breathe again.
>
> And how on earth could you write about a country where you have lived for thirty years, thirty years associated with boredom, contradictions, petty concerns, failures, daily routine – a country about which you no longer know anything. (Michaux 1933: 99).

The Barbarian-narrator is even granted a privileged position: 'the naive gaze of a passer-by can sometimes pin down the essential' (Michaux 1933: 101), as if the outsider – intent on seeking experience of elsewhere rather than confirmation of pre-formed impressions – can avoid being a passive, superficial observer and can present in textual form the experience of being faced with a radically different, even unassimilable culture.

Because of the context from which it emerges, Michaux's innovation of seeing the travelling self as other goes beyond the conceit of an earlier tradition of a metamorphosed or reversed ethnographic gaze. The exoticization of Europe no longer depends on literary games with mirrors, but becomes in 1930s France an integral element in accounts representing the autonomous voices of formerly silenced exotic subjects. My conclusions will centre on the implications of these initial French stages of what has now come to be known as the 'Empire Writing Back'. The 1930s saw the growth of a Black culture rooted in Paris whose importance can be seen in a series of journals and reviews set up in that decade.[12] Far from being simply the creator of mythical universes elsewhere, France found itself to be the centre of a mythical universe and, for many Africans and Caribbeans, a stage in a journey of apprenticeship or even initiation. A novel in which these aspects are particularly apparent is the Senegalese author Ousmane Socé's *Mirages de Paris*. Inspired by and structured around a journey from Africa to Europe, it is an account of the protagonist Fara's stay in Paris during the *Exposition coloniale*.[13] The text focuses on the processes of recuperation of the exotic, considering how the trappings of empire – from the imposition of town planning right down to pencils, exercise books and women's shoes – are radically other for the Senegalese child for whom Paris becomes a longed for 'El Dorado': 'a dangerous love of exoticism was taking shape in his youthful conscience, already inclined to believing in gilded illusions' (Socé 1964: 15).

For the French reader, the adult Fara's journey from Africa entails distinct defamiliarisation, as it depends on the traditional devices of the travel narrative to describe France itself: demonization of white characters; use of catalogue of exotic-sounding names – 'Angoulême ... Poitiers ... Tours ... Blois ... Orléans ...' (Socé 1964: 27) – to give an impression of space crossed; and disappointment at the moment of arrival. However, Socé does not simply replicate or reverse these aspects of the European text. His work is a critique of the superficiality of literary exotic, a superficiality which emerges in particular in descriptions of the *Exposition* itself: 'He walked along the main avenue of the French Colonies. On the right were Martinique, Réunion and Guadeloupe, conjuring up images of these islands according to the classical features which literature grants them' (Socé 1964: 35). The meaning of the 'mirages' of the title is, therefore, double-edged, for it refers not only to Fara's expectations of Europe but also to France's projection of elsewhere. The protagonist's disappointment at slippage between the imagined and the discovered is accentuated by his growing awareness of metropolitan ignorance of cultures outwith Europe: one character asks if Dakar is the capital of Madagascar (Socé 1964: 41), colonial reporters and lecturers are cast as 'manufacturers of exoticism' (Socé 1964: 66), in a conversation over dinner with the parents of his would-be fiancé Fara describes in detail the mechanisms of colonial exoticism:

> He spoke about the French ignorance of Africans. On the whole, their friends in Africa only talked about the Africans' little failings and their funny actions, and they dwelt on these at length and turned them into dominant character traits.
>
> Cinema and literature come to the rescue and produce preconceived effects with 'exoticism' and 'documentation'. As a result, those Europeans who thought they knew Africans well were those who in fact knew them the least.
>
> The paradoxical result was that a Frenchman faced with an African thought he was dealing with a big child whilst the African thought he was in the presence of a big white child (Socé 1964: 90–91).

Fara's failure to fit in to Parisian society – and his parallel inability to return to Senegal – result in his ultimate death, with the tragedy of his suicide becoming the protagonist's only means of freeing himself from exile. The apparent pessimism of this text, however, can be attenuated and even be seen to conceal traces of a more positive model of meetings of cultural differences when read in the light of contemporary French texts offering a similar analysis of and a similar challenge to the mechanisms of exoticism.

Michel Leiris's *L'Afrique fantôme* falls into this category, and a contrapuntal reading of this text together with Socé's would form a substantial paper in its own right, with the contradictory vectors of the two authors' journeys illuminating each other. For the purposes of this article, however, *L'Afrique fantôme* can only be referred to as a concluding illustration of the complex understanding of 1930s exoticism this study has begun to outline, as a means of pulling together a number of strands.[14] Leiris's account of the Dakar to Djibouti ethnographic expedition, the principal aim of which was the collection of artefacts for the Musée de l'Homme, is problematic because of the dependence of its narrative on repeated acts of salvage, recuperation or theft.[15] There is a slippage, however, between such description of the institutional practice of 1930s ethnography and Leiris's personal exploration of the failings of colonial exoticism. Leiris eschews accounts of landscape or specific scenes and seems to prefer everyday, sedentary situations – such as transcribing oral narratives in a railway depot – to the progress of travel. In his own terms: 'It is a major war against the picturesque, a laughing in the face of exoticism' (Leiris 1934: 89). In *Mirages de Paris*, Fara suffers from the denial of coevalness: both his own dreams of Parisian progress and his reception in the French capital relegate him to an imaginary past on which the primitivist overtones of colonial exoticism can depend. Repeatedly in his African journey, Leiris also finds traces of such denial – not only in the expectations of the Western traveller, but also in the expedient African response to such touristic expectations: at one point, the narrator decries the artificiality of exchanges and claims that the only link between him and Dogon informants is 'a shared duplicity' (Leiris 1934: 131).

What is apparent in both of these texts – even in their titles alone – is their authors' wariness about the phantasmagoric versions of elsewhere which can emerge from an exoticism founded on an earlier tradition of recurrent tropes and stereotypes. Socé's text emphasizes, however, the reciprocity of the encounter represented by exoticism, and his exoticisation of metropolitan France is echoed by Leiris's own emphasis, in a preparatory article for the Mission Dakar-Djibouti, on the need for the traveller to be aware of his status as the other's other (Leiris 1992a: 34). This is one of contemporary paradoxes of Leiris's ethnographic text, for any academic aspirations to objectivity are eclipsed by an overwhelming sense of subjectivity: 'writing subjectively, I add to the value of my account' (Leiris 1934: 263). The texts of Leiris and Socé both mark the demolition of a certain variety of exoticism dependent on superficial differences of climate, pigmentation and landscape; in their exploration of the profoundly problematic nature of journeys between cultures, they endeavour to point to a new understanding of exoticism which is focused on sustained consideration of more radical differences between cultures.

What has emerged from these beginnings of a contrapuntal reading of two 1930s travel texts are the foundations of a new understanding of the concept of exoticism. The term 'exotic' is recovered as a linguistic shifter, no longer describing a restricted series of fixed locales and a bank of often jaded images; the notion of exoticism becomes dependent on reflexivity and reciprocity and develops into a potential tool for considerations of intercultural contact and of one of the principal modes of such contact: travel itself. With this understanding of exoticism as a form of interaction or exchange, there is a further shift from the notion's pejorative overtones of cliché and control to a potentially more complex understanding of the interaction between individual and place. There is an emphasis on experience and in particular on the interplay between the real and the imaginary inherent in meetings with radical otherness. Exoticism is salvaged and reasserted not simply as a literary theme or device, but also as a means of reading and understanding texts; it is no longer exclusively a non-systematic marker of imperial displays of power, but becomes instead a means of exploring such displays and the context from which they emerged.

NOTES

1. For a discussion of Williams's notion of the 'structure of feeling', see O'Connor 1989: 83–85, and Williams 1979: 156–65.
2. On this subject, see Moura 1998a: 37.
3. For a discussion of this colonial critique of exoticism, see Moura 1998b: 112–19.
4. For an analysis of the context and subsequent implications of Huysmans's reflections of travel, see Przybos 1988.
5. On the *Croisière Jaune*, see Baldensperger 1981 and Le Fèvre 1990.
6. For a full discussion of Morand and the ideological/aesthetic implications of his analysis of interwar travel, see Thibault 1992.
7. On the implications of the Popular Front for leisure and tourism, see Bodin and Touchard 1972: 136–45, Jackson 1989, Jackson 1988: 131–38, and Lavenir 1999: 337–61. As Eugen Weber makes clear in his study of fin-de-siècle France, popular aspirations to paid holidays – and opposition to such aspirations – emerged in the late nineteenth century (Weber 1986: 190–94). 1936 represents, therefore, more a symbolic stage in the democratization of travel than an actual turning point. Most travellers benefiting from the Popular Front's paid holidays stayed relatively close to home as 'the first paid holidays represented less a "discovery of France" than a "*retour au pays*"' (Jackson 1989: 236).
8. On anti-tourism, see Buzard 1993 and Urbain 1993.
9. For a discussion of Simenon's *Touriste de bananes*, see Faessel 1997.
10. For a consideration of uses of travel in Céline's *Voyage*, see Loselle 1997: 127–57.
11. For a fuller consideration of Michaux's travel accounts and their implications for contemporary 1930s exoticism, see Alexandre 1995, Broome 1985, and Thibault, 1990.
12. On the role of the journey to and stay in Paris as a key element in the emergence of the francophone literatures of Africa and the Caribbean, see Fonkoua 1998 and Jack 1996.
13. Socé's novel has received little critical attention. See, however, Joppa 1970 and Ní Loingsigh 1998.
14. For a fuller account of Leiris's attitude to conventional exoticism, see Pierrot 1986.
15. For recent readings of Leiris's account which consider the inherent contradictions of 'salvage ethnography', see Larson 1997 and Shelton 1995.

Bibliography

Ageron, C.-R., 'L'Exposition coloniale de 1931. Mythe républicain ou mythe impérial?', in *Les Lieux de Memoire*, Vol. I, ed. P. Nora. Paris, 1997: 493–515.
Alexander, M. S. and Graham, H., eds. *The French and Spanish Popular Fronts. Comparative Perspectives.* Cambridge, 1989.
Alexandre, D., 'Henri Michaux, le barbare', *Revue d'Histoire Littéraire de la France* vol. 95, no. 2 (1995): 199–217.
Ashcroft, B., Griffiths, G. and Tiffin, H., eds. *Key Concepts in Post-Colonial Studies.* London, 1998.
Baldensperger, D., 'Citroën lance la Croisière Jaune', *Historia* vol. 413 (1981): 93–101.
Barkan, E. and Bush, R., eds. *Prehistories of the Future. The Primitivist Project and the Culture of Modernism.* Stanford, 1995.
Bodin, L. and Touchard, J., *Front Populaire, 1936.* Paris, 1972.
Bongie, C., *Exotic Memories. Literature, Colonialism and the Fin de Siècle.* Stanford, 1991.
Broome, P., 'Henri Michaux and Travel: from outer space to inner space', *French Studies* vol. 39 (1985): 285–97.
Buzard, J., *The Beaten Track: European Tourism, Literature and the Ways to Culture.* Oxford, 1993.
Cadilhac, P.-É., 'Promenade à travers les cinq continents', *L'Illustration*, 23 May 1931, 73–76.
Clifford, J., *Predicament of Culture.* Cambridge, Massachusetts, 1988.
Constantin-Weyer, M., *Le Flâneur sous la tente.* Paris, 1935.
Faessel, S., 'Simenon, Gary: deux lectures du mythe de Tahiti. *Touriste de bananes* et *La Tête coupable*', *Travaux de littérature* vol. 10 (1997): 379–95.
Fonkoua, R., 'Le "voyage à l'envers". Essai sur le discours des voyageurs nègres en France', in *Les Discours de voyages.* Paris, 1998: 117–45.
Gide, A., *Journal, 1889–1939.* Paris, 1951.
Girardet, R., *L'Idée coloniale en France de 1871 à 1962.* Paris, 1972.
Huysmans, J.-K., *À Rebours.* Paris, 1978.
Jack, B., '"Mirages de Paris": Paris in Francophone Writing', in *Parisian Fields*, ed. M. Sheringham. London 1996: 150–61.
Jackson, J., '"Le temps des loisirs": popular tourism and mass leisure in the vision of the Front Populaire', in *The French and Spanish Popular Fronts. Comparative Perspectives*, eds. M. S. Alexander and H. Graham. Cambridge, 1989: 226–39.
———, *The Popular Front in France: defending democracy, 1934–38.* Cambridge, 1988.
Joppa, F., 'Situation de *Mirages de Paris* d'Ousmane Socé dans le roman néo-africain', *Présence Francophone* vol. 1 (1970): 219–32.
Larson, R., 'Ethnography, Thievery and Cultural Identity: a rereading of Michel Leiris's *L'Afrique fantôme*', *P.M.L.A.* vol. 112 (1997): 229–42.
Lavenir, C. B., *La Roue et le Stylo. Comment nous sommes devenus touristes.* Paris, 1999.
Lebel, R., *Histoire de la Littérature Coloniale en France.* Paris, 1931.
Lefèvre, F., 'Une heure avec [Paul Morand]', *Carnets de l'exotisme* vol. 10 (1992): 79–80. [First published in *La Nouvelle Revue française*, 1924].
Le Fèvre, G., *La Croisière Jaune – expédition Citroën Centre-Asie Haardt-Audouin-Dubreuil.* Paris, 1990.
Leiris, M., *L'Afrique fantôme.* Paris, 1934.
———, 'L'Œil de l'ethnographe (À propos de la Mission Dakar-Djibouti)', in (1992), 26–34.
———, *Zébrage.* Paris, 1992.

Loselle, A., *History's Double. Cultural Tourism in Twentieth-Century French Writing*. New York, 1997.
Michaux, H., *Ecuador*. Paris, 1929.
———, *Un Barbare en Asie*. Paris, 1933.
Mesnard, J., ed. *Les Récits de voyage*. Paris, 1986.
Morand, P., *Éloge du repos*. Paris, 1996. [First published as *Apprendre à se reposer* Paris, 1937].
———, *Flèche d'Orient*. Paris, 1932.
———, *Le Voyage*. Monaco, 1994. [Originally published 1927].
Moura, J.-M., *La Littérature des lointains. Histoire de l'exotisme européen au XXe siècle*. Paris: 1998a.
———, *L'Europe littéraire et l'ailleurs*. Paris, 1998b.
Ní Loingsigh, A., 'Exil et perception du temps chez Tilli et Socé', *A.S.C.A.L.F. Bulletin* vols. 16–17 (1998): 3–21.
Nora, P., ed. *Les Lieux de mémoire*. 3 vols, Paris, 1997.
Norindr, P., *Phantasmatic Indochina. French Colonial Ideology in Architecture, Film and Literature*. Durham and London, 1996.
O'Connor, A., *Raymond Williams. Writing, Culture, Politics*. Oxford, 1989.
Pierrot, J., '*L'Afrique fantôme* de Michel Leiris ou le voyage du poète de l'ethnographe', in *Les Récits de voyage*, ed. J. Mesnard. Paris, 1986: 189–241.
Przybos, J., 'Voyage du pessimisme et pessimisme du voyage', *Romantisme* vol. 61, (1988): 67–74.
Ramal-Cals, J., 'Souvenir de l'Exposition Coloniale', *Les Œuvres libres*, vol. 126, (1931): 7–22.
Said, E., *Culture and Imperialism*. London, 1993.
Saint-Pol-Roux., *Vitesse*. Limoges, 1973. [Written 1932–34].
Sartre, J.-P., *Situations II*. Paris, 1948.
———, 'D'une Chine à l'Autre', in *Situations V*. Paris, 1964, 7–24.
Schwartz, V., *Spectacular Realities. Early Mass Culture in Fin-de-Siècle Paris*. Berkeley, 1998.
Segalen, V., *Essai sur l'exotisme*. Paris, 1986. [Written 1904–1918].
Shelton, M.-D., 'Primitive Self. Colonial impulses in Michel Leiris's *L'Afrique fantôme*', in Barkan and Bush (1995), 326–38.
Simenon, G., *Touriste de bananes*. Paris, 1938.
———, *À la Recherche de l'homme nu*. Paris, 1976.
Socé, O., *Mirages de Paris*. Paris, 1964. [Originally published 1935].
Thibault, B., '"Voyager contre": la question de l'exotisme dans les journaux de voyage d'Henri Michaux', *The French Review* vol. 63 (1990): 485–91.
———, *L'Allure de Morand. Du Modernisme au Pétainisme*. Birmingham, Alabama, 1992.
Urbain, J.-D., *L'Idiot du voyage*. Paris, 1993.
Wasserman, R., 'Re-inventing The New World: Cooper and Alencar', *Comparative Literature*, vol. 36, no. 2 (1984): 130–45.
Weber, E., *France Fin de Siècle*. Cambridge, Massachusetts, 1986.
———, *The Hollow Years. France in the 1930s*. London, 1995.
Williams, R., *The Country and the City*. London, 1985.
———, *Politics and Letters*. London, 1979.

PART 2

JOURNEYS IN EUROPE

Chapter 3

TRAVEL AND AUTOBIOGRAPHY
GIOVANNI COMISSO'S MEMORIES OF THE WAR

Derek Duncan

Giovanni Comisso (1895–1969) was one of the numerous prominent Italian writers of the 1930s who wrote extensively about travel and place. Major literary figures as diverse as Emilio Cecchi, Alberto Moravia, Corrado Alvaro, and Carlo Emilio Gadda contributed to a substantial body of travel writing that accumulated as the decade advanced. They travelled extensively both in Italy and abroad, most commonly writing articles for newspapers or magazines which would subsequently be edited and published together as a travel journal. It is generally accepted that the intensity of interest in foreign locations had been encouraged by the fascist regime as part of a drive to foster an imperialist spirit in the Italian people and produce a population more readily disposed to the colonialist project. This promotion of the exotic went hand in hand with the desire to instil in Italians a stronger sense of national identity. Domestic travel writing was one means of encouraging Italians to develop a securer sense of their native land by making it more familiar, and creating a point of identification with other Italians in disparate corners of the peninsula. A similar interest in place, both foreign and domestic, is evinced in other forms of cultural production at that time – novels, magazines, school-textbooks, films, newsreels, photography, and advertizing all enhanced the Italian nation's sense of place. In some respects, this creative work paralleled the activity of government statisticians of the period whose aim was to use the information they acquired to map the nation in a project that combined the search for knowledge and the production of a national identity (Tomasello 1984; Ipsen 1996).

At the upper end of the literary scale, the Italy that was invoked through travel writing was utopian. The recreation of the glorious Italian past, the eulogizing of Italy's great men, and the unstinting praise of the nation and national character all, by implication at least, lauded the regime. Little direct mention was ever made of politics, let alone fascism, yet such writing was saturated with its values. Writers expressed their support for the regime indirectly through the places they chose to visit, and the details they used to describe them. They also shared a common discursive framework, or repertoire of imagery, in which to situate their perceptions. However much the experience of travel might have varied in its details, the overall intention of the writer/traveller was to stabilize and consolidate the meaning of Italy. On a more personal level, their work also mapped out a version of subjectivity that appeared authoritatively and coherently male (Burdett 1999: 178–206).

It is perhaps difficult to argue, however, that the discursive strategies of travel writers in Fascist Italy were in themselves unique. Their idealization of the nation reflects the more general tendency of travel writing to create a sense of place through projecting pre-existing values onto specific sites, and a sense of identity for the writer/traveller through consolidating a particular relationship with place. This tendency has contributed much to its critical devaluation, and paradoxically, to its attraction. For the theoretically minded, the appeal of travel writing seems to be that its status as 'discourse' is so clearly telegraphed. To the theorist of travel writing nothing is more redundant than the notion that these texts might actually have a referent in the real world that in some arcane way could influence the content of what is written. Place assumes meaning through the various ways in which it is rendered intelligible, a precocious intelligibility that necessarily precedes its articulation. Travel writing is about cultural perception in the broadest sense yet its most acute aperçus are indirect, offering insight into what is to be found at home, in the text's culture of origin rather than away, in the terrain of discovery. Authors are clearly compromised by this state of affairs. Stripped of all authority they are the mere mouthpieces for the commonplace, scriveners of the conventional and rightly perhaps their work is afforded scant literary value. Yet their labour does not simply betoken the passive reinscription of the already known, for as Foucault also argued discourse is not separable from power. The ways in which the world is made intelligible have concrete and material, if not necessarily predictable, effects. The act of putting place into discourse is already expressive of a hierarchical relationship of cultural authority. This question of authority has been most insistently explored in relation to the kind of travel writing that can be encompassed by the dual projects of Western imperialism and Western colonization. The vastness and diversity of these enterprises seem to find some homogeneity of expression in the kind of diverse discursive mappings that accompanied more brutal acts of territorial and economic conquest to the extent that they are now sometimes viewed as the most emblematic instances of colonial authority rather than simply as relatively innocuous by-products. Indeed the producers of such texts are no longer seen as the transmitters of tired clichés, but are transformed into the most ardent purveyors of imperialist values. The conflation of a certain type of masculinity with the rigours of Empire building ensures in addition that individual male travel writers have come to bear a special burden of representation.

Such a parodically strong reading of travel texts underlines the risks in overlooking specificities of both texts and contexts, and the resultant homogenization of important differences of period, place, subjectivity, and genre. David Spurr points to the initial similarities between, and stakes involved in, writing and colonizing: 'The problem of the colonizer is in some sense the problem of the writer: in the face of what may appear as a vast cultural and geographical blankness, colonization is a form of self-inscription onto the lives of a people who are conceived of as an extension of the landscape. For the colonizer as for the writer, it becomes a question of establishing authority through the demarcation of identity and difference' (1993: 7). How such authority is established and maintained is a hazardous and unpredictable enterprise, for its success is never assured. Mary Louise Pratt's concept of the 'contact zone', which has become fundamental to recent thinking on colonialism, moves toward a recognition that the colonial encounter is always, albeit unevenly, negotiated (Pratt: 1992). It is not simply about the imposition of force although this is clearly its prime effect. Travel writing is a nodal site of colonialist discourse, yet it needs to be considered as a point of reception as much as one of propagation. To pursue the idea that the text is a site of discursive reception opens up more complicated ways of investigating how its particularities resist as much as underwrite hegemonic modes of thought. This is perhaps particularly the case if travel writing is read as part of an autobiographical project where the writing of place is in fact a displaced mode of self-inscription.

Recent criticism of autobiography has shifted the conventional focus on the autonomous individual to examine the self in its social context as an entity that is created through relationships with other people (Eakin 1999; Miller 1994; Gagnier 1991). The move refers at once to the constitution of identity in the real world, and to its emergence in the autobiographical form where it is constructed through the play of recognition and identification between author and reader (Gilmore 1994: 71). On a textual level, autobiography draws on a variety of genres and styles of writing with the result that it is difficult to argue that it constitutes a genre in its own right. Such an understanding of autobiography usefully opens the way to a re-examination of the autobiographical self in travel writing which is constructed precisely in terms of the fraught negotiation of relations between self and other. Similarly, while critics would tend to agree that travel writing is articulated through a strong set of generic conventions, there is also a consensus that it does not exist in total isolation from other ways of thinking about and representing places. Travel writing intersects with other historically and culturally specific practices that engage with issues of subjectivity and textual production as well as those more visibly focussed on colonialism and the occupation of space.

Sara Mills picks up the question of the links between constructions of identity and travel when she argues for a variegated recognition of the unexpected interplays and strange dependencies between power and resistance as she examines colonialist travel literature from the perspective of gender (Mills 1993). She demonstrates how diverse and contradictory positions of cultural hegemony can become in a context where European women occupy conflicting positions of authority and subordination. She also interrogates the ways in which women participated in the masculinist rhetoric of imperialist domination. Did their own gendered subordination within it result in a more benign, or even contestatory, perspective on the colonial situation? Her inquiry can be extended to investigate further examples of otherness within colonialist discourse. Do differences of class provoke allegiances across lines of racial difference? Do dissident forms of sexuality necessarily disrupt an adherence to imperialist domination? Similar issues can emerge at the level of international politics. For example, while Italy in the 1920s and 30s was attempting to join the ranks of Europe's imperialist nations, justifying its aims through the now familiar rhetorics of racial superiority, the civilizing mission, and demographic need, it was also waging its own quite particular battle of resistance against the British Empire from which it was keen to distinguish itself. Italy was both complicit, and at odds, with the project of European colonization.

However these questions are broached, the fact that they are asked at all is at least a tacit avowal that the parameters of hegemonic discourse may be, in some way, shifted by the subjectivity of those who occupy a structurally dissident position within it. Mills takes issue, however, with critics who have resorted to autobiographical fact as a prism through which to read travel texts (1993: 36–43). While recognizing that such writing seems to demand some kind of acknowledgement of the author and of biography as a means of framing textual interpretation, Mills argues that biographical detail is often deployed as a means of simplifying the subjectivity of the author. Residues of difference are eliminated through anchoring the authorial perspective to an already encoded, and implicitly, wholly transparent position. This approach underestimates the theoretical problems of self-representation, and construction. While Mills is doubtless correct to be suspicious of overly facile gestures of interpretation based on the presumption of autobiographical fact, I would suggest that autobiographical writing and recent reflection on it has much to offer the reader seeking to disentangle the webs of complicity and resistance in a travel text. Autobiography, like travel writing, is not self-evident and many of the questions about cultural authority that are asked of travel writers are also posed to, and by, those who try to convey a sense of their own lives in writing. Like travel literature, autobiography can appear the most codified, static, authoritarian, and masculinist of genres. In its conventional form, it shapes lives according to its own aesthetic criteria. It is not life-like at all. Yet resistance to this textual model is possible even as it is acknowledged. Autobiographical writing allows for the production of resistant subjectivities even as they are compromised by their acquiescence to what is a socially and culturally specific medium. Similarly, the generic constraints of travel writing shape, but do not wholly determine, how place is constructed. Autobiography and travel writing become spatial exercises in the complex elaboration of self-inscription and authority, the cultural mappings of reciprocities and dissonances between self and the world. My contention is quite simply that rather than avoiding the autobiographical dimension of travel writing, one should actively pursue it. If travel writing is read as autobiography, bearing in mind all the hazards that such a procedure entails, a more accurate understanding of how narratives of the self are embedded in narratives of place and of how place provides the parameters for self-inscription might be achieved.

Comisso's work offers rich pickings for those interested in the confluence of travel writing and autobiography. He wrote prolifically throughout the 1930s, publishing novels and collections of short stories as well as several travel journals. In addition, he completed a substantial quantity of other writing that would only be published after the fall of fascism. What this body of writing shares is an undeniable autobiographical imprint that makes rigid genre classification very difficult. Yet critics tormented by the questions of the purity of the genre disagree over how to interpret the apparent overtness of his self-reference. Rosanna Esposito maintains that 'His narrative autobiography is one of the most immediate and transparent amongst twentieth century writers as its literary veneer is reduced to a bare minimum and its narcissism is so obvious as to dispel any doubt over the authenticity of Comisso's self-portrait' (1990: 48). Aurelia Accame Bobbio, however, is less convinced that Comisso's work can be read in this way. Conceding that all his work is 'to some degree autobiographical' (1973: 5), she notes that Comisso shunned the direct transcription of life into art. For Accame Bobbio, this aversion led almost to the 'projection onto the page of a life that had not been led' (1973: 9). Her position is close to that of Gilbert Bosetti, in an article comparing Comisso with Gide, who contends that autobiography serves to mask as much as reveal the author, and makes an explicit link between Comisso's narrative strategies of concealment and the repressive climate of fascism in which he wrote (1983: 216). Bosetti's suggestion is appealing for it resists the temptation to pathologize Comisso's generous, yet also repetitive and sometimes random, inclusion of incidents apparently drawn from his own life. Instead, he allows it to be understood as a resource or tactic of resistance to prevailing narratives of identity. Comisso's own comment that 'Narrating life is like trying to depict the constant flight of light itself' (Naldini 1985: 135) points to an aesthetic of the autobiographical that cannot commit to direct representation, that is grounded in the sense of the impossibility of restoring an always fleeting, and already past, moment.

Although nowadays Comisso has none of the cultural prestige of Gide, Lorca, or even Robert Byron, he was hugely successful and well-known as a writer in Italy in the 1930s. Like them, he was a homosexual who travelled extensively in politically fraught times. He had participated in the tail end of the First World War before becoming involved in D'Annunzio's occupation of Fiume. He was, however, far more impressed by the sensualism of D'Annunzio's assistant Guido Keller under whose influence he cultivated a pastoral eroticism that would colour much of his later work. He began his career as a travel journalist in 1928 and, for the next few years, travelled extensively in North Africa and Europe (including Italy itself). Probably his most significant trip was the one he made at the end of 1929 to China and Japan via Eritrea, India and Ceylon. His reports from the East were published in the pro-fascist Milanese newspaper, *Il corriere della sera*, and, in slightly amended form, as the volume *Cina-Giappone* [China-Japan] in 1932. Interest in his work no doubt increased as a result of the nomination of Galeazzo Ciano, Mussolini's son-in-law, to the position of Italian ambassador in Shanghai. After his return, he invested his money in a farm outside his native Treviso in a place called Zero Branco. Following some extensive renovations to the property, he set up home there in the company of Bruno, the son of a fisherman from Chioggia. Recently released from prison where he had become an adept of the 'strange caresses' of his fellow inmates, Bruno had willingly repaired to Zero allegedly nostalgic for the 'caresses in the darkness of his cell' (Naldini 1985: 117).

Despite having become something of a home-body, Comisso still travelled widely in Italy and a collection of his Italian writings came out in 1937 as *L'Italiano errante per l'Italia* [The Italian Wandering in Italy], which Comisso described as 'a discovery of the hidden Italy' (Naldini 1985: 133).[1] In the same year he was commissioned to report from Ethiopia after the declaration of Empire, but traumatized by the experience was unable to write very much about it. His final trip before war broke out was to Libya at the invitation of the proconsul, the leading fascist Italo Balbo, himself renowned as a very modern traveller having led a squadron of flying boats over the Atlantic to Chicago in 1933.

Notwithstanding his homosexuality, in many respects, Comisso stood at the heart of fascism. His introduction to the biography of his mother's brother, Tomasso Salsa, in which he praised the exploits and the daring of this turn of the century colonial pioneer, appears to celebrate Italy's imperial ambition (Canevari and Comisso 1935). Yet his support could be ambivalent. The shocking racism of remarks he made about the indigenous inhabitants of the new Empire in 1937 go hand in hand with expressions of disdain for the venal ambition of the colonial project and of the colonizers themselves (Comisso 1951: 244-63). Works such as *Cina-Giappone* can easily be accommodated within the traditional discourse of Western orientalism (Duncan 2002), but Comisso himself was entirely conscious of their ideological limitations, and finally came to reject the cynical manipulation of his talents. In 1938, Leo Longanesi, the editor of the successful cultural magazine, *Omnibus*, had offered him the chance to go to Spain as a travel correspondent, but Comisso rejected the proposal. He told Longanesi he could no longer bring himself to write 'articles totally at odds with my own impressions…If I could write them as I saw fit my job would be easier, but I'm sure that what I had to do would be pointless and tiresome, tiresome for you too as you'd have to send the articles back to me because I'm not allowed to say this, and can't say that' (Naldini 1985: 138). Comisso also poured scorn on *Omnibus*'s bourgeois readership, its conventional tastes and hollow intellectual pretensions. He expressed similar reservations in an unpublished diary two years later, where he reflected bitterly on his involvement with *Il corriere della sera*: 'This was a newspaper that had lots of resources but no taste and it was vile of me to agree to adapt my own style to theirs. I was writing for *Il corriere della sera*. The handbook of the average middle class Italian, it was there I published the articles that later came out as *Cina-Giappone*, a book I loath. When I returned as a reaction to my literary cowardice I wrote *Gioco d'infanzia* [Childhood Game] and *Amori d'Oriente* [Loves of the Orient] completely free and opposed to the taste of that newspaper's readers; as yet I haven't been able to publish them'

(Naldini 1989: 21, also Comisso 1951: 197). Here, Comisso quite explicitly attributes a compensatory and contestatory role to his unpublished manuscripts, alluding also to the problems of censorship he encountered throughout the 1930s. *Amori d'Oriente* would appeared in 1948 while *Gioco d'infanzia* was not in fact published until 1965 and even then in a much abridged version. The fairly explicit sexual content (both homo- and heterosexual) is an obvious reason. Yet it was not just sex that had caused Comisso's work to be censored in the 1930s, but principally his anti-militarism. His refusal to glorify what he saw as brute carnage led to a series of conflicts throughout the decade in which Mussolini was preparing the nation for military success, creating a sense of national identity through the deification of Italy's war dead and advocating the figure of the warrior hero as the standard for masculine identity (Gentile 1993; Spackman 1996). Comisso's unfashionable pacifism was, as will become apparent, inseparable from his erotic imagination.

In 1935 Comisso succeeded in publishing *Avventure terrene* [Earthly Adventures], a collection of short stories, after a series of skirmishes with the fascist censor (Comisso 1951: 220). Even after the less acceptable elements had been excised, what remained was a representation of Italy and its recent past that far exceeded fascist notions of propriety. These are stories of murder, alcoholism, wife beating, visits to lunatic asylums, and homosexuality. Set mostly in the countryside, these largely autobiographical pieces make no direct mention of fascism, yet they are clearly silent indictments of the state of the nation. Possibly the most interesting story is 'Viaggio in Toscana' ['Journey to Tuscany'] in which Comisso recounts a meeting with Guido Keller his mentor in Fiume. Keller's decline is the embodied evidence of the nation's decay since the heady days in Dalmatia. Intriguingly, the past's allure is fleetingly recaptured through the body of a young peasant lad they meet in an inn: 'We couldn't help ourselves from stretching out our arms, grabbing him by the waist and squeezing him, fighting over who should kiss him. We were intoxicated as though we had rediscovered in him something of our lost youth' (1937: 93). I would juxtapose this fascinated and nostalgic reading of the boy's bodily text with a excerpt from another of the stories, 'Tempi di scuola' [School Days], in which the narrator remembers how the contemplation of his school atlas allowed him to escape the tedium of Latin grammar lessons (1937: 113]. This incident is in fact recounted elsewhere in Comisso's work in somewhat more explicit terms in which the atlas very handily acts as cover for episodes of mutual masturbation with his schoolboy neighbour (1987: 147, Naldini 1985: 8). What connects both episodes is the metonymic link between memory, homosexuality and place. The privileging in autobiography of metonymy over the more commonly deployed trope of metaphor is commented on by Leigh Gilmore (1994: 69). Her contention is that while metaphor solidifies notions of identity through an emphasis on sameness, metonymic structures of autobiographical narrative display an identity in the making. Comisso's identity then might be said to emerge in the connections he forges from apparently disparate elements, a set of connections that do not allow the reader to pin him down on the basis of irrefutable fact, and that will be employed in turn to displace the fascist discourse of nationalism.

In *L'Italiano errante per l'Italia* (1937), Comisso pieces together a map of 'his' Italy. The book consists of a set of travel vignettes written over a period of almost ten years, yet assembled in such a way as to imply they are scenes from a single journey. Comisso begins in his native Veneto, crosses to Genoa on the west coast, before travelling to Sardinia, the southern mainland and Sicily, then finally returning to the north east. In the course of his travels, he visits practically none of the sights familiar from other travel accounts of the period.[2] Instead of being described as a modern fascist utopia, Italy assumes the contours of a pastoral fantasy in which the writer's own sense of identity is happily obliterated. For example, the charm of the boys of Naples is such that 'Gradually we abandon our own sense of self in imitation of them, sure of the state of perfection they'd reached' (Comisso 1937: 69).

Comisso's Italy is sparsely populated and most of his attention is focussed on the creation of a bucolic and timeless haven. The isolation and novelty of Sardinia particularly lends itself to the excesses of his imagination. He fancies that the island has just risen from the 'sea's womb', a world in which 'pure, untamed, sublime ecstasy still exists.' He surrenders to the Sardinian landscape as he would to an 'ozio musicale' [musical idleness], in a move that allows him to flee the 'costed miseries' (Comisso 1937: 53) of everyday life. The motif is picked up again in the course of a visit to the Villa Adriana that in a more committed writer might have led to some contemplation of imperial grandeur, if not luxuriance, at a time when Empire was to the forefront of the fascist mind. Comisso, however, stresses the idyllic nature of the setting, remarking in passing that 'The Emperor Hadrian is dead, but beside this villa, there stands a shepherd idle as he. There is nothing to be sought elsewhere' (1937: 55–56).[3] The networks of imagery constructed by Comisso throughout his work undercut the fascist idea of Italy in other ways. The description of Naples in *L'Italiano errante per l'Italia* that appears simply to highlight the life and vitality of the city – 'The streets appear beyond measure, full of people'; ' The crowd is immense, confusing' (1937: 63, 64) – echo with the more disturbing resonances of the cities of the East. China's 'cities that are beyond measure' (1951: 189) typify the menacing formlessness and indifference to boundary that unsettles the traveller. What Comisso saw at the Villa Adriana he had already seen in China. Empires, he seems to intuit, are not destined to endure; neither are Emperors: 'The Emperor and his princes are dead, the foreigner has taken their place' (1932: 116). The foreigner may have replaced the Emperor in China, yet it is the idle shepherd that straddles time in Italy.

The notion of 'idleness' recurs throughout Comisso's tour of Italy, and indeed throughout his work as a whole, and its association with the figure of the shepherd boy creates a pattern of meaning that seems to unite, but also breach the boundaries of both time and place. In the autobiographical journal, *Le mie stagioni* [My seasons], Comisso recalls his first meeting with the painter Filippo de Pisis in 1922: 'I recited some of my little prose poems to him; they were about summer rivers and naked shepherds taking their oxen to water' (1951: 33). De Pisis was obviously charmed for the two would become great friends. Some thirty years later in *Approdo in Grecia* [Landing in Greece], Comisso claims to have found the idyllic pastoral landscape of his imagination, and indeed feels himself to be the 'wandering shepherd' (Comisso 1991: 26). His trip concludes with the confirming sight of 'a young shepherd boy who was standing on a hillock with his herd grazing around him, he blew us a kiss and then followed us for a long stretch waving his hand' (1991: 80–81). His Arcadian fantasy is, however, given a more political slant because of its association with the period spent with D'Annunzio and Keller in Fiume which Comisso experienced with an 'idle spirit' (1951: 48). It finds expression in the deeply right-wing, anti-bourgeois political programme he invents with Keller which, amongst other things, envisaged 'a nation of shepherds, peasants, seafarers, artisans and artists' (1951: 81). It would be difficult to argue that Comisso had a concrete political agenda of any sort. At most, it is expressed as an ill-defined resistance to conventional standards and expectations. In *Gioco d'infanzia* Alberto, the main protagonist, thinks back on his adolescence as a time of 'sublime idleness'. Yet society's repression of these 'moments of sublime idleness' leads Alberto to the conclusion that perhaps memory itself is a tool 'for resistance in a world grown sad because of the persecution of laws, work and man-made social systems' (1987: 162). Memory as a possible means of resistance recurs throughout Comisso's work and finds echoes in his anti-militarism and homosexuality.

In *L'Italiano errante per l'Italia* there is little sense of what the we might imagine 1930s Italy to have been like. The pastoral framing seems to obliterate history, yet history has not been expunged. Comisso's approach to Sardinia is mediated by the memory of the Sardinian soldiers he knew during the First World War and of the perfumed sweets they would bring back from their periods of leave: 'I didn't know anything else about Sardinia: this island was drawing me back, the songs, sweets, faces of my Sardinian soldiers with the passing of time ended up belonging to a world that was lofty, isolated and unreachable' (1937: 52). This lyrical evocation of the soldiers is juxtaposed with much harsher reminiscences in the first and final chapters of the collection named after the places he visits. Asolo and Gorizia are both located in the north east of Italy, Comisso's home region, where he himself endured the experience of trench warfare. In the opening chapter, 'Asolo', he begins with a conventional description of the medieval town and its past grandeur. He is interrupted and repulsed, however, by the arrival of a group of cyclists 'covered in dust, sweat and smelling like a regiment on the march' (1937: 8). From this point on, memories of the war flood his mind: 'Forgotten faces, phrases, smells and tastes all came back to me: slices of life like torn up pieces of a letter each containing a word of deep emotion; yet the letter can barely be put back together' (1937: 9). The chapter concludes with this stifled recollection that only finds articulate expression at the volume's conclusion.

The final chapter sees him in Gorizia. It is 1936, the year Empire was declared, and the rustic idyll of the intervening chapters has vanished: 'I was going back to woods and countryside that I'd seen destroyed by artillery fire, the earth was red and broken' (1937: 155). Yet, he realizes that it is only in his memory that the horror of war lives on : 'Here everything speaks to me and relives for me, but says nothing to those who weren't born when the woods and the land were being destroyed' (1937: 156). His final memory is a lamentation: 'Youth was offered up to death without respite for thirteen months. The blood went home back to the earth' (1937: 159). This vision of the Italian landscape scars irrevocably the bucolic fantasy: 'Like primroses or flowers of the dew I see the colours of the soldiers' flashes on the damp earth: all the yellows, blues, and whites' (1937: 160).

Comisso's image of a wasted meadow stained with the blood and emblems of patriotism indicts the bellicose rhetoric of the Empire. In 1935 he had been saddened that after 17 years of peace soldiers were setting off to war (1951: 220). He mocked the fact that for fascism 'A war had to be all triumph, bliss and free of danger' (1951: 232). His return to Gorizia in 1936 had, however, been erotically motivated for, as he reports in his journal, he had gone to visit Bruno who was completing his military service there. This sparked another memory of a different order:

> Return to this countryside where I lived as a boy. Like being brought back to life. I find the same trees, the hills, the fruit, the same eggs, the same figs, the same apples, bram-

bles; the old people still alive after the war that changed everything; the boys who played with me are fathers now and seem older than me; and those who weren't born then or were children are fathers themselves. And the river Piave, sun drenched and stony welcomed me with the joy of swimming and playing with its waters. And naked boys, sublime on the islands of sand. Oh time! Oh life! What will become of me? (Naldini 1985: 132).

Comisso returns as a ghost to this bucolic fragment of the past, and it is this sense of the past that he attempted to recreate at his new home at Zero Branco. In *La mia casa di campagna* [My House in the Country], his account of his years there, he describes the 'earthly paradise' he discovers with Bruno when they come across a spot on the river where the local peasant boys swim 'completely naked' (Comisso 1984: 47). Both these bathing scenes need to be linked to the memory invoked in *Gioco d'infanzia* where Alberto reflects on the effects of an intense, casual, sexual encounter with a young soldier during the war: 'And for years, even after the war, when he felt the summer coming to an end, he would feel again the desire for that place, for that canal and for those yellowing acacias, the naked soldiers running followed by the joyful dogs, and the dried up river bed; and the unknown man' (1984: 143). Comisso's erotic memory is cathected both to a pastoral landscape and the War, and the collusion of personal fantasy and desire becomes a melancholic statement of political dissidence. His declarations of remembrance are acts of mourning and refutations of the fascist rhetoric of war that promoted a nationalistic cult of death and self-sacrifice that occluded any sense of loss.

In my view, Comisso is one of the few Italian writers of the period to use travel writing implicitly to critique the regime rather than to lend it support. He achieves this by reworking the conventions of other travel writing of the period, choosing for example to visit places that did not underwrite the values of the regime, and by writing about them in ways that put him and them at odds with how fascism wanted Italy and Italians to appear. In a sense, Fascist Italy does not appear in Comisso's work, at least not in the way in which it was envisaged by the regime. As already noted, when Comisso returned from the Far East he purchased a farm outside his native Treviso with the proceeds. Set amidst the Italian countryside, the farm and its landscape remind Comisso of the beauty of Asia – the ash coloured mountains, the cherry trees in flower, the yellow fields of rape seed, the sloping roofs. He concludes: 'the similarities began to convince me that the whole world lies in one square metre, but I felt this also as a new formula for living; without travelling so much, staying put in order to go deeper into myself' (1951: 204; 1984: 13–14). Comisso's claim to depth may appear to set him at odds with those critics for whom discourse is all surface. He did not of course bring the Orient home in any material sense. The fetish of the souvenir was not for him. Fascist censorship prevented Comisso from writing what he wanted about his experience of travel even though it did not exactly silence him. The deployment of colonialist rhetoric had, after all, given him financial security. Yet, what he did achieve was the undermining of the colonialist project through the creation of a network of superficial associations linking place, homosexuality and himself that reinvents Italy as the space of inadvertent resistance to Fascism.

James Duncan and Derek Gregory have argued that the networks of power that travel writing instates should also be seen in terms of 'the play of fantasy and desire, and the possibility of transgression' that inhabit them (1999: 3). Perhaps this is nowhere more necessary than when travel writing, which they also claim to be 'inherently domesticating' (1999: 5), turns its attention directly onto the home. Unlike many travel writers, Comisso is almost obsessively interested in constructing a home for himself in both his writing and his life. Yet, the home he constructs turns out to be entirely foreign to fascist expectation. While it is not uncommon for critics to grant that the 'other' place is inevitably conceived of in terms of the already familiar, it is less usual to allow that this familiarity is already ambivalent, 'unheimlich' in a different register of critical thought. As an imagined and desired place, home is entirely unfamiliar, and in a sense, undomesticated. It is what Comisso had to say about the subjective construction of home in the political context of fascism's imperialist rhetoric that his work is most challenging. It has been said that because of the way Comisso was able to 'disperse the self, he could make the reader forget not only him but fascism too' (Alvaro 1995: v). I would contend that on the contrary the apparent obliteration of fascism and the dispersal of the self are reminders of Giovanni Comisso's covert, yet relentless, resistance to fascism.

Notes

1. An expanded and significantly re-ordered edition was published as *La favorita* in 1945. In the later volume the chapters mentioned above do not open and close the narrative so attenuating the significance attributed to them here.
2. Charles Burdett (2000) discusses a range of these ideal places in terms of Foucault's notion of the 'heterotopia'. Travellers experienced the religious dimension of fascist ideology through contact with sites such as the prison or new town which seem to give physical substance to fascist belief.
3. Comisso's desire to find and indeed construct an 'elsewhere' as antidote to the claustrophobia of life under fascism can usefully be read in terms of Bongie's discussion of the 'exotic' (1991). While Comisso demonstrates characteristic nostalgia for the utopian ideal, he differs from those traveller/writers discussed by Bongie in attempting to recover this exotic elsewhere at home.

Bibliography

Accame Bobbio, A., *Giovanni Comisso*. Milan, 1973.
Alvaro, C., *Itinerario italiano*. Milan, 1995. [Originally published 1941]
Bongie, C., *Exotic Memories: Literature, Colonialism and the Fin de Siècle*. Stanford, 1991.
Bosetti, G., 'Gide e Comisso', in *Giovanni Comisso*. ed. G. Pullini, Florence, 1983, 215–39.
Burdett, C., *Vincenzo Cardarelli and his Contemporaries: Fascist Politics and Literary Culture*. Oxford, 1999.
———, 'Journeys to the *other* spaces of Fascist Italy', *Modern Italy* vol. 5 no. 1 (2000): 7–23.
Canevari, E., and G. Comisso., *Il Generale Tomasso Salsa e le sue campagne coloniali*. Milan, 1935.
Comisso, G., *Cina-Giappone*. Milan, 1932.
———, *Avventure terrene*. Florence, 1935.
———, *Un Italiano errante per l'Italia*. Florence, 1937.
———, *Le mie stagioni*. Treviso, 1951.
———, *Amori d'Oriente*. Milan, 1957. [Originally published 1948]
———, *La mia casa di campagna*. Milan, 1984. [Originally published 1958]
———, *Gioco d'infanzia*. Milan, 1987. [Originally published 1965]
———, *Approdo in Grecia*. Rome, 1991. [Originally published 1954]
Duncan, D., 'The Queerness of Colonial Space: Giovanni Comisso's Travels with Fascism' in *In a Queer Place: Sexualities and Belongings in British and European Context*, eds. K. Chedgzoy, E. Francis and M. Pratt, Aldershot, 2002 (forthcoming).
Duncan, J., and D. Gregory, eds., *Writes of Passage: Reading Travel Writing*. London and New York, 1999.

Eakin, J.P., *How Our Lives Become Stories: Making Selves*. Ithaca and London, 1999.

Esposito, R., *Invito alla lettura di Comisso*. Milan, 1990.

Gagnier, R., *Subjectivities: A History of Self-Representation in Britain, 1832–1920*. Oxford, 1991.

Gentile, E., *Il culto del littorio*. Rome and Bari, 1993.

Gilmore, L., *Autobiographics: A Feminist Theory of Women's Self-Representation*. Ithaca and London, 1994.

Ipsen, C., *Dictating Demography: The Problem of Population in Fascist Italy*. Cambridge, 1996.

Miller, N. K., 'Representing Others: Gender and the Subjects of Autobiography', *differences*, vol. 6 (1994): 1–27.

Mills, S., *Discourses of Difference: An Analysis of Women's Travel Writing and Colonialism*. London, 1993.

Naldini, N., *Vita di Giovanni Comisso*, Turin, 1985.

———, ed. *Giovanni Comisso: Vita nel tempo (lettere 1905–1968)*. Milan, 1989.

Pratt, M.L., *Imperial Eyes: Travel Writing and Transculturation*. London and New York, 1992.

Spackman, B., *Fascist Virilities: Rhetoric, Ideology and Social Fantasy in Italy*. Minneapolis and London, 1996.

Spurr, D., *The Rhetoric of Empire: Colonial Discourse in Journalism, Travel Writing and Imperial Administration*. Durham, N.C., 1993.

Tomasello, G., *La letteratura coloniale italiana dalle avanguardie al fascismo*. Palermo, 1984.

Chapter 4

BRINGING HOME THE TRUTH ABOUT THE REVOLUTION
Spanish Travellers to the Soviet Union in the 1930s

Mayte Gómez

In the early and mid-1930s, before the outbreak of civil war in Spain, the Soviet Union represented to many around the world one of the greatest symbols of political utopia.[1] In 1928, eleven years after the triumph of the Bolshevik revolution and after a postwar period marked by social and economic rebuilding, the revolutionary state opened its doors to the rest of the world. With some of the most renowned intellectuals, writers and artists of the time visiting the Soviet Union, the pilgrimage to the newly organized state became the subject of a large and rich body of political travel writing.

The writing of Western travellers to the Soviet Union in the 1930s has been studied from a number of perspectives. Various scholars have looked at the collective reasons that moved communist and pro-communist intellectuals and artists – the so-called 'fellow-travellers' – to visit the country, analysing the social and political dreams these travellers shared and the common patterns in their intellectual and political behaviour. In a landmark study of these questions, Paul Hollander has suggested that these intellectuals travelled to the Soviet Union and wrote favourably about what they saw because of a previous disenchantment with Western society and a predisposition to see what they wanted to see, that is, their 'selective perception, combined with projection' (1981: 109). According to Hollander, 'the most distinctive trait of a large segment of contemporary Western intellectuals [was] the fluctuation in their attitudes between estrangement and affirmation'(1981: 4).

In 1917 no other European country was so different from and yet so similar to Russia as Spain, if only because both were backward and semi-rural nations weighed down by an oppressive organization of society. Though geographically distant from Russia, Spain was deeply affected by the political events there from 1917 onwards through the 1920s and 1930s. Some recent academic work has shown how national politics in Spain were influenced by the way in which the press and a number of travel books portrayed the Russian revolution and the building of the Soviet Union during such hugely significant periods in Spanish history as 1917, 1931 and 1936-9. Other scholars have studied the content of the early (relatively few) travel books written in the mid-1920s, while some attention has also been given to the political analysis found in the travelogues of well-known travellers such as Ramón J. Sender or Fernando de los Ríos.[2] What follows is an overview of the explosion of travel books about the Soviet Union that took place in Spain between 1928 and 1936. Coming from a country that was very quickly inundated by radical visions of the Bolshevik revolution and by strong currents of what historian Rafael Cruz has called 'rusophobia' and 'rusophilia' (1997: 274), Spanish travellers to the Soviet Union endeavoured to search for ideological balance and political objectivity. In the following pages, I aim to explore how these travellers approached that self-imposed goal, the kind of 'observable reality' they found in the Soviet Union, how they saw themselves as travelling subjects and how they emerged from that exercise relatively unaffected and intact as political subjects.

BETWEEN HEAVEN AND HELL: EARLY SPANISH IMAGES OF RUSSIA AND THE BOOM OF THE TRAVEL BOOK.

At the turn of the twentieth century, Spain was still a rural country where the power of a semi-feudal oligarchy was sustained by an absolute monarchy, and any dreams of a bourgeois revolution remained unrealized. Until 1931 Spaniards had only known two forms of government: either a mockery of parliamentary democracy staged by the political parties of the oligarchy or a military dictatorship. Neither had saved them from suffering the highest levels of poverty and illiteracy in Europe. In a year when the Spanish workers' movement had already failed in its attempt to lead the working class towards a national uprising, the Bolshevik revolution had a tremendous impact in the country. It marked the start of three years of renewed political upheaval that came to be known as the '*trienio bolchevique*', the end of which coincided with the founding of the Communist Party in 1920.

As soon as news of the revolution in Russia filtered through to Spain (mostly via foreign publications), the press became divided into two hostile camps that nurtured utterly incompatible versions of the events (Cruz 1997: 274). The 'news poisoning' (Ruiz 1988: 121) and 'war without mercy' (Cruz 1997: 273) that ensued, lasting over two decades, cannot be overemphasized. The Spanish political establishment (represented by publications like *ABC* and *El Debate*) was happy to welcome the bourgeois-democratic reforms brought about by the first revolutionary wave in February 1917, because they were often interpreted as a 'political mistake' that would benefit Germany in the war (Avilés 1999: 20). As the democratic reforms of February gave way to class struggle in October, however, the conservative press gave free rein to both its disappointment and its fear. Conservative newspapers interpreted the October revolution as the triumph of evil over good, and thus a model for the future that one had to protect oneself against. As far as these publications were concerned, revolution represented nothing less than social chaos (Lazo 1975: 105).

On the other hand, most political groups to the left – anarchists, communists, and radical socialists – believed that the Bolsheviks had provided the rest of the world with a revolutionary model that could be applied universally and that was bound to shake the grounds of 'civilization'. For them, the Bolshevik revolution was a 'new dawn' for humanity, a 'kingdom of light' on earth, a 'redeeming utopia' that was going to save Western civilization from all the evils and wrongdoings of capitalism (Cruz 1997: 287). Although *Solidaridad Obrera*, the official publication of the anarcho-syndicalist wing of the National Confederation of Workers (CNT), was quite cautious in its initial reactions, by the end of the war the entire anarchist union was participating in a 'wave of pro-Bolshevik enthusiasm', in the belief that the Bolsheviks had put into practice the principles of justice and equality of libertarian communism (Forcadell 1978: 263). They were joined by the Communist Party (PCE), whose official publications (*El Comunista*, *La Antorcha*) welcomed the October revolution as the realization of a utopia: the first dictatorship of the proletariat in history.

Caught in between these two radical approaches, the Spanish Socialists (PSOE) – who believed that Spain needed to experience a democratic revolution before it could sustain a proletarian one – welcomed the bourgeois-democratic revolution in February as a 'liberal' uprising against the ancien regime (Araquistáin 1917: 3) but were rather unenthusiastic towards the October events, since they believed Russia was 'mature for democracy' but not for socialism (Huysman 1917: 1). As they watched their dream of a democratic Russia slip away, their publications (most importantly, *El Socialista*) chose to keep a dignified silence until the end of the European conflict.

The publication of a few titles on Russia between 1917 and 1920 did very little to break through this radical but misinformed perception, as they were either translations of foreign titles or original Spanish titles documented from foreign sources.[3] Only three books published between 1921 and 1925 – Fernando de los Ríos' *Mi viaje a la Rusia sovietista* [My Journey to Soviet Russia] (1921), Isidoro Acevedo's *Impresiones de un viaje a Rusia* [Impressions of a Journey to Russia] (1923), and Ángel Pestaña's *Setenta días en Rusia. Lo que yo vi* [Seventy Days in Russia. What I Saw] (1925) – were written by political leaders who travelled to the country personally. Rather than classic travel books, these three were *'informe-relatos'* (Cruz 1987: 91), a mixture of political report and travel writing dealing first with the immediate effects of the Bolshevik revolution and later with the creation of the Soviet Union and the Communist International. The publication of these landmark books was followed by a few other titles in the next two years, the most influential of which was *La nueva Rusia* [The New Russia], written by Socialist leader Julio Álvarez del Vayo in 1926.

After 1928 and until the outbreak of civil war in Spain in 1936, as the Soviet Union opened its doors to foreign travellers and as the political climate in Spain became more open to writing of a political kind, many more Spaniards travelled to the Soviet Union: writers, poets, journalists, teachers, business people, tourists, even priests. The result of these journeys en masse was a true explosion of travel books[4] that very often offered a rather superficial description of life or politics in the Soviet Union, but that also 'unfolded [...] with great fluency the range of possibilities between [the two radical visions of the country] as hell and [...] as heaven' (Egido 1988: 141). This explosion became even greater after 1930.

Despite international and national economic crises, the 1930s began in Spain as a decade of great promise. In 1931 both the military dictatorship and the monarchical regime fell and a Republic was proclaimed, with an alliance of Socialists and progressive Republicans taking the reins of government and setting out to bring social justice, education, culture and freedom to a country devastated by decades of class war and centuries of political instability. The proclamation of the Republic coincided with the coming of age of a generation of revolutionary intellectuals who had also been key players in the struggle against the Monarchy and the dictatorship, and who believed that the construction of socialism in the Soviet Union could be a solution to the crisis of international capitalism as well as to the fascist threat in Europe. This generation played a decisive role in the new national political scene via their leadership in a number of left-wing publishing houses that inundated the Spanish book market with titles on Marxist theory and left-leaning politics. Among the new titles, books about the Soviet Union became instant best-sellers.

What is most remarkable about these travel books is not the description of Soviet life and culture they contain, but the way in which they became a vehicle for discussing the goal of travelling to the Soviet Union, as travellers elaborated on the original reasons that moved them to go and on why they believed it was necessary to write 'yet another book' about the revolutionary country. Invariably, the reasons were the same. Whether authors wrote a few explanatory lines before the travel account or indulged in a fully-fledged narration of the vicissitudes of preparing their journeys, most of them had only one reason to go: to bring home a 'true' account of the revolutionary country, to produce the kind of 'truthful', 'objective' and 'balanced' reporting the Spanish press had failed to give for so long. They declared it clearly, loudly, eloquently and unapologetically. Prefaces, forewords and afterwords were filled with justifications of the travel book itself as a desperately needed exercise in objective and scientific observation. Objectivity was the means and the attainment of truth was the goal. More than mere possibilities or literary aims, both were considered social and historical duties. Travellers had different reasons for seeking such goals, but they all believed that they would attain them, as long as they were able to 'inform' with 'honesty' (Llopis 1929: 9). Travel writing on the Soviet Union thus reached, or purported to reach, a degree of restraint, fairness and equanimity that would have been impossible to find in the press or in earlier titles. To use David Caute's terms, these travellers were given an image the Soviet Union as a 'symbol' but they wanted to make of the country an 'observable reality' in order to make it more accessible, both for themselves and for the public they purported to represent (1964: 124–5).

Yet, for all the self-awareness in their discussion of objectivity as a goal, these travellers were also extraordinarily unaware of the political and cultural implications, not to mention the contradictions, of their obsession with truth. More in the role of classical anthropologists than modern travel writers, and obviously untroubled by much more contemporary questions of identity, representation, self, and otherness, they believed reality was decipherable by the mere presence of a coherent and objective self who was going to carry out a straightforward inquiry through the exercise of fair observation in a world dominated by objective political change. Most of them also assumed that their experiences as travellers, reporters and 'eyewitnesses' would be unmediated, that there would be some kind of straight, unproblematized relationship between themselves as the observers and the others as the observed.

Despite the efforts made by most travellers to portray Soviet citizens as part of the same observable, objective reality they seemed to find everywhere, their encounter was not merely an interaction between a (travelling) subject and a 'foreign other', or what Marc Augé has called 'absolute otherness' (1993: 18). At a time when social struggle had reached levels unknown in Spain and the rest of Europe, what happened as a result of that encounter was more a question of 'internal' or 'social' otherness. Indeed for these travellers 'otherness' was not a question of race or nationality. It was a question of class. Thus their writing created social 'others' as much as social 'equals', depending on whether they rejected or identified with the people of the Soviet Union.

The intention to 'inform honestly' was clearly a subjective enterprise, and each group of travellers conceived that mission differently, despite similar claims to objectivity and fairness. The Second Spanish Republic was a political regime that raised passions everywhere. On the one hand, it raised the hopes of the socialist and Republican élites who had been key players in making political change possible and whose dream was to make Spain a truly liberal, democratic country on a par with the most advanced European nations. On the other, it brought a great deal of disillusion to a workers' movement run by communists and anarchists eager to take Spain directly towards a proletarian revolution. Needless to say, it brought much political and financial anxiety to a conservative upper bourgeoisie that was losing its social privileges and its control over political life. The travel books written by Spaniards who travelled to the Soviet Union while these passions were affecting Spain so deeply, were the result of a fragile negotiation between a conscious desire for objective observation and the relatively unconscious influence of a pre-determined political ideology. In most cases the balance between these two forces was extraordinarily difficult to maintain. As a result the political conclusions these travellers reached were not in the end so different from those that had been expounded, much more noisily and without any scientific pretensions, by the national press in the years immediately after 1917.

'WALKING AND SEEING': THE JOURNEYS OF THE SOCIALIST INTELLIGENTSIA.

In *Mi viaje a la Rusia sovietista* (1921), Fernando de los Ríos, a member of the learned, progressive bourgeoisie, and a well-known leader of the Socialist Party, provided an analysis of Russia which focused specifically on political and cultural questions, and offered conclusions that were far from positive. He was the only one among early travellers to admit that his 'judgement' of political events in Russia was tainted by his own conception of history, a humanist vision in which socialism was defined as 'a moral imperative grounded in the problem of man [sic]' (1921: 15). He thus criticized the early Bolshevik system for sacrificing individual freedom and for lacking real democracy.

After keeping a long silence on Russia as a result of the drastic turn of events in October 1917, socialist newspapers welcomed the publication of de los Ríos' book with a mixture of admiration for the writing and repulsion for the reality it portrayed. A familiar claim of the Socialists in the early to mid 1920s was that communist policies went against human rights and democracy. Towards the end of the decade and into the 1930s *El Socialista* and other socialist mainstream publications were able to express a good deal of enthusiasm for the great material progress made in the Soviet Union in the course of the Five Year Plans. They chose to place the emphasis not on political ideology but on statistics and numbers: the references may have been 'cold', but they were significant in pointing to an economic model that Western countries could imitate.

In line with this model established by the press, the Socialist leaders who travelled to the Soviet Union after 1928 (Rodolfo Llopis (1929), Julián Zugazagoitia (1932), Enrique Díaz-Reitg (1932)) believed a factual study of the Soviet system was bound to result in the dissemination of the truth about the country. Accordingly, they wrote *informe-relatos*, focusing on specific questions such as Soviet agrarian reform, the national economy or cultural/educational issues. Zugazagoitia argued that travellers should simply 'walk', 'see' and later 'report' on the 'social value' of Soviet institutions and the 'goals they [were] trying to achieve' in the attempt to answer a very simple question: did the Soviet 'harvest' that created schools, factories, clubs, laboratories, health centres and hydroelectric plants 'impoverish or enrich the country?' (1934: 28). The answer to such a question could hardly be 'arbitrary' given the fact that economic growth was both objective and measurable. Like a modern St. Thomas, the traveller was thus 'forced to believe' upon seeing the facts (1932: 141).

In order to prove that what they said was scientific observation rather than the product of their imagination, wishful thinking or mere utopian projection, these travellers wrote about their experiences with what Patrick Holland and Graham Huggan refer to as 'cool detachment' (1998: 7). They wanted to be, as Lutwack has argued in another context, not 'principal[s] in the story' but, like their own readers, 'interested witness[es] of the action' (1984: 61). The rhetorical strategies which they deployed were used to persuade the reader of the truth of what was being reported (Holland and Huggan 1998: 129). The abilities of this kind of writer contributed greatly to showing the importance of the Soviet model. But it also served to create the myth of Soviet citizens as passive recipients rather than active agents of political and economic change. While engaged in social or economic research, or simply too absorbed by their social commitments with the Soviet intellectual élites, socialist travellers failed to interact with ordinary Soviet people and to report on their role in the extraordinary changes which they were so keen to report. In these travel books, the proletarian 'other' appears both lifeless and voiceless. Workers' statements are rarely found in print, and are much more often hidden underneath the narrator's reported speech.

Although the strategy adopted by socialist travellers of 'walking and seeing' in order to discover truth had apparently been chosen as a means of departing from the model of straightforward ideological analysis that had been established by de los Ríos in 1923, there were a number of ways in which the later socialist travellers proved to be the faithful heirs of de los Ríos. Having accomplished their 'fieldwork' in the Soviet Union, these travellers went back to Spain convinced that it was still worthwhile believing in the value of utopia and in the future of the country. The utopia in which the socialist travellers believed was that of a democratized Soviet Union; in every aspect of the country they studied, they managed to see a promise of democracy. Their hope was that if the country survived the current difficult crossroads, socialist education would prevail and citizens would learn to live in a true democracy, finding a 'synthesis' between the 'inflexib[ility]' of 'communism' and the 'useless[ness]' of capitalism (Díaz-Reitg 1932: 407). Socialists thus found in the Soviet Union of the 1930s the promise of what they believed the bourgeois-democratic revolution in February could have ushered in.

'PROLETARIAN TRUTH': THE JOURNEYS OF WORKING-CLASS TRAVELLERS.

In his *Impresiones de un viaje a Rusia* (1923), Isidoro Acevedo, one of the founders of the Communist Party of Spain, declared his approval of the Soviet regime and his allegiance to the Communist International. However, in *Setenta días en Rusia. Lo que yo vi*, Ángel Pestaña, an anarchist leader, wrote about the difficulties of daily life in the Soviet Union and the lack of democracy in the Party, and concluded – as early as 1925 – that the popular (read anarchist) spirit of the October revolution had been betrayed by the Bolshevik Party. Despite their different interpretations of events in the Soviet Union, both Acevedo and Pestaña made an effort to leave their own proletarian ideologies aside and see themselves as objective observers of a political process. While Acevedo was inspired by the motto that 'Truth is supreme beauty' and thus believed his mind could be 'free of all possible prejudice' (1923: 17), the editors of Pestaña's book argued that they had published a 'documented' and 'irrefutable [...] book of facts' for those readers who were interested in 'objective truth' (Pestaña 1925: 5).

Once the doors of the Soviet Union opened wide, a multitude of communist and anarchist militants followed in the footsteps of these proletarian leaders and early travellers. The journeys of Spanish communist intellectuals or fellow-travellers to the country did not inspire a great deal of travel literature. Poets like Rafael Alberti, Emilio Prados or Miguel Hernández wrote either journal articles narrating their journeys or poems singing the glories of the Soviet system,[5] but did not venture into any sustained political analysis and produced no book-length travelogues. Ramón J. Sender (*Madrid-Moscú*, 1933) and César Vallejo[6] (*Rusia en 1931*) were the only communist intellectuals to publish books of political analysis in the tradition of the *informe-relatos* of the 1920s. For the most part those communists and anarchists who travelled to the Soviet Union were militant workers, just as Pestaña was.

These working-class travellers (A. Eulogio Díes, Vicente Pérez and the many individuals going as part of workers' delegations, publishing their travel accounts both in the workers' press and in book format) went to the Soviet Union on behalf of their political parties or unions and focused on describing the organization of work, the daily life of the working class, the role of unions, and the like. Their journeys developed from a premise that was quite similar to that of the socialist intelligentsia: to search for 'truth, honesty, and impartiality', and they were equally confident that they could simply 'gather' the information they saw and heard (Eulogio Díes 1934: 1). For these travellers truth was to be found less in the solid objectivity of factual information and more in the eye of the beholder, since they believed that the Soviet revolution could only be interpreted correctly from the point of view of the working class. According to *Mundo Obrero* – the official publication of the Communist Party after 1930 – workers could understand the changes taking place in the Soviet Union in a way that 'journalists sent by the bourgeoisie in order to discredit [the country]' could not (*Mundo Obrero* 1931: 3). The communist publication encouraged workers to combat the 'bourgeois lies' about the Soviet Union printed in the bourgeois press with the weapon of their 'proletarian truth'.

This 'proletarian truth' seemed to be the prerogative of communist workers alone. According to *Mundo Obrero*, anarchist workers like Vicente Pérez (aka Combina), who had 'sold their soul' to the bourgeoisie and no longer supported the Soviet system, had told so many lies that they could no longer claim to have any 'moral weight' with the Spanish working class. While communist workers were committed to 'Truth, Truth, Truth', anarchist workers were 'serving imperialism' with their 'opportunistic lies', 'deceit' and 'fiction' (*Mundo Obrero* 1933: 2).

Since working-class travellers found truth in their very own gaze, they had a tendency to confuse their desire for objectivity with their passionate attachment to the events they reported. Unlike Socialist leaders, workers did not cultivate self-effacement for the sake of credibility. Instead, they sought to be immersed as much as possible in the scene and to speak with passion about what they saw, for the sake of reporting fairly about the political dream unfolding before their very own eyes. 'I can't go on' – a working-class delegate wrote in *Mundo Obrero* – 'because I'm overtaken by enthusiasm and I might exaggerate. I can't wait to be back among my fellow workers again in order to explain to you everything these courageous people have done' (*Mundo Obrero* 1932b: 4).

Through passionate attachment, workers attempted to efface all 'otherness' from Soviet workers, transforming them into social 'equals' with whom they sought complete emotional and political identification. In the books and newspaper reports written by these travellers Soviet workers speak for themselves for the first time, although their speeches are sometimes slightly polluted by the use of ready-made political slogans. Their voice sounds more authentic as they speak about the glories and the miseries of their daily lives.

Despite repeated calls from the anti-Stalinist communist press asking other proletarian organizations to report dispassionately on the Soviet Union,[7] communist workers affiliated to and sent to the country by the pro-Soviet Communist Party continued to speak of the revolutionary country as paradise, while anarchist workers were already describing a place like hell. In line with many other articles coming out of pro-Soviet communist publications (*Nosotros, Nueva Cultura, Octubre*), communist workers wrote their reports in grandiloquent prose, idealising the lot of a nation of workers who were building a truly communist society with 'admirable enthusiasm' while being 'conscious of their historical responsibility' and enjoying complete freedom as a class (*Mundo Obrero* 1932a: 4). Like Acevedo, communist travellers hoped that the Soviet Union would be able to liberate itself completely from its bourgeois inheritance, survive the delicate negotiations currently taking place between the old and the new systems and move forward to a pure dictatorship of the proletariat. Upon returning home, they were happy to confirm that a concept that had previously been utopian was no longer so. On the other hand, anarchist workers described a country of 'desolation and death', exposing the lack of political freedom and the harsh reality of forced collectivization (Pérez 1932: 15). Anarchists returned to Spain displaying a certificate that utopia was already dead and that dystopia had taken its place; they expressed the hope that the Soviet Union would take several steps backward in order to embrace again the libertarian spirit of the Bolshevik revolution.

THE NOSTALGIA OF HOME: CONSERVATIVE TOURISTS IN THE SOVIET UNION.

Upon the proclamation of the Spanish Republic in 1931, the conservative press still believed there were signs of communist sabotage and conspiracy almost everywhere, and openly challenged the Republican government to keep such forces under control lest 'the agents of the Third International' should take over Spain (Alcalá Galiano 1930: 4). In a somewhat histrionic tone, most articles in the conservative press focused either on the anti-religious nature of communism or on the misery of the daily life of Soviet citizens (*ABC* 1935: 29). Not surprisingly, the travel books written by conservative and ultraconservative travellers (Hoyos Gascón (1933), Eloy Montero (1935), Félix Ros (1936), Vizconde de Eza (1931)) emphasized three things about the Soviet system: the lack of freedom, the environment of fear and the intransigence of the Bolshevik leadership. Thus they foregrounded the 'moral and material poverty' of a nation that moved them to compassion (Egido 1988: 141).

Most conservative travellers (Vals i Taberner (1928), Terrasa (1932), Tapia Bolívar (1935), Ramón de Rato (1935), Amado Blanco (1932), Diego Hidalgo (1929), Pedro Segado (1935)) went to the Soviet Union as tourists, driven by a 'terrible curiosity' rather than political interest (Hidalgo 1929: 46). Like working-class travellers, bourgeois tourists believed that truth would be found not in factual descriptions but in the eye of the beholder. They were convinced that the source of their 'objectivity' was precisely their own apolitical point of view (Hoyos Gascón 1933: 3). Unlike the 'curious' travellers who had returned from the Soviet Union saying that it was all 'horrible' and those to the 'opposite extreme' who had come back saying it was all 'marvellous', these travellers proudly announced that they had not reached any conclusions a priori and 'purely and simply' asked a very direct question: 'What is happening in Russia?' (Hoyos Gascón 1933: 3).

In fact, many of these tourists were candid enough to confront what Hollander has called 'the self-evident limitations' of their experience (1981: 20), rebelling against the scientific pretensions of other travellers by foregrounding their subjectivity as observers and their status in the

Soviet Union as mere foreign visitors. Perhaps because they were politically unattached and uncommitted, they were intelligent enough to admit that their experience as travellers was always mediated, since they depended on the services of guides and translators whose explanations and comments they often perceived as 'schematic and grotesquely simplified' (Terrasa 1932: 9). Since their experience was so constrained, they argued they could only share with the public a number of personal impressions that should not be considered objective, because they were the result of chance and not of reflection. Yet perhaps because these travellers were outsiders, with little access to official institutions and information, they were in a better position to come to terms with the fact that the Soviet Union was 'neither heaven nor hell' but a 'country struggling through a painful historical experience' (Blas i Vallespinosa 1929: 10–11), a country where there were 'good and bad things, like everywhere else' (Hidalgo 1929: 279).

In a similar way to socialist intellectuals, these tourists grounded their objectivity in keeping emotionally unattached. Despite their lack of involvement it was clear that the Soviet revolution was, in Dennis Porter's phrase, the 'phobia that threatened to disable' them (1991: 13). They were not willing to show their fear. Busy enough taking photographs and complaining about the tourist guides they so loved to hate, these visitors were rather unmoved by the collective sentiments of the Soviet people. They went so far as to treat the proletarian 'other' with contempt: 'Once you've seen ten proletarians, you've seen ten thousand', said Félix Ros in a rather emotionless description of a workers' march in Red Square (1936: 1).

In line with their emotional distance, the political conclusion of these tourists was that 'Western civilization should not be afraid of Marxism' (de Rato 1935: 74). For these tourists the 'longing to leave' for the Soviet Union, to use Porter's words, was matched only by the 'longing to return' home (1991: 12) in the hope that the whole trip had been but a bad dream and that the world would soon return to normal (Segado 1935: 107). Their 'nostalgia' for home was unsurprisingly grounded in illusion. In the act of going back to the apparent safety of home and pretending to leave the revolution safely behind they were ignoring the complicated reality of a country, their own, where class struggle and revolution were tearing social and historical identity apart. Indeed, these travellers returned safely and solemnly to a dream, to a Spain that no longer existed.

On history and revolution: Spanish travellers and the Soviet space

Caren Kaplan has suggested that in a great deal of travel writing space is simply 'assumed to be *there*' as if it were 'a substance [...] relatively immune to the workings of time unless culture perpetrates its crimes against space by spoiling, crowding, polluting, and inscribing its presence onto or into that blank expanse' (1996: 147). All Spanish travellers to the Soviet Union were intelligent enough to understand that they were observing the complex reality of a country in motion. The place which they observed had not been 'immune' to time: rather it was a space marked by huge social and political change. They could not escape from seeing the Soviet Union not only as a 'place on a map' but also as what Adrienne Rich has called a 'place in history' (1986: 212).

One of the most obvious incongruities all travellers pointed out had to do with the relationship between people and space: while the new generations of Soviet citizens could feel they belonged to a new space that was called the Soviet Union, older generations were, in the view of many travellers, symbolically and literally out of place, completely unattached to and in constant struggle with the new revolutionary space. This lack of connection was most obvious in the ongoing negotiation between a generation of older people unable and unwilling to give up their religious beliefs and a new revolutionary state struggling to enforce drastic change. Thus Spanish travellers witnessed apparent oddities such as a bourgeois woman praying passionately in church, while outside a revolutionary banner assured citizens that religion was the opium of the people; or workers who had just attended a revolutionary march crossing themselves on the street as a hearse went by.

In pointing out these contradictions, Spanish travellers seemed to be making an effort to portray the Soviet Union as a space that was unstable and which could be said to be experiencing a mixture of the worst things of the past and the best things of the future or, depending on the viewpoint of the observer, a mixture of the best things of the past and the worst things of the future. On the one hand, many travellers understood the influence which space exerted in defining the identity of Soviet subjects. But on the other, they tended to perpetuate the myth of an essential, pre-revolutionary Russian identity by emphasising not how this identity was evolving but how it experienced conflict when subjected to the transformation in the physical appearance and ideological basis of the space it occupied.

The battles being waged between two different generations of citizens fighting for their own historical and political space did not seem to unsettle in any way the travelling subjects' perception of the congruity and solidity of their own identities. Many of the Spanish visitors to the Soviet Union acknowledged the uneasiness they felt either before departure or during the journey itself. Before leaving Spain, Rodolfo Llopis wondered whether or not he would be able to 'penetrate into the conscience' of the Soviet people or to understand the 'tragic drama' they were living (1929: 33). He expressed an awareness of the complexity of the Soviet reality and acknowledged that a European mind could not understand Soviet society, and that his own bourgeois education with its emphasis on individualism was no help in trying to understand the collective enterprise of the Soviet revolution (1929: 16).

Like most other travellers describing similar reservations, the diffidence expressed by Llopis was rather superficial. Writing his book on his return from the Soviet Union, he concluded that he had succeeded in gaining some knowledge of the major contradiction of a civilization 'grounded in rigid dogmas but living in the midst of an experimental stage' and he was confidently able to predict that the Soviet Union would eventually become a democracy (1929: 277–8). His conclusion effectively weakened the contradictions he had attempted to confront, turning an unfamiliar political process into a more familiar one that his Spanish socialist mind could comprehend.

While the travelling subject of most Spanish texts written about the Soviet Union remained unproblematically stable and coherent, there was one dissident voice in the collection of books published between 1928 and 1936. Unlike any other Spanish travel book of the period, Leon Villanúa's *La Rusia inquietante* [Worrying Russia] (1931) – a travelogue written as a novel – was dominated by self-conscious parody and irony, achieving what Holland and Huggan have called a 'self-reflexive construction of the travelling subject' (1998: 158). By drawing the reader's attention to the construction rather than the content of the travel story, Villanúa acknowledged his own limitations as a writer, debunking the myth of the congruous identity (political or otherwise) of the travelling subject.

To begin with, Villanúa did not allow the protagonist of his novel and alter ego – who, incidentally, does not seem to have a name – to indulge in any feelings of self-importance. Villanúa's protagonist is an ordinary human being and a no less ordinary journalist: he is opportunistic, unreliable, and unscrupulous. He has no sound political analysis, let alone a stable political affiliation. In fact, he can sell his soul to the devil and a newspaper article to the highest bidder. He decides to go to the Soviet Union simply because he is bored and has nothing better to do, yet when he has made his decision he finds that everyone around him wanted him to go including, unsurprisingly, the Communist Party of Spain. He expects to make no discoveries, to have no encounter with utopia. Once he arrives in the Soviet Union he has no queries, he asks nothing, he approaches no one. He acquires information purely by chance. More importantly, he is manipulated by circumstances and by other people. The implication of his work is clearly that if a person like him can go, so can anyone.

La Rusia inquietante is a self-conscious play on the obsession with objectivity that typified other examples of the travel text. The book is precisely about all the barriers that the protagonist finds in his way, making it impossible for him ever to 'tell the truth'. 'I am a journalist' – he says in an effort to present a dignified image of himself – 'I see, I listen, I write, and I comment' (1931: 234). Yet his articles are routinely fiddled with by the Soviet authorities to the point that he could hardly recognize them as his own when they are published. Thus he is forced to admit, much more honestly and humbly, that he cannot have his own opinion, that other people have paid him and he has simply written what he was told (1931: 234). *La Rusia inquietante* is certainly the funniest and most readable travel book about the Soviet Union published in Spain during the 1930s and the only one that dares to take a humorous look at a country that had become the object of some extremely solemn reflections.

Spanish travellers to the Soviet Union had never claimed that they wanted to see the world with new eyes, but that they wanted to see it 'objectively'. As a result, their journeys were not so much journeys of discovery but of re-affirmation. After their experiences in the Soviet Union these travellers understood things better, cleared up a number of myths and verified facts, but very few of them experienced any kind of political or personal change. Rather than investing in a dialogic encounter with an 'other', they went through a monologic process of re-affirmation of their own identity. In the travel books published in Spain, and despite all claims to the contrary, the Soviet Union was imagined before it was seen, defined before it was explored, and judged before it was fully understood. As a result the introductions to these books were, in many ways, already their conclusions, and afterwords were but the chronicles of political summaries that had already been announced. In the way they chose to interpret events in the Soviet Union these books were a vivid reflection of the Spanish national political scene and of the different expectations different visitors to the Soviet Union had for their own country.

Very few of these travellers saw their political dreams come true. It is not by chance that the bulk of Spanish travel books about the Soviet Union was published before 1936. There were some remarkable journeys to the country during the years of the Spanish Civil War, like that of communist poet Miguel Hernández, a guest at the Soviet Theatre Olympics of 1937. After 1936, however, the train rides of political pilgrimage were going in the opposite direction, with many illustrious and ordinary passengers going to visit Spain and even to fight as members of the International Brigades. By then Spain had already undergone a great deal of political change. In an ongoing struggle against Spanish fascism, the fragile Republic expanded its horizons via a political alliance with the groups to its left, including the Communist Party, and national politics radicalized even further, a process that led directly to the Civil War. As the possibility of a bourgeois democracy started to fade away there were only two visions of Spain at play: either a popular democracy or the return to the rule of the oligarchy. Since the Soviet Union was one of the only two countries in the world that gave their unconditional moral, political and military support to the Spanish Republic, it was only a matter of time before the Spanish press (now divided unequivocally into pro-Republican and pro-Nationalist camps) would go on to portray the Soviet Union as either heaven or hell, with no possible positions in between, moved by a passion and anger unknown since 1917.

Notes

All translations from Spanish original sources are the author's own.

1. Although this essay deals mostly with books and newspaper articles written in the late 1920s and throughout the 1930s, when the Soviet Union had already been established, it also makes reference to books and articles released in 1917 and the very early 1920s, when the name 'Soviet Union' was still not official and travellers still spoke of 'Russia'. Spanish travellers themselves used the terms 'Russia' and 'the Soviet Union' indiscriminately after 1923. For the sake of clarity, I will refer to 'Russia' when making reference to journeys undertaken or books published until December 1922, and to the 'Soviet Union' for those accomplished from 1923 onwards.
2. In addition to the academic pieces quoted elsewhere in my essay, see also Pablo Sanz Guitián's *Viajeros españoles en Rusia* (1995), Luis Lavaur's 'Socialismo y turismo: El viaje a la Rusia soviética (1919–1939)' in *Ayeres. Cuadernos de Historia*. Year III, no. 7 (March 1993): 12–20; and Antonio Elorza's *Queridos camaradas: La Internacional Comunista en España, 1919–1939* (1999).
3. These early books were Rafael Calleja's *Rusia, espejo saludable para uso de pobres y ricos* (1920), Quintiliano Saldaña's *La revolución rusa: la Constitución rusa de 10 de julio de 1918* (1919) and Sofía Casanova's *La revolución bolchevista* (1920). Casanova was the Moscow correspondent for *ABC* and thus one of the first Spaniards to travel to Russia. The other two titles were documented from foreign sources. Among the translations of foreign titles, Alfons Paquets' *En la Rusia comunista: Cartas desde Moscú* (1921) was widely read by the Spanish intelligentsia.
4. I have found records of at least forty travel books on the Soviet Union written by Spaniards between 1925 and 1935, a considerable number if one takes into account the conservative political climate until 1931 and the relatively poor publishing industry in the country. Rafael Cruz has found fifty books or series of press articles about journeys to revolutionary Russia or later to the Soviet Union, and more than four hundred titles of books and pamphlets written about the country in general (1997: 279). Juan Avilés has pointed out that between 1917 and 1925 there were sixty books published about the political transformations taking place in the Soviet Union, and that half of them were published in 1920 alone (1999: 131).
5. See Alberti in *Luz* (22 July to 8 August 1933) and Hernández in *Nuestra Bandera* (21 November 1937).
6. Vallejo was a Peruvian poet and founding member of the Communist Party of Peru. He spent some time in Spain and his travel book about the Soviet Union was first published there.
7. See Julián Gorkín's 'La verdad sobre Rusia' in *La Batalla* 6 September 1934: 3; and a book review of Boris Souvarine's *Stalin* in *La Nueva Era* May 1936: 100.

Bibliography

Primary Sources

'Impresiones de unos turistas que regresan de Rusia', *ABC* 20 January 1935: 29.
'*Stalin (Aperçu historique du bolchevisme) Paris, 1935*' by Boris Souvarine. *La Nueva Era* May 1936: 100.
'Una delegación obrera en Rusia', *Mundo Obrero* 23 December 1931: 3.
'Una impresión auténtica de la Rusia soviética', *Mundo Obrero* 2 January 1932b: 4.
'La infame campaña de los líderes anarquistas contra la URSS'. Mundo Obrero 18 March 1933: 2.
'La verdad obrera frente a la mentira burguesa. Lo que ven los delegados obreros españoles en la Unión Soviética'. Mundo Obrero 7 December 1932a: 4.
Acevedo, I., *Impresiones de un viaje a Rusia*. Oviedo, 1923.
Alberti, R., 'Noticiario de un poeta en la URSS'. *Luz* (22, 26, 28 July, 1, 8, 23 August 1933).
Alcalá Galiano, A., 'Ni dictadura ni demagogia', *ABC* 1 April 1930: 4–7.
Álvarez del Vayo, J., *La nueva Rusia*. Madrid, 1926.
Amado Blanco, L., *8 días en Leningrado*. Madrid, 1932.
Araquistáin, L., 'La revolución rusa: pan, guerra, libertad', *España* 22 March 1917: 3–4.
Blas i Vallespinosa, F., *Viatge a Russia passant per Escandinavia*. Barcelona, 1929.
Calleja, R., *Rusia, espejo saludable para uso de pobres y ricos*. Madrid, 1920.
Casanova, S., *La revolución bolchevista (diario de un testigo)*. Madrid, 1920
Díaz-Reitg, E., *En Rusia la revolución empieza ahora. Informaciones y estudios objetivos llevados a cabo en Rusia, en plena ejecución del Plan Quinquenal, hasta enero de 1932*. Madrid, 1932.
Eulogio Díes, A., *Un obrero español en Rusia (Film de un viaje)*. Alicante, 1934.
Gorkín, J., 'La verdad sobre Rusia', *La Batalla* 6 September 1934: 3.
Hernández, M., 'La URSS y España fuerzas hermanas'. *Nuestra Bandera* 10 November 1937: 3.
———. 'Miguel Hernández nos habla del V Festival de Teatro Soviético y de su fé en pueblo español'. *Nuestra Bandera* 21 November 1937: 4.
Hidalgo, D., *Un notario español en Rusia*. Madrid, 1929.
Hoyos Gascón, L., *El meridiano de Moscú, o la Rusia que yo vi*. Preface by D. Hidalgo, Madrid, 1933.
Huysman, C., 'Juicio socialista sobre la revolución rusa', *El Socialista* 12 April 1917: 1.
Llopis, R., *Cómo se forja un pueblo. La Rusia que yo he visto*. Madrid, 1929.
Montero, E., *Lo que vi en Rusia*. Madrid, 1935.
Paquets, A., *En la Rusia comunista: Cartas desde Moscú*. Madrid, 1921.
Pérez, V. (Combina), *Un militante de la C.N.T. en Rusia*. Barcelona, 1932.
Pestaña, Á., *Setenta días en Rusia. Lo que yo vi*. Barcelona, 1925.
Rato, R. de., *Vagabundo bajo la luna. Rápida visión de Europa y sus problemas*. Madrid, 1935.
Ríos, F. de los., *Mi viaje a la Rusia sovietista*. Madrid, 1921.
Ros, F., *Un meridional en Rusia*. Barcelona, 1936.
Saldaña, Q., *La Revolución rusa: la Constitución rusa de 10 de julio de 1918*. Madrid, 1919.
Segado, P., *El camarada Belcebuf: Un 'pequeño burgués' en la U.R.S.S.* Madrid, 1935.
Sender, R.J. *Madrid-Moscú*. Madrid, 1933.
Tapia Bolívar, D., *Ha llovido un dedito*. Madrid, 1935.
Terrasa, J., *URSS, La república de treballadors. Notes de viatge*. Barcelona, 1932.
Vals i Taberner, F., *Un viatger català a la Russia de Stalin (1928)*. Preface by d´Erhard Zurawka. Barcelona, 1985.

Vallejo, C. *Rusia en 1931.* Madrid, 1931.
Villanúa, L., *La Rusia inquietante. Viaje de un periodista español a la U.R.S.S.* Madrid, 1931.
Vizconde de Eza., *Rusia, un peligro o una leccion?* Madrid, 1931.
Zugazagoitia, J., *Rusia al día.* Madrid, 1932.
———, 'Notas de andar y ver', *Leviatán* no. 3 (July 1934): 27–31.

SECONDARY SOURCES

Augé, M., 'Espacio y alteridad', *Revista de Occidente* 140 (January 1993): 13–34.
Avilés Farré, J., *La fé que vino de Rusia. La revolución bolchevique y los españoles (1917–1931).* Madrid, 1999.
Caute, D., *Communism and the French Intellectuals, 1914–1960.* New York, 1964.
Cruz, R., *El Partido Comunista de España en la Segunda República.* Madrid, 1987.
———, '¡Luzbel vuelve al mundo! Las imágenes de la Rusia Soviética y la acción colectiva en España', *Cultura y movilización en la España contemporánea.* eds. R. Cruz, M. Pérez Ledesma, Madrid, 1997: 273–304.
Egido L., Ángeles, M. de los. 'Del paraíso soviético al peligro marxista. La Unión Soviética en la España republicana', *Cuadernos de Historia Contemporánea* vol. 10 (1988): 139–154.
Forcadell, C., *Parlamentarismo y bolchevización. El movimiento obrero español, 1914–1918.* Barcelona, 1978.
Holland, P., Huggan, G., *Tourists with Typewriters: Critical Reflections on Contemporary Travel Writing.* Ann Arbor, 1998.
Hollander, P., *Political Pilgrims: Travels of Western Intellectuals to the Soviet Union, China and Cuba, 1928–1978.* New York, 1981.
Kaplan, C., *Questions of Travel: Postmodern Discourses of Displacement.* Durham, 1996.
Lazo, A., *La revolución rusa en el diario ABC de la época.* Sevilla, 1975.
Lutwack, L., *The Role of Place in Literature.* Syracuse, NY, 1984.
Porter, D., *Haunted Journeys: Desire and Transgression in European Travel Writing.* Princeton, 1991.
Rich, A., *Blood, Bread and Poetry: Selected Prose, 1979–1985.* New York, 1986.
Ruiz, D., 'Escépticos y creyentes ante la revolución: los primeros viajeros españoles al país de los Soviets'. F. Carantoña, G. Puente, eds. *La revolución rusa 70 años después. Actas del segundo coloquio de Historia contemporánea.* León, 1988: 119–136.

Chapter 5

THE POLITICS OF THE EVERYDAY AND THE ETERNITY OF RUINS
Two Women Photographers in Republican Spain (Margaret Michaelis 1933-7, Kati Horna 1937-8)

Jo Labanyi

I should like to start by putting together three quotations from disparate sources, all of them on the subject of ruins.

In her travel book *Farewell Spain*, written in London from October 1936 to February 1937 (that is, in the early months of the Spanish Civil War), Kate O'Brien, in her first chapter titled 'Adiós, turismo', lamented the end of the sentimental tourist in a world of 'forward marchers, who read no epitaphs' (1985: 13):

> Let us reflect with sadness that Macaulay's New Zealander, so exciting to us all at school, will almost certainly never stand on Westminster Bridge to view the ruins of St Paul's [...] because in his day [...] ruins will not be tolerated, for reasons of physical and mental hygiene. (1985: 14-15)

I shall come back to O'Brien at the end of this essay, for in many ways her travel writing provides a verbal analogue to the photographs of Republican Spain – also by women – which I shall be discussing.

The second quotation is from the Spanish anarchist leader Durruti. When interviewed shortly before his death in 1936 during the Civil War by a foreign journalist who remarked that, even if victorious, the workers would be sitting on a pile of ruins, Durruti magnificently replied:

> We've always lived in slums and holes in the wall. We'll manage. You mustn't forget, we can also build. It was the workers who built these palaces and cities [...]. We can build others to take their place. [...] We're not afraid of ruins. (cited by Cleminson in Graham and Labanyi 1995: 117)

Margaret Michaelis, one of the two Central European women photographers discussed in this essay, photographed Durruti's funeral in Barcelona. The other photographer studied here, Kati Horna, photographed Durruti's portrait in a Valencia shop window in October 1937 (Figure 5.1). The portrait, mass-produced for public consumption, is displayed amid a jumble of cultural relics which mix the political (the Marianne-like embodiment of the Spanish Republic) and the personal (the portrait of a baby, a sentimental landscape, a mallard). Both Michaelis and Horna were anarchists; I shall return to the significance of this for their attitude to ruins, and to photography.

FIGURE 5.1 Kati Horna, 'Shop window', Valencia, October 1937. Reproduced by permission of the Ministerio de Educación y Ciencia, Archivo General de la Guerra Civil Española.

My third quotation, the most famous, is Walter Benjamin's passage on the 'angel of history' in his 'Theses on the philosophy of history' (Benjamin was, of course, a key commentator on the historical significance of photography):

> This is how one pictures the angel of history. His face is turned towards the past. Where we perceive a chain of events, he sees one single catastrophe which keeps piling wreckage upon wreckage and hurls it in front of his feet. The angel would like to stay, awaken the dead, and make whole what has been smashed. But a storm is blowing from Paradise; it has got caught in his wings with such violence that the angel can no longer close them. This storm irresistibly propels him into the future to which his back is turned, while the pile of debris before him grows skyward. This storm is what we call progress. (1992: 249)

I should like in this chapter to explore the ways in which the photographs of Republican Spain of Michaelis and Horna, by focussing on the debris and incompleteness of everyday experience, 'blast open the continuum of history' (Benjamin 1992: 254) in order to produce 'a past charged with the time of the now' (Benjamin 1992: 253). As Hannah Arendt notes in her preface to Benjamin's collection of essays, *Illuminations*, Benjamin had wanted to write a book that consisted solely of a montage of quotations (Benjamin 1992: 51) true to his unorthodox notion of historical materialism as the juxtaposition of motley fragments from the debris of the past, lifted out of their context in order to release them from the grip of tradition, thereby creating new constellations of meaning or what he called 'the transfiguration of objects' (Benjamin 1992: 46). Benjamin's refusal of causal explanation in order to liberate the 'materiality' of things is based on the idea that the past reveals itself in those things which have been forgotten and which thus elude incorporation into grand causal narratives of progress. As Arendt puts it (Benjamin 1992: 45), for Benjamin 'the past spoke only through things that had not been handed down'. Benjamin's fascination with the imagery of ruins is a fascination with that which refuses the notion of history as a sequential continuum; that is, as progress. In similar fashion, Benjamin noted that photography can liberate things from our preconceived notions of them by drawing our attention – through the freezing of the image in a moment of time, and its isolation from its context – to elements that elude the notice of those present at the time. Thus, as he notes, 'The camera introduces us to unconscious optics as does psychoanalysis to unconscious impulses' (Benjamin 1992: 230). The reference to Freud should be taken seriously, for, in Benjamin's analysis, the past – as revealed by photography – obeys the structures of the dream logic: a materialist dream logic ruled not by subjective fantasy projections but by the capacity of objects to interpellate us: to make us theirs. Like Benjamin's collector, the excavator of the debris of history does not 'possess' the past but is 'possessed' by it. The historical excavator – likened by Benjamin to a ragpicker or *bricoleur* – is thus driven not by a desire for rational mastery but by personal engagement.

Benjamin's major essays were, of course, written in exile from the threat of fascism in the 1930s, as befits a 'nomadic' thinker in Deleuze's and Guattari's sense of the term (1998) as one who refuses to be 'territorialized' by 'master narratives'. Benjamin's unorthodox version of historical materialism, which aims to release the multiple potential of the past by freeing it from the 'master narratives' of historicist causal explanation (whether orthodox marxist or liberal), in some senses shares with anarchism its refusal of a single, rational authority and its celebration of the heterogeneous: history at the micro- rather than the macro-level. Michaelis and Horna were also refugees from Nazism, who had sought refuge in Republican Spain from Austria and Hungary respectively. Margaret Michaelis, of Jewish origin, was born in Austria in 1902, and had worked as a photographer in Vienna, Prague and Berlin since 1929. In December 1933 she fled Berlin for Barcelona with her husband after both had been separately arrested for their involvement with the anarcho-syndicalist Freien Arbeiter-Union Deutschlands (FAUD), all of whose members ended up in Republican Barcelona. Her husband, Rudolf Michaelis, was head of the FAUD's cultural branch, as well as an archaeologist who had worked on excavations in the Middle East (and hence an expert on ruins). She separated from him in Barcelona in 1934, thereafter earning her living as a professional photographer. She had photographed the Barrio Chino (red-light district and old popular quarter) of Barcelona during a previous stay in 1932. Her 1932 photographs and those taken during her later stay in Barcelona from 1933–7 were published in the magazine *AC* of the architectural group GATEPAC, which included the famous Bauhaus-linked modernist architect Josep Sert. These published images included a large number of architectural photographs commissioned by GATEPAC, as well as photographs of southern Spanish popular architecture taken on a trip with Josep Sert and the painter Joan Miró. She also did some commercial photography for advertising. In October 1936 she accompanied Emma Goldman, of whom she took an impressive portrait, on a tour of the anarchist collectives in Aragon. Between 1936 and 1937 she was commissioned by the Propaganda Commisariat of the Catalan Autonomous Government (the Generalitat) to take photographs for its magazine *Nova Iberia*. In 1937, as the tide turned against the Republic in the Civil War, she left Spain, settling in Australia in 1939. Her photographs of Republican Spain remained forgotten or unknown till, on her death in 1985, they were donated to the National Gallery of Australia. Kati Horna, born in Hungary in 1912, came to Spain as a freelance photographer in 1937 expressly to photograph the Civil War, though she did not sell her photographs commercially and did not work for any official Republican organization. However, many of her photographs were published in anarchist magazines such as *Mujeres Libres, Libre Studio, Tierra y Libertad, Tiempos Nuevos*, and *Umbral*; she worked for the latter as a graphic artist. She photographed life on the Aragonese front, and in the major cities, as well as rural areas, of the Republican zone. Most of her photographs have been lost; the only ones to survive are the 270 she took with her in a box when she left for second exile in Mexico in 1938. In 1979, after Spain's return to democratically elected government, she donated her photographs to the Spanish Ministry of Culture.

As Josep Vicent Monzó notes in his introduction to the exhibition catalogue of Horna's photographs (Horna 1992: 10), the work of women photographers in Republican Spain has been eclipsed by that of better known male photographers linked to the major international agencies such as Magnum: Robert Capa during the Civil War, but one thinks also of Henri Cartier-Bresson's photographs taken in Republican Spain before the war's start. While I do not wish to suggest that female photographers have an essentially 'feminine' vision, it is noticeable that both Michaelis and Horna stress the everyday, with particular – but not sole – emphasis on women and children caught in the midst of some banal (but, for that reason, expressive) activity. However, this emphasis on women and children is not a privileging of the private over the public; on the contrary, these women and children are captured in the course of public interchange in the street, or in some cases in public institutions such as refugee centres. I prefer to read these photographs through Benjamin's insistence on everyday material culture as that which, precisely because it is not handed down through official records and discourses but is forgotten, thus forms the 'stuff' of the past. As Benjamin notes (1992: 248), historicism – which stands back from the past in order to produce a supposedly rational account of it – in practice empathizes with the victors by editing out the multiple potential of the everyday which, at the time, is experienced as a 'now' and not as part of a causal chain. The order in which I shall discuss the photographs is not that of their publication, which in turn does not follow the sequence in which they were taken. In keeping with Benjamin, and with the anarchist rather than Marxist orientation of Michaelis and Horna, I prefer to concentrate on their photographs as single statements, irreducible to causal explanation as part of a grand historical narrative, but revealing the material 'stuff' of history in all its triviality and specificity. Their concentration on individualized human figures (particulary in the work of Horna) also matches the visual style of Spanish anarchist posters produced during the Civil War, by contrast with the constructivist influenced communist posters which represent the human body in the mass as machine. Many of Michaelis's photographs were taken before the Civil War, and she photographs the effects of war only at a distance via its refugee camps, Red-Cross workers, demonstrations and posters. But if war tells us anything about history, it is that it does not make sense at the time (or after) and is perceived in a fragmentary, partial manner, for in the midst of war one simply does not know what is going on elsewhere. Thus in their insistence on the everyday moment interrupted in midstream – suspending any possibility of explanatory narrative – the photographs of Michaelis and Horna capture a sense of the materiality of history (objects that are used; bodies engaged in social exchange) and of its impermanence (as in those photographs where humans beings are absent but implicit in the object captured within the frame).

Benjamin argues that:

> Thinking involves not only the flow of thoughts, but their arrest as well. Where thinking suddenly stops in a configuration pregnant with tensions, it gives that configuration a shock, by which it crystallizes into a monad. [...] In this structure, [the historical materialist] recognizes the sign of a Messianic cessation of happening, or, put differently, a revolutionary chance in the fight for the oppressed past. He takes cognizance of it in order to blast a specific era out of the homogeneous course of history [...]. (1992: 254)

The fact that so many of Michaelis's and Horna's photographs capture social encounters in mid flow allows us to perceive the past moment not as a 'fact' but as a crystallization of tensions whose outcome is still undecided. In this sense they can be seen as constituting what Benjamin calls 'a politics of remembrance' which is not geared towards prophecies of the future, but towards producing an experience of the past as a 'now' which stands outside of time and yet forms the 'matter' of history. Benjamin has talked of this 'resurrection' of the past in the now as a Messianic project, as opposed to historicism which constitutes the past as dead and immutable: hence his insistence that the historicist notion of history as a causal continuum does not, in fact, link the past with the present except insofar as it subjects the past to a providentialist vision which legitimizes the victors (1992: 248). It is, I think, possible to relate Benjamin's concept of Messianic time (in his case, derived from Jewish thought) to an anarchist tradition strongly influenced by millenarianism. I would also suggest that Benjamin's insistence on wrenching the fragments of the past out of their context – explicitly described by him as a form of creative destruction – maps quite closely onto the anarchist concept of the need to destroy the old in order to usher in a new dawn which is not so much a destruction of the past, as a destruction of those contextual configurations which prevented the potential of the past from realizing itself. Benjamin's angel of history, blown towards the future while facing the wreckage of the past, sounds remarkably like the anarchist Messiah – incarnated for many in Spain in the figure of Durruti, especially after his sacrificial death in the defence of Madrid.

In effect, Benjamin replaces the historian – in the historicist sense – with the figure of the collector, whose passion he describes as 'anarchistic' and 'destructive' because he destroys the context of the objects which he collects at random (Benjamin 1992: 49). Unlike the historian, the collector is driven by passion for the objects which he assembles in new arbitrary configurations that infuse them with a personal meaning or 'transfiguration' (Benjamin 1992: 47–8). As Hannah Arendt comments:

> The figure of the collector [...] could assume such eminently modern features in Benjamin because history itself – that is, the break in tradition which took place at the beginning of this century – had already relieved him of this task of destruction and he only needed to bend down, as it were, to select his precious fragments from the piles of debris. (Benjamin 1992: 49)

One may note here that the Spanish Civil War played a decisive role in the destruction of the grand historical master narratives – as Orwell's *Homage to Catalonia* shows so well – not just because liberalism and socialism were defeated, but because both found it necessary to turn on the anarchists and the Trotskyists as a prerequisite for fighting fascism. Both Michaelis and Horna were in Spain during the events of May 1937 in Barcelona, described by Orwell, when the communist authorities turned their guns on the anarchists and Trotskyists, though they did not photograph them. Their focus on the trivial and the everyday allows a 'resurrection' of that which lies forgotten beneath the debris of history, at a time when history seemed to be constituted by ruins – for what else does one think of when one conjures up an image of the Spanish Civil War?

This was, of course, the first war to see the systematic aerial bombardment of civilian targets, by the Nationalist forces aided by the German Condor Legion. Horna returned repeatedly in her photographs to the ruins left by the Nationalist bombing of Barcelona. In the photograph reproduced here as Figure 5.2, the mound of debris on the right comprises a miscellany of domestic appurtenances from which protrudes what appears to be a truncated female shop-window mannequin. The Republican soldiers keeping guard look the camera directly in the eye, interpellating us; while the statue of the Virgin carefully placed to one side of the debris is reminiscent of Benjamin's angel of history: unlike the latter, her back is turned on the rubble but she nonetheless stands as a forlorn image of redemption which, rather than reject the past for the future, takes the burden of the past on its shoulders. Such photographs invite us to occupy the position of Benjamin's ragpicker who confronts

92 JO LABANYI

us with the materiality and immediacy of the past precisely by refusing to order and explain it. It is the fact that the debris in the picture is wrenched out of its context by war that makes it speak to us so eloquently.

Michaelis did not photograph ruins but she photographed a great deal of rubbish. Her major project was her photographs for GATEPAC's 1934 exhibition *Nova Barcelona*, whose aim was the reconstruction of Barcelona's old popular quarters on rational modernist lines. In practice, Michaelis's photographs document the chaotic heterogeneity of Barcelona popular street life, stressing its rubbish for sanitary reasons – as in the aerial view of an inner courtyard in the Barrio Chino reproduced here as Figure 5.3 – but in effect replicating Benjamin's excavation of the

Figure 5.2 Kati Horna, 'On guard after the air raid', Barcelona, March 1938. Reproduced by permission of the Ministerio de Educación y Ciencia, Archivo General de la Guerra Civil Española.

debris of history. These photographs could not be more different from her architectural photographs of new modernist apartments in Barcelona, whose functionalist structures appear dehumanized in their geometric lines and uniformity, and whose very cleanness has a spartan quality; indeed, with one exception these photographs of 'model' modernist

Figure 5.3 Margaret Michaelis-Sachs, 'Untitled', Barcelona, 1933–4. Used here on the cover of J. Grijalbo's and F. Fàbregas's book *La Municipalització de la propietat urbana* (1937), published by the Socialist trade union UGT. Reproduced by permission of the Arxiu Historic del COAC (Col.legi d'Architectes de Catalunya), Barcelona.

Figure 5.4 Margaret Michaelis-Sachs, 'Kitchen, 24 Calle San Rafael', Barcelona, c.1933–4. Reproduced by permission of the National Gallery of Australia, Canberra.

housing show no signs of human habitation. By contrast, it is the filth of the working-class kitchen in the Barrio Chino photographed by her (Figure 5.4) that betrays the traces of human presence.

Michaelis's emphasis on street life makes her a female version of the Baudelairean *flâneur* who provided Benjamin with a model for the historian of everyday material culture. Her photographs of the Barrio Chino create a sense of arrested narrative, of random constellations that exist

Figure 5.5 Margaret Michaelis-Sachs, 'Untitled (woman in doorway)', Barcelona, c. 1934. Reproduced by permission of the National Gallery of Australia, Canberra.

entirely in the now. Loaves are caught about to be shovelled into the baker's oven; meat is captured about to be carved in a bar as a guitarist plays; one extraordinary photograph 'arrests' a pickpocket in the act of snatching a handbag from a table where a woman and a man sit engaged in animated conversation: the thief is fixed forever at the edge of the frame trying to steal out of it into oblivion. In a large number of these

Figure 5.6 Margaret Michaelis-Sachs, 'Untitled', Barcelona, 1932. Reproduced by permission of the Arxiu Historic del COAC (Col.legi d'Architectes de Catalunya), Barcelona.

Figure 5.7 Margaret Michaelis-Sachs, 'Comisariat de Propaganda postcard (woman with line of children in Barcelona Stadium'), Barcelona 1936–7. The caption reads: 'Young teachers know how to teach through play'. Reproduced by permission of the National Gallery of Australia, Canberra.

Figure 5.8 Kati Horna, 'Refugee Centre in the Alcázar de Cervantes (Alcázar de San Juan)', undated. Reproduced by permission of the Ministerio de Educación y Ciencia, Archivo General de la Guerra Civil Española.

street photographs, as in Figure 5.2 by Horna discussed above, at least one human figure is looking at the camera: that is, at Michaelis and at us. These figures looking at us are not communicating any message – we cannot guess what they are thinking – but their function is simply that of interpellating the spectator. A particularly poignant photograph of a sick-looking boy (suffering from rickets?) is shot from above (from a balcony?), with his crooked head staring vacantly up at us as if interrogating us: this photograph was used on the cover of volume 6 of *AC*, next to a statistic indicating the 20% mortality rate in the Barrio Chino. In the photograph reproduced here as Figure 5.5, the boy peering at us from

98 JO LABANYI

Fugure 5.9 Kati Horna, 'Centre for pregnant women from Madrid in Vélez Rubio', August 1937. Reproduced by permission of the Ministerio de Educación y Ciencia, Archivo General de la Guerra Civil Española.

between the two figures – whose unexplained, arrested encounter provides the picture's main focus – serves to draw us into the photograph, resurrecting the past in the present. In the street-life scene reproduced as Figure 5.6, parts of bodies are cut off by the frame, producing a sense of the fleeting moment captured in its arbitrary materiality. The lack of unity in the photograph's composition (the various figures are each involved in some individual activity) creates a sense of the heterogeneity of history as it is experienced at the time. This immediacy is increased by the fact that we do not know what the child in the middle and the woman seated with her back to us on the right are looking at outside the picture's frame: the historical moment is not explained but is reproduced as an interrogation. Similarly, Figure 5.7 gives us a high-angle shot of a teacher leading a trail of refugee children across the Stadium in Barcelona to an unknown future, present in the photograph through their various gazes at the unrepresented (unrepresentable) space ahead (positioned somewhere behind us). The ragged line formed by their shadows contrasts with the geometric formations found in fascist (and in many Spanish communist) pictorial representations: this is history left ragged at the edges (and, in many of these photographs, literally in rags).

Figure 5.10 Kati Horna, 'Field hospital at Grañeu', March–April 1937. Reproduced by permission of the Ministerio de Educación y Ciencia, Archivo General de la Guerra Civil, Española.

In Horna's photographs, we have a similar sense of the 'now' interrupted in mid flow. Again many of the photographs contain one or more human figures looking at us, or looking at something that is beyond representation off frame. The photograph of a group of children in a refugee centre reproduced as Figure 5.8 combines both modalities, with one girl and one boy interpellating us, and the boy in the centre of the picture looking at something off frame to the right, while the boy on the far right hides his gaze altogether. In Figure 5.9, the nursing mother photographed at a maternity centre for pregnant women evacuated from a besieged Madrid gazes anxiously at something off frame to the left: an image of new life undercut by the impossibility of knowing the future. In another photograph, the crowd (mostly women and girls) is shot staring expectantly at something off frame to the left, with the camera held at a tilt as if tipping the figures into the uncertainty ahead. In a further photograph – reminiscent of Michaelis's photograph of the teacher and children in the Barcelona Stadium but bleaker – a small group of refugees, clutching infants and suitcases, marches towards us round a bend in a desolate country road, in a landscape empty save for a few pollarded trees, bound for an unknown future that exists off frame somewhere to our rear. As spectators, we find ourselves occupying the position of Benjamin's angel of history, our gaze fixed on the human relics and ruins, and impelled with them into the future to which our backs are turned.

Horna frequently chooses as subjects situations of impermanence and incongruity. One photograph portrays a makeshift hospital installed in a requisitioned church, with the letters CNT for the anarchist trade union painted on the bare wall where the altar once stood. Another depicts piles of furniture in the street after a bombing raid in Valencia in 1937: the centre of the picture is occupied by a large framed photograph of a little girl who is staring directly at us. This interpellating gaze from within the 'photograph within the photograph' draws us not only into the 1937 street scene represented, but also further back into the earlier private historical moment when this family portrait was taken. Here, as in the first photograph by Horna discussed (Figure 5.1), the jumble of randomly assembled objects recalls the collages of *objets trouvés* so beloved of the surrealists, and through them by Benjamin. Several of Horna's photographs use montage, superimposing a human face over a street scene or, on an anti-fascist poster produced for the Federación Anarquista Ibérica, over the ruined shell of a house destroyed by bombing. This use of montage has the effect of giving human figures a spectral quality, as ghosts of the past who return to haunt the present. A similar effect is produced in several photographs shot through shop windows, where the reflection on the glass superimposes a ghostly outside world onto the objects displayed – which always represent human figures: photographic portraits, busts of Durruti. Perhaps nowhere is this sense of a haunting human presence stronger than in the photograph of a field hospital in Grañeu taken by Horna in March-April 1937 (Figure 5.10), where the human presence is felt all the more poignantly because of its absence from the photograph, present only through its traces: the suitcases, the pin-ups on the wall, and the imprint of a body still left on the empty bed. Here it is not the human figure that interpellates us, but its absence, evoking the fragility of the moment and recognition of the fact that the historian can never fully recover the past but only its fragmentary traces.

The isolation of a human figure interpellating us, who is not symbolic of anything but simply 'there' as a guarantee of presence, is found similarly in Kate O'Brien's *Farewell Spain*. Provoked by a newspaper photograph of Irún burning, while writing in London, she evokes a vision of the sight of Irún on crossing into Spain from France, which corresponds to no particular date but is emblematic without being symbolic:

> There was apparently nothing else to see at Irún – except just beyond the bridge, a man in black. He was standing quite still in the roadway, with his back to the train. A solid man of fifty, of respectable mien, and wearing his black overcoat slung as if it were a cape. Wearing a black beret, too. Apparently unaware of the train and indifferent to the weather.
>
> They saw this identical man that morning, because wherever or however one enters Spain, he is the first living object that catches the eye. (1985: 8)

If this testimonial figure has his back turned, on other occasions, O'Brien singles out a human figure who is looking at her and who thus also interpellates us: for example, the six-year-old Enrique in Santiago who, as 'the type of all these little boys', is seen by her and her companion Mary every day, and is seen again by Mary the following year. O'Brien ends her chapter on Santiago: 'So Rome of the Middle Ages fades from me again, its baroque towers clear and noble in the background and in the foreground a little smiling boy' (1985: 88).

Just as Benjamin exalts the idle wanderings of the *flâneur* (he notes the particular advantages of being transient in another country), so O'Brien exalts what she calls 'pottering memory': 'Santander is comparatively safe for pottering memory' (1985: 20), she nicely writes. And just as Benjamin insists on the random encounter, wrenched from its context, that produces the 'shock' of the real, so O'Brien seeks 'the quickened sense of life, the accidents that jab imagination' (1985: 16); she writes repeatedly of how the places she visits do not fit her expectations, almost always focusing not on the predictability of place but on some chance encounter that throws things awry. Like Benjamin, she too refuses linear sequence and historicist accuracy:

> my journey will be a composite one, made up of many, and without unnecessary chronological reference. The route will be a plaiting together of many routes; seasons and cities will succeed each other here in reminiscence as almost certainly they did not in fact [...]. (1985: 21)

Knowing that Spain is in flames as she writes, she remembers and mourns 'the new ruins', recalling 'a million things not set down in this book or anywhere – moments and places without name or date' but filled with the everyday: 'Rich in sun, children and acacia-trees' (1985: 226–7) and with:

> The junk we have accumulated and so obstinately loved and sought to increase. Temples, palaces, cathedrals; libraries full of moonshine; pictures to proclaim dead persons; [...] odds and ends of two thousand silly years [...]. (1985: 5)

That is, a vision of history based on the everyday which does not fit the grand master narratives of 'the forward marchers, the right-minded' (1985: 6) whose rational vision is set on the future. By contrast O'Brien insists: 'Let us praise personal memory, personal love', insisting that 'our protective dullness is only really penetrated, our nerves only really ache when that which we have personally known, that which has touched ourselves, takes the centre of the stage awhile' (1985: 7). O'Brien is convinced that she has lived the last decade – the 1930s – when it was possible to be a 'sentimental tourist', for the 'hour of full authority' of the scientific vision is dawning: 'There will be no point then in going out to look for a reed shaken in the wind' (1985: 4). She was wrong because, as Benjamin predicted despite his dislike of prophecy, there are still plenty of ruins and we are still fixated on them while being blown backwards into the future. If the Spanish Civil War still arouses such passions it is perhaps because it figures so tangibly the possibility that history could have been otherwise; that is, as the photographs of Michaelis and Horna show, it provides an emblem of the eternity of ruins – not in the sense of a universalist belief in timeless essences, but in the sense that ruins, if one looks among the debris, contain the unrealized potential of forgotten material lives and objects.

Note

1. We are grateful to the Ministerio de Educación y Ciencia, Archivo General de la Guerra Civil Española for permission to reproduce the photographs by Kati Horna; and to the National Gallery of Australia, Canberra and the Arxiu Historic del COAC (Col.legi d'Architectes de Catalunya), Barcelona for permission to reproduce the photographs by Margaret Michaelis-Sachs.

Bibliography

Benjamin, W., *Illuminations*, introd. H. Arendt. London, 1992.
Deleuze, G., and F. Guattari., *A Thousand Plateaus: Capitalism and Schizophrenia*. London, 1998.
Graham, H., and J. Labanyi., eds. *Spanish Cultural Studies: An Introduction. The Struggle for Modernity*. Oxford, 1995.
Horna, K., *Fotografías de la guerra civil española (1937–1938)* (exhibition catalogue). Salamanca, 1992.
Michaelis, M., *Fotografía, vanguardia y política en la Barcelona de la República* (exhibition catalogue). Valencia, 1998.
O'Brien, K., *Farewell Spain*. London, 1985.

Part 3

Liminal Spaces

Chapter 6

SIGNS OF ROMAN RULE
ITALIAN TOURISTS AND TRAVELLERS IN GREECE AND EGYPT

Charles Burdett

If, as Paul Fussell contends, the years between the wars represented a prolific period in the history of travel writing in English, then the same can, with some qualification, be said of the interwar years in Italy (Fussell 1980). The journeys of well known writers and critics, such as Arnaldo Cipolla, Corrado Alvaro, Orio Vergani or Margherita Sarfatti were frequently sponsored by newspapers whose readership gained the opportunity of following one writer or another through cities and countryside different from those to which they were accustomed. The written accounts of journeys were often supplemented by a rich array of photographs, so that the reader was offered not only a literary but a visual experience, one that could be enjoyed first in the pages of a newspaper or magazine and subsequently in the form of a travelogue. Many leading publishers, including Mondadori and Treves had long lists of travel series. The established travel writers of the time were willing to explore relatively unfamiliar territory: the national daily, the *Corriere della sera*, for example, did its best to keep pace with Italian colonial expansion while sending its correspondents to explore such far away places as Central America and the Far East (Cecchi 1932; Comisso 1932). In 1930 the Touring Club Italiano decided to publish a new magazine to accompany the already existing *Le Vie d'Italia*, the new and expensively produced magazine was entitled *Le Vie del Mondo*.[1] As well as representing the stages of Italian imperial development, offering elegantly mediated versions of the exotic or stimulating a desire for journeys of an adventurous kind, all literary travellers made excursions to more familiar and more easily accessible territory. A common destination was, unsurprisingly, the eastern Mediterranean and more specifically, Greece and Egypt. In 1930 Arnaldo Cipolla travelled down the Nile (Cipolla 1930) and three years later he organized a similar journey by following the footsteps of Alexander the Great (Cipolla 1933); Mario Praz (1942) collected his impressions of Greece in his published diary of 1931; Domenico Tumiati and Emilio Cecchi represented an Arcadian version of Greece in 1934 and 1936 respectively; as a correspondent for *La Stampa*, Margherita Sarfatti travelled through Egypt in 1937; G. Bobich (1939) and F. Milone (1941) wrote on Egypt and Greece respectively as correspondents for *Le Vie del Mondo*.

Journeys to places within Egypt and Greece were recorded not only by travel writers who were paid to capture their impressions, but also by some of the many tourists who visited the same locations. One of the tourist itineraries which was most often followed for motives of pleasure was the tour of the eastern Mediterranean. Tour operators organized cruises which went to Alexandria, Palestine, Rhodes, Istanbul and Athens. The cruises allowed, for the most part wealthy, Italians to mingle with the privileged classes of other European nations and to see such places as the pyramids of Giza, Jerusalem, Knossos or the Acropolis. The writings to emerge from this kind of tourism derived their narrative structure from the interrelation of the various stages of the cruise: one object of desire after another was first anticipated, then enjoyed and finally remembered. In the recorded journeys of such occasional writers as Maria Benzoni, Emma Bona or Carlo Manzini (1934), the first person narrator frequently rushed from one site to another, managed briefly to visit a famous tomb or museum but found time to muse at leisure on recent impressions as the cruise liner sailed towards its next destination. While the writings of those who travelled principally as tourists may display fewer linguistic innovations or metaphorical constructions than the books or articles which better known writers were able to produce, they nevertheless share a great deal of common features: they obey the same generic conventions, they draw on the same precedents and they attempt to address the same kind of public – those who have not seen the sites that are described. Despite the emphasis which authors placed on the individuality of perception, it is thus appropriate to speak of a fairly homogeneous body of texts. The various travelogues mapped the boundaries of the itineraries that determined the movements and impressions of their writers, they illuminated the abstract, scripted meanings that one place after another assumed in the travellers' system of cultural recognition. The recorded journeys serve as valuable indications of the complex processes whereby certain sites were constructed and experienced. What follows is an attempt to read the written accounts of journeys to Greece and Egypt in the light of recent work (Culler 1988; Rojek 1997; Gregory 1999) on the hidden dynamics of travel writing and tourist perception.

The intention is to examine the structures at work in the texts and to explore their relation to the wider context of Italian fascism and colonial expansion.

The spectacular archaeological excavations in both Egypt and Greece in the late nineteenth and early twentieth centuries certainly inspired a great many travellers from all over Europe, eager to see for themselves the monuments and artefacts which Schliemann, Evans, Carter and others had recently uncovered as well as more established sites on the tourist route. In the narration of her trip to Egypt, Annie Vivanti had even described a mesmerizing conversation with Howard Carter (Vivanti 1925: 26–33). The expressed desire of most Italian visitors to either country was not to see the present but to discover the ancient past, though an interesting exception to the rule was Filippo Tommaso Marinetti's *Il fascino dell'Egitto* [The Fascination of Egypt] (1933) which displayed a Flaubertian interest in the pleasures, erotic and other, that contemporary Egypt had to offer. The desire to travel primarily through time rather than through space was not only the motivation of most tourists and travel writers, it was also the conceptual assumption on which almost all itineraries were predicated. The privileging of an interest in the material remains of the past over the reality of the present had several important implications for the ways in which the travellers viewed the countries that they toured. To begin with, their perception of place was organized along strictly hierarchical lines. Whether consciously or not, they were all the time involved in making or reinforcing distinctions between the sightworthy and the invisible (Rojek 1997: 52). The anxiety to see the tomb of Tutankhamen and the temple of Luxor (Cipolla 1930: 65–70) or the rush to see the pyramids (Benzoni 1935: 51–5) was accompanied by a comparatively superficial interest in the social structure of modern Egypt. The automatic selection of sights hinted at another perceptual strategy common to professional and improvised travel writers alike: both tended clearly to relate the temple or monument which stood before them to images or descriptions of the same place which they had previously encountered. Emma Bona began the narration of her visit to the pyramids by listing the various travelogues which had, for her, given life to a vision of North Africa (Bona 1938: 137), just as Pina Ballario's journey to Greece began with her reading of the Thomas Cook booklet, *How to See Greece*. The sight, to use Johnathon Culler's terms (Culler 1988: 160), was continuously related to its markers, reality was measured against its representations.

Thus by touring monumental or archaeological sites the Italian travellers of the 1930s revisited their preconceptions of the ancient world. They were able to feel or assert a presence within the tortuous history whereby these sites had come to be marked as culturally extraordinary. Such an impression was enhanced by the wealth of comparisons which it was possible to make with the observations of celebrated literary travellers. Emilio Cecchi chose frequently to frame his comments on Greece as a response to the earlier appreciations of Goethe, Raynal, Byron or Chateaubriand (Cecchi 1997: 723), Domenico Tumiati's journey to Greece was motivated in part by the desire to relive scenes from D'Annunzio's macabre Greek drama *La città morta* [The Dead City] (1898) and from his celebrated *Viaggio in Grecia* [Journey to Greece] (1895), while less solitary travellers were informed by the learned opinion of Italian archaeologists. Travelling with the Royal [Italian] Geographical Society, Maria Benzoni commented: 'The whole country is swarming with Homeric and Virgilian recollections' (Benzoni 1935: 153). The indulgence in literary reminiscences as well as the relation of the sight to its markers points quite clearly at the citationary structure in which the travel texts were involved: expectations of what the traveller would see were shaped culturally and commercially, past journeys provoked present excursions which would, if narrated, encourage others to travel. Despite the physical reality of the journey, its discomforts and obstacles, the travellers moved as much through a constructed, orientalizing fantasy (Said 1991) as they did through any real locality. Their movements said as much about the contemporary reception of archaeology as a discipline (the position adopted by the tourist was often that of the keen student of recent discoveries) or the mechanics of the burgeoning tourist industry as they did about either Greece or Egypt. The many photographs which were reproduced as a kind of visual commentary on the texts served the unintended function of pointing to the circle of repeated experiences around which the travellers moved. One photograph after another represented the tourist or professional travel writer close to the pyramids or the sphinx, standing on or near to the Acropolis, or in the middle of a Greek amphitheatre. This sort of archetypal photograph can be seen, as Kowalewski (1992: 1–16) has suggested, as the modern equivalent of etching one's name on a monument, of declaring a personal presence in the history of a ruin. The many repetitions of the same panorama also provide a peculiarly striking indication that the various travellers to celebrated places in the eastern Mediterranean, whatever their cultural preparation or social standing, travelled in the same kind of space, one which was, to paraphrase Barthes (1973: 75), made up of a web of temples, tombs, palaces, sculptures and museums.

As they moved from one point on their itineraries to another, the tourists of the 1930s sought to experience not only a sense of the ancient societies whose surviving sites they saw, they also endeavoured to develop an imaginative understanding of the mythic or transcendental beliefs that animated those societies. They explored the layering of symbols, fantasies and legends which surrounded a given site. Indeed, all the texts tended to be structured around the narration of intense moments when the writer recorded a sense of reality being eroded by a perceived engagement with myth. The physical feeling could be heightened by night time visits to Greek temples or to the interior of Egyptian tombs. Recounting her visit through the chambers of the royal palace of Knossos by candle light, Emma Bona wrote of the 'oriental night mixing its fantastic shadows with the shades and glimmering light of a living legend' (Bona 1938: 132). A similar experience of 'ecstatic contemplation' was recorded by Maria Benzoni, who visiting the pyramids by night wrote of seeing the ghostly double of one of the dead pharaohs and of remaining perfectly still, anxious to hear the echo of voices from within ancient tombs (1935: 55). Most travellers saw Greek vases or Egyptian sepulchral engravings as a means of entering the mythical world of the past (Benzoni 1935: 141; Cecchi 1997: 789), but the figurations of ancient myth could be sensed with varying degrees of explicitness. At successive stages of his journey through Greece, Tumiati wrote of his encounters with the characters of Greek myth: he saw the Graces appear with the first rays of dawn (1934: 12), witnessed Maia descend from the constellation of the Pleiades (1934: 61), and encountered Athene in personified form (1934: 99). With less poetic licence, Cecchi (1997: 748) sought to view reality with the eyes of the heroic or mythical dead. He wrote:

> Mycenae transposes myth into physical sensation. [...] From the very point where your eye looks down the steep curve of the mountain and sees every blade of grass and every rock with such clarity that they seem within your grasp, Clytemnestra watched out for ten years, nurturing both hatred and passion. And for an instant it seems as though you can see the same things through her serene yet ferocious eyes.

Though the attempt to gain an imaginative apprehension of past beliefs may have inspired some of the most intriguing passages of the travel literature of the time, the attempt in itself could inhibit the investigation of realities that were closer to hand. Various cultural critics speak of tourism being an exercise in type construction (Culler 1988; Rojek and Urry 1997) in so far as the tourist sees in the country that he or she visits living or concrete examples of preconceived ideas. The type that is already familiar to the tourist is simply confirmed by the act of travelling. When they gazed at the inhabitants of the communities that they toured, the Italian travellers of the 1930s tended to see ancient features on contemporary faces. The present, at least as it was evoked in their prose, was in the grip of the distant past. For Pina Ballario, the Egyptians who farmed the land close to the Nile seemed as though they had stepped out from the tomb painting of Giza or Sakkara or from the *Book of the Dead* (Ballario 1936: 363), while Cecchi constantly saw in the features of the latter day inhabitants of Greece the semblance of a hero or demi-god (1997: 722). He went on to make the observation that in Greece the ancient and the modern were not easily separable and that everyday reality seemed both fantastic and remote (1997: 704). Thus to read any one of the many accounts of journeys to the eastern Mediterranean, is to read of the experience of temporal dislocation, of a journey which takes its traveller to 'the threshold of a world that is supernatural' (Cecchi 1997: 733). The guided but obsessive concentration on the sight, often to the exclusion of its twentieth-century context, increased the sense of the transcendental, the unfamiliar and the other. What the travelling subjects did, perhaps unwittingly, was to view the countries they visited as a museum or as a kind of interwar equivalent to the theme park.[2]

The responses that I have so far indicated might be said to be common to most tourists who made, or indeed who make, organized visits to sites within the Mediterranean. There is certainly a great deal which links the recorded observations of the travellers of the 1930s with those made by travellers to Greece and Egypt in the late nineteenth and early twentieth centuries. Both display the same sense of a privileged initiation into the mysteries of ancient culture and both are indications of the evolving reception of antiquity in Western Europe. For most tourists the thrill of seeing a particular sight resided in the depth of associations that it allowed the viewer to make. When in front of the Acropolis, the Lion Gate or the Pyramids at Giza, the sightseer's sense of the relation between the site and its markers encouraged, at some level, an awareness of the importance which certain places assumed within the symbolic language of his or her own culture. In fairly obvious ways, past or ancient societies are often exploited as emblems of contemporary identities. The British Museum, for example, is a symbol of British culture though it has significant Greek and Egyptian components. It is precisely the concealed expression of the traveller's own sense of cultural identity expressed through a particular appreciation of another culture that makes apparently vague or timeless identifications all the more specific and significant. As they moved through the monumental attractions of Greece and Egypt, the Italian tourists of the 1930s drew analogies, explicit or otherwise, between the ancient world and the political and cultural reality that they inhabited. In the process of attributing certain meanings to given signifiers, they pointed at some of the key semiotic mechanisms of Italian fascism.

The desire of many travellers to experience the physical and mental sensation of journeying through time may have generated the momentary illusion of living in the ancient past, but that illusion was never independent from the present. The past was consistently seen as graspable because of the repeated belief in the cyclical nature of history: for the majority of the Italian observers, the ancient monuments were the material evidence of a tremendously powerful cycle of decline and regeneration. If such ruins provided contradictory evidence of both grandeur and decline, the tourists themselves expressed the conviction of belonging to a civilization that, under the guidance of Mussolini, was on an upward curve. Thus Arnaldo Cipolla could confidently affirm that: 'The language of the remotest antiquity is closer to our spirit than we may dare to suppose' (Cipolla 1930: 35). Other tourists remained deeply fascinated by symbols of death, renewal and resurrection or, when confronted by the stone or golden effigies of the ruling figures of antiquity, indulged in comparisons with iconographic representations of the Duce (Benzoni 1935: 77). Accompanying the assimilation of ancient ruler with modern dictator was the inclination on the part of the tourist to see the evidence of past cultures as a reflection of Italian society under fascism.[3] Standing by the pyramids, Emma Bona wrote of the connection she perceived between the evidence of the society she saw and the reality of the society of which she felt herself to be a part. The pyramids were, in her words, the work of 'a superior civilization', of 'a people dominated by a dream of greatness and power', they were, 'mile stones along the path of a great people' (Bona 1938: 138).

The reading of the ancient world through a palingenetic conception of history and a faith in the eternal endurance of the 'spirit' of a people (Benzoni 1935: 62) was substantiated by the apparent merging of the myths of the ancient world with those of fascism. Nowhere was this more clearly represented than in the reported visits to the Greek amphitheatres or stadia. At one level, the response of the various tourists to these sites was simply one of awe for the surviving examples of architectural perfection. But at another level, most tourists dwelt on a disorienting sense of acquaintance with these unfamiliar places. The impression of familiarity derived from the recent completion of one of the most famous building projects of the regime, the Foro Mussolini. Planned by Enrico del Debbio and completed in 1934, the Foro was designed as an athletics stadium on the south bank of the Tiber, close to the centre of Rome. Built in the oval shape of an amphitheatre, its ascending rows of white stone were surmounted by huge male statues, each in a sporting or martial pose and each representing, in personified form, a town or city in Italy. The Foro was intended to be a place where the youth of Italy could display its physical agility and prowess. Part of the complex that was to form the *Scuola superiore fascista di educazione fisica* [The Fascist Academy for Physical Education], the Foro was a site where subjectivities could be moulded and where mass celebrations could be held. The instant comparison made between the Greek structures and the contemporary building was accompanied, in the writings of one figure after another, by the suggestion that Mussolini's Italy was nothing less than the astonishing apparition in the present of the monumental grandeur of the ancient past.[4] In a way that was both uncanny and at the same time exalting, the boundaries between the ancient and the modern were for the viewer erased. The future which fascism seemed to herald had its model in the past, while travellers of the 1930s could temporarily believe that they inhabited the same spiritual climate as an ancient people. The effect of gazing at the marble of Epidaurus or Delphi was similar to that of attending the spectacular public displays of the regime: most travellers journeyed as much through fascism's 'official symbolic discourse' (Falasca-Zamponi 1997: 2) as they did through the physical reality of Greece.[5] The experience of seeing the future reflected in the past nurtured the belief that gigantic projects like the Foro Mussolini would themselves conquer time and eternalize the values of 'la civiltà fascista'.[6]

If travelling to Greece in the 1930s granted many tourists a privileged perception of the significance of the monumental architecture favoured by the regime, then it also encouraged a vision of humanity fully in accordance with the fascist project to redefine the character of ordinary Italians. By piecing together the descriptions of Greek statues contained within the many texts a coherent picture emerges. Domenico Tumiati wrote of an 'ideal of man' being born in the stadia of antiquity, of feeling a pulsating sense of 'the youthfulness of the race' (1934: 7, 91), of divine statues gloriously perpetuating the human form (1934: 93). Similarly, Emma Bona, comparing the Foro Mussolini with the monuments of the Acropolis, spoke of an impression of beauty fused with force, and, imagining the statues of the Foro to be momentarily alive, of an atmosphere of youthfulness and future promise (1938: 60–3). Writing in exactly the same florid but assertive style, Maria Benzoni described remembering the Foro Mussolini while at the Olympic stadium in Athens:

> The statues of athletes seem to move in the space with a bearing that is decisive, Roman, unmistakable. [In] Athens […] the man-god was the ideal. In the Foro Mussolini, the Roman spirit dominates the beauty of the scene. It is the figure of the athlete who predominates, not that of the ephebe: it is the cult of intelligent force, of incessant action. (1935: 229–30)

The most interesting feature of these comparisons is not the precise repetition of the same key words or the intensity of the male chauvinism that circulates within the repetition. Rather, it is the way that belief in a core element of fascist thinking is couched, perhaps unknowingly, as appreciation of a purely aesthetic kind. The exaltation of the statues' perfection hints at a preference for the monumental over the human, for ideological homogeneity over individuality. The writing paradoxically suggests that the spirit of a people finds its most sublime expression through lifeless simulacra (Milone 1941: 391). As Tumiati wrote: 'Thousands of men descended to decay in their tombs, while the divine statues gloriously perpetuated human form' (1934: 93).

Analysing the system of quasi-religious beliefs and liturgical practices that were central to Italian fascism, Emilio Gentile has drawn attention to the importance of a notion of history as the perpetual struggle between destiny and the power of the will. Ardent supporters of the regime were, he writes, convinced that it was this 'struggle that decided the ascendancy and the decline of civilizations' (Gentile 1993: 153). The vision of the ancient world offered by the travel texts of the 1930s certainly displayed an interest in narrative history. The process of birth and decline that all tourists could not help but witness had its resolution in the story of Roman dominance. On the itinerary of every traveller were the sites of the Roman Empire, sites that were explored in detail and that were the object of veneration since it was there that a direct contact with the spirit of the ancient Romans could supposedly be felt. To write about a journey to the eastern Mediterranean was thus to participate in a form of literary production that proliferated in the late 1930s, though it had a much longer history, namely the dramatic discovery of signs of Roman rule.[7] Any reader of magazines aimed at the touring public, like *Le Vie d'Italia* or *Le Vie del Mondo*, read a seemingly endless stream of articles with titles like 'Traces of the Legionnaires beyond the seas' (Pozzi 1940) or 'Traces of Rome in the Fezzan' (Magaldi 1938). Articles such as these served a purpose within a culture that sought antecedents for an aggressive policy of territorial expansion. Like such writings, the travel texts were documents that both indicated the reception of the cult of Romanità [Romanness] and served as part of an apologia for Mussolini's imperial ambitions. Maria Benzoni speculated on the 'outstanding fortune' that the last pharaohs enjoyed in living under the guidance of Rome (1935: 77) and wrote that, 'through marble even Athens renders eternal the memory of Roman conquest' (1935: 227). Similarly, on the trail of Alexander the Great, Arnaldo Cipolla discovered one example after another of the extent of Roman power. Drawing on her own heady experience of witnessing the signs of Roman domination, Benzoni claimed it was the duty of 'every new Italian to travel the paths of the sea' (1935: 250).[8] Cipolla, meanwhile, suggested that his journey in the wake of the hero of antiquity might prove 'to young people how the destiny of nations has always been decided by the courage, the moral and physical qualities of a few men of exceptional valour [and] indomitable will' (1933: 12).

It is easy to see how many of the claims made by travellers to the eastern Mediterranean simply repeated official thinking on the need for Italy to develop the extent of its overseas territory, while framing such a repetition as unmediated observation. It is precisely this grafting of the symbolic language of imperialism onto an already existing and quite clearly defined genre that characterizes most Italian texts written on travel in the 1930s. What lends a more sinister overtone to the majority of writings on Greece is that they deployed many of the same concepts that were used in the propaganda that preceded and accompanied Italy's invasion of the country in October 1940. Decided upon directly by Mussolini, the invasion began disastrously with Greek resistance forcing Italian troops back into Albania. The invasion was only concluded successfully in 1941 with the aid of German forces (Rochat 1997: 350–1). The occupation of much of Greece was to last until the 8 September 1943, the date of the Italian surrender to the Allied forces. Many of the hurriedly compiled publications on modern Greece that appeared between 1939 and 1941 emphasized a radical disconnection between the ancient past and the present. In his book *Grecia d'oggi* [Greece Today] (1941), Sergio Grático argued that it was clear that present day Italians were the direct descendants of Rome, but suggested that the people who had inhabited Greece 'twenty centuries ago' had, at a certain point, simply disappeared for ever (1941: 1). Relying on an explicitly racist theory of degeneration, he went on to affirm that: 'the population which now lives on the area once occupied by the ancient Greeks are, through blood, race and lineage, entirely foreign to them' (1941: 3). Icilio Bianchi, a poet and novelist of some fame and a prolific commentator on Italy's imperial foray into Greece, echoed the same theory of degeneration. Writing a triumphal account of the start of the invasion, he contended that the distant past and the present of Greece were linked only by a 'geographical coincidence' (*Le Vie d'Italia* 1940: 1415).

In all such writing a stark contrast was made between the narration of the demise of Greek civilization on the one hand and the story of Rome's decline but renewal on the other. The invasion of Greece was legitimated not only by the former presence of Rome, but also by the later colonial successes of the Venetian Republic. The conquest of

Greece was thus represented as a *return*, while present day Italians could *relive* the assertion of Roman dominance. In this kind of propaganda, Italian intervention would serve a redemptive function. In the words again of Icilio Bianchi, the Italian presence provided the means for Greece to enter:

> Once more the cycle of civilization that in antiquity united the two countries. [...] The Greek people may thus evade their age-old decadence and decline. [...] Once more European civilization follows the consoling path of Rome. [...] Once more imperial legions open the way [...] to the restoration of justice. (*Le Vie d'Italia* 1940: 1422)

Notes

1. During the 1920s and 1930s the state was keen to encourage tourism to Italy's recently acquired possessions. For a detailed study of the impact of the regime on the tourist industry see Bosworth (1997a), for a discussion of the origins and development of the Touring Club Italiano and its endeavour to retain some autonomy under the pressure of state intervention, see Bosworth (1997b).
2. For a discussion of the dynamics of the theme park see Craik (1997). Craik makes the important point that to be successful the theme park, or earlier equivalent, must tap into a theme that has particularly wide appeal.
3. The association between the ancient ruler and the modern leader was one that fascist propaganda and iconography was keen to exploit. The most common comparison that was drawn was between Mussolini and Augustus, see Kostof (1978).
4. The Foro Mussolini provides a good example of the way in which the regime liked to frame modern institutions as the expression of a Greek or Roman ideal (Piacentini 1933: 65). In the words of another commentator: 'Once more in Italy there reappears the gymnasium of the Greeks and the Romans, the most perfect expression of the Mediterranean spirit and of the Latin world at its greatest moment' (Magi-Spinetti 1934: 91).
5. On the remodelling of Rome as a theme park of Roman grandeur see Stone (1999).
6. On the anticipated posthumous narcissism that is part of most building projects of the regime see Magi-Spinetti (1934: 101). On the ways in which the fascist culture aimed to exploit collective and individual experiences of time see Griffin (1998).
7. Two good examples of texts where the travel writer is uniquely concerned with uncovering the ancient and long established presence of Rome in the context of a new manifestation of Italian colonial power are Ciarlantini (1928) and Orano (1930).
8. Benzoni also refers to journeys of fascist youth organizations to Rhodes. In her words, travel gives a sense of 'our place in the world', it engenders a 'faith in the qualities of our race' (1935: 250).

Bibliography

Ballario, P., *Come ho visto la Russia e altri paesi del mondo*. Milan, 1936.
Barthes, R., 'The *Blue Guide*' in *Mythologies* (1957) trans A. Lavers, London, 1973: 74–8.
Benzoni, M., *Oriente mediterraneo: memorie di viaggio*. Milan, 1935.
Bianchi, I., 'Le aquile romane tornano in Grecia', *Le Vie d'Italia*, December 1940: 1408–22.
Bobich, G., 'Il Cairo, centro dell'Islam', *Le Vie del Mondo*, February 1939: 124–51.
Bona, E., *Tappe a capriccio, prose di viaggio*. Rome, 1938.
Bosworth, R.J.B., 'Tourist planning in Fascist Italy and the limits of a totalitarian culture', *Contemporary European History*, vol. 6 (1997a).
———, 'The *Touring Club Italiano* and the nationalisation of the Italian bourgeoisie', *European History Quarterly*, 27 (1997b).
Cecchi, E., *Messico*. Milan, 1932.
———, *Et in Arcadia ego*. Milan, 1936.
———, *Et in Arcadia ego* in *Saggi e viaggi*, ed. M. Ghilardi. Milan, 1997.
Ciarlantini, F., *Africa romana*. Milan, 1928.
Cipolla, A., *Sul Nilo*. Turin, 1930.
———, *Sulle orme di Alessandro Magno*. Milan, 1933.

Comisso, G., *Cina-Giappone*. Milan, 1932.
Craik, J., 'The Culture of Tourism', in C. Rojek and J. Urry, *Touring Cultures*, London, 1997: 113–37.
Culler, J., 'The Semiotics of Tourism', *Framing the Sign: Criticism and its Institutions*, Oxford, 1988: 153–67.
D'Annunzio, G., *Viaggio in Grecia*. Milan, 1895.
———, *La città morta*. Milan, 1898.
Falasca-Zamponi, S., *Fascist Spectacle*. Berkeley, 1997.
Fussell, P., *Abroad: British Literary Travelling Between the Wars*. Oxford, 1980.
Gentile, E., *Il culto del littorio*. Rome-Bari, 1993.
Gratico, S., *Grecia di oggi*. Milan, 1941.
Gregory, D., 'Scripting Egypt: Orientalism and the cultures of travel', in *Writes of Passage: Reading Travel Writing* eds. J. Duncan and D. Gregory, London, 1999.
Griffin, R., '"I am no Longer Human. I am a Titan. A God!" The Fascist Quest to regenerate Time', Electronic Seminars in History, History of Political Thought at http://ihr.sas.ac.uk/ihr/esh/quest.html (May 1998).
Kostof, S., 'The Emperor and the Duce: the Planning of Piazzale Augusto Imperatore in Rome', in H. Millon and L. Nochlin, eds. *Art and Architecture in the Service of Politics*, Cambridge, Mass, 1978: 317–45.
Kowalewski, M., *Temperamental Journeys: Essays on the Modern Literature of Travel*. Athens, Georgia, 1992.
Magaldi, E., 'Orme di Roma nel Fezzan', *Le Vie d'Italia*, March 1938: 322–5.
Magi-Spinetti, C., 'Il Foro Mussolini', *Capitolium* X (1934): 85–101.
Manzini, C., *Di qua e di là del Nilo*. Milan, 1934.
Marinetti, F. T., *Il fascino dell'Egitto*. Milan, 1933.
Milone, F., 'Splendore e declino di un popolo: dall'antica ellade alla Grecia moderna', *Le Vie del Mondo*, April 1941: 391–9.
Orano, N., *Le vigile ombre del passato, note di viaggio nell'Africa romana*. Rome, 1930.
Piacentini, M., 'Il Foro Mussolini in Roma', *Archittetura*, XII (1933): 65–74.
Pozzi, A., 'Orme di Legionari sulle terre d'Oltremare', *Le Vie d'Italia*, June 1940.
Praz, M., *Viaggio in Grecia. Diario del 1931*. Roma, 1942.
Rochat, G., 'La guerra di Grecia', in *I luoghi della memoria: strutture ed eventi dell'Italia unita*, ed. M. Isenghi. Rome-Bari, 1997: 347–63.
Rojek, C., 'Indexing, dragging and the social construction of tourist sights', in *Touring Cultures: Transformations of Travel and Theory*, eds. C. Rojek and J. Urry, London, 1997: 52–75.
Rojek, C. and J. Urry, eds. *Touring Cultures: Transformations of Travel and Theory*. London 1997.
Said, E., *Orientalism*. London, 1991. [Originally published 1978]
Stone, M., 'A flexible Rome: fascism and the cult of romanità', in C. Edwards, ed., *Roman Presences: Receptions of Rome in European Culture, 1789–1945*, Cambridge, 1999: 205–21.
Tumiati, D., *La terra degli Dei*. Milan, 1934.
Vivanti, A., *Terre di Cleopatra*. Milan, 1925.

Chapter 7

TRADITION AND MODERNISM IN GUSTAV RENE HOCKE'S TRAVEL BOOKS, 1937–9

Helmut Peitsch

The 1930s publications of Gustav Rene Hocke, who became famous in the fifties as an essayist on literary and art history, were, in the decades following the war, presented as a form of resistance. It was suggested that the books represented the defence of a 'supranational', 'humane' tradition (Gärtner 1997: 201) and that they preserved, in their toned-down aesthetic modernity, a certain autonomy or distance from fascism (Schäfer 1997: 225–27). At first glance, the three books published by Hocke between 1937 and 1939 appear to confirm this picture. The travel book on Paris during the World Exhibition of 1937 contains the names of representatives of a Modernism which has been canonized as classical: Proust, Gide, Modigliani, Chagall, Braque, Picasso, Leger (Hocke 1937: 6; 18). His 1938 essay on the French spirit adds other foreign names to this list: Valéry, Ortega y Gasset, Prezzolini and T.S. Eliot (Hocke 1938: 24). His Italian travel book of 1939 – which will be at the heart of what follows – makes a point of discussing Futurism. All three works display the same strategy of interpreting what is foreign as his own. In both France and Italy the essayist and travel writer can perceive 'a law' at work in contemporary culture, 'which can be summed up in the formula: Tradition combines with objective Modernity' (Hocke 1937: 21).

Gustav Rene Hocke's *Das verschwundene Gesicht. Ein Abenteuer in Italien* [The Vanished Face. An Adventure in Italy] was one amongst many travel books on Italy which appeared between 1933 and 1945. This specific version of the genre was particularly favoured under German fascism by authors who were associated with those newspapers, periodicals and publishing-houses which aimed at leading elements within the formerly liberal, educated middle class. In the *Frankfurter Zeitung* and the *Societäts-Verlag* which was connected with it (witness the publishers' adverts in Hausenstein 1934), accounts of Italian journeys by Kasimir Edschmid, Hans E. Friedrich, Bernhard Guttmann, Wilhelm Hausenstein, Theodor Heuss, Benno Reifenberg and others were printed. Atlantis published the travel books of Margret Boveri, the *Frankfurter Zeitung* journalist. Karl Rauch, who had originally taken over Willy Haas's *Die literarische Welt*, published accounts of Italian journeys by Eugen Gottlob Winkler and Hocke. In the *Kölnische Zeitung*, of which Hocke was editor (1934) and Rome correspondent (1940), Italy was the main focus of its travel supplement; descriptions of Italian journeys were most frequently reviewed in the periodical *Die Literatur* under the direction of W.E. Süskind of the Deutsche Verlags-Anstalt. The DVA's second periodical, Joachim Moras's *Europäische Revue*, which was more openly political, looked favorably upon these authors, and especially their Italian journeys, as we see in a collective review by Horst Rüdiger (1940). In the same publication, Theodor Heuss (1939) discussed, among other works, Hocke's book under the title: 'Our Tradition'. In the same volume of the *Europäische Revue* Roberto Farinacci (1939) proved that it was an illusion to assume that Italian fascism was not anti-Semitic (Jesi 1984: 118).

Farinacci's friend, Ugo Ojetti, published *Italienische Variationen* [Italian Variations] in the Godmann press in 1942. The travel writer, formerly an editor with the *Corriere della Sera* (Burdett 1999: 205), emphasized, 'that there is more of Greece, I mean of Magna Graecia, in Italy than in Greece itself' (Ojetti 1942: 170). The fascist claim that contemporary Italy was more Greek than Greece fascinated German travellers in the 1930s. This is evident in the central image of their texts, which Ojetti also points to: 'We can still see Greece in that which Rome conquered, plundered, imitated and absorbed from that land; in fact the greatest Doric temples are here in Italy, from Paestum to Selinunte, from Segesta to Agrigento' (1942: 170).

Although authors of travel feuilletons, essays and accounts of journeys in book form stay loyal to the topic of the journey in Italy by Germans, their fixation on Magna Graecia did give their texts a special quality which is visible in the prominence they give to the image of the Doric column and to an associated concept of order. For example, in the *Neue Rundschan*, where the genre of travel writing had replaced the political essay since 1934 (Schwarz 1972: 1385), Eugen Gottlob Winkler's travel account ends with a hymn to the temple at Segesta: 'But what endured, endured magnificently, despite all the ruin, was this order which vanquished the chaos, reposing in its own self-produced law, was beauty, the eternal presence, the permanence and the immutability, the marvelous conquest of nothingness' (Winkler 1973: 44). Ernst Jünger's description of the same temple in 1944 in the quarterly *Deutschland-Frankreich*, which was directed against intellectual collaborators, praised 'the union of power and the Muses':

> Segesta. The temple combines with the landscape to form a whole of raw power and harmony. The day was dark and blustery; the procession of clouds and the balance of the mountains seemed to be controlled by the shrine. If this temple were not there, then natural forces would join in the titanic battle against each other. The ideal relationship of power and order is achieved in the balance of horizontals and verticals; the spirit, as it gazes on this, feels secure and at peace (Jünger u.d., IV: 96–7).

The fixation on what is Greek (on column and on order) alters the meaning of the three topoi of German accounts of Italian journeys identified by Grimm (1990): the rebirth experienced by the hero of such journeys, the primacy of nature and art as the objects for the traveller's contemplation, and the conscious striving on the part of the narrator to summon up the past.

In his travel book, Hocke justifies his insistence on portraying the unique worthiness of Magna Graecia by distancing himself from Goethe. The traveller is emphatically introduced as a man whose goal is a country, 'which lies off the beaten track of the classical routes of the Italian journey'. The comparison of Greek Italy to an 'island in the stream of foreigners going East and West' is put on the same level as the image of the 'two Doric columns standing in the little yard, cut off from the world in the ancient city of Byssus (Taranto)' (1939: 31):

> And there, packed in tiles and mortar, hemmed in on all sides by later masonry, the plain silver-grey column rises up amidst the corpse-like chalk colour, haughty and proud, as if it were still supporting the sky of Jupiter. Almost undamaged, the body with its massively curved Doric capital lies in its coffin, proclaiming the pure sense of beauty of Magna Graecia's Taranto. [...] This Doric column, the most exemplary of columns, with its shallow flutings, tapers toward the capital, as if it wanted to mock the sheer weight of the material, and with trembling breath it breaks through the weight and swoops up to heaven, whose breadth it reflects. (1939: 27–28)

The distinction between the traveller who is interested in the Doric column as an image of Greek order in Italy, and the stream of foreigners going East and West, is not restricted to criticism of tourists. In the introductory sections of the text, the observation is frequently made that the tourist is a representative of contemporary Europe; they are materialistic, egoistic, democratic, violent, and, in the mass, just a part of a machinery of meaningless activity (1939: 9; 115–7). Such a view is indicative of Hocke's intellectual landscape. It is certainly no accident that Greece is detached from the East-West axis and – apparently – moved well away from it. Hocke cites as his authority, his teacher, the Romance scholar Ernst Robert Curtius, who gave the following definition (quoted in Hoeges 1990: 45) of the function of a journey to the Greek area of Italy:

> Whenever a modern Westerner [...] comes into contact with the ancient world, this process involves [...] a return to the origin, a restorative and invigorating immersion in the wellsprings of our own life. Such self-validation and self-discovery is nothing less than a spiritual ritual for our accidental humanity.

Hocke's travel book claims to be a narrative of such a self-discovery. To achieve exemplary status, Hocke reports his journey in the third person. At the end, his fictionalized hero, Manfred, arrives at Manfredonia (Hocke 1939: 187). Hocke's narrative method in *The Vanished Face* conforms to the claim made in the title itself: on the one hand, 'to examine without prejudice' – the face; on the other, to communicate 'an almost forgotten knowledge of the past' – that which has vanished. The evidence he uses therefore consists of the visible evidence of Greek art, including descriptions of it, and above all the evidence of architecture (referred to in 15 of the 38 chapter-headings). His method of proof is the narrative of the traveller's adventure, which is explicitly described as a 'myth of mythical renewal' (1939: 119).

The structure of this mythical tale of self-discovery as a return to the origin entails that the traveller can only ever recognize himself, the true essence of the German as the Westerner bearing the Hellenic stamp. He distances himself in principle from the modern world on the very first page of the text, in an allegorical condemnation of the modern megalopolis of Naples, over which there presides, 'a faceless, a-historical god of basic life-instincts, hunger, thirst, desire and money' (1939: 7). From this point on, the only experiences he relates are ones in which the hero is reflected in the Greek world defined as spirit, art and history, and can identify himself with it. Only right at the end of the journey, in Bari, the 'favourite city of fascism' (1939: 206), does the traveller find himself exposed to the modern world: 'If the skyscraper-like buildings were taller, the sky less clear, and the striking colour of the stone duller, one could not prevent oneself thinking of New York, of Chicago, of another version of Americanism in south-eastern Italy' (1939: 204). This city is 'personified' by Hocke as a woman: a 'chic, vaguely nervous young lady', who 'drives a racing car', prefers Marinetti to Virgil, 'pays more attention to planes and ships than to the pedantries of Vitruvius', and each morning studies 'not sonnets, but stock-market reports from London, Paris and Berlin. [...] Greece – for her that means the Balkan markets' (1939: 205).

The relationship between native and foreign, origin and present day, myth and modernity, a relationship articulated in terms of a national dichotomy, can nevertheless accommodate compromise; the travel-plot itself shows us that after the 'regeneration' we return to everyday concerns. Here the typical characteristics of the hero acquire significance: the traveller does not just appear as the representative of the young generation; rather, and most importantly, he sees and thinks what 'every German' (1939: 198), or indeed 'only the German' can perceive and ponder. At Castel del Monte, Hocke contrasts the behaviour of German and non-German travellers:

> Here [...] Manfred witnessed a beautifully symbolic scene. After all the visitors from a wide variety of European countries had gone off to a nearby restaurant, and from some way off one could soon hear the laughing voices of people enjoying their wine, the Germans stayed behind. [...] Each one was soon walking about on his own, attracted over and over again by the octagonal harmony as if by a friendly spirit. Each one felt the power which penetrated his soul and wanted to be alone, wanted to try and explain the meaning of this incomprehensible phenomenon in a solitary review. [...] To any outsider the sight of these Teutons, sitting all around, with fixed gazes, not saying a word, would certainly have appeared grotesque. They themselves were unaware of the icy melancholy of the process, the cause of that unfulfilled yearning for a form of the German spirit which was *valid* and *common* to *all*. (1939: 226–7)[1]

The fact that this German experience of a sense of European identity occurs in front of Castel del Monte, which acted as model for the fascist memorials to the dead of the First World War, indicated the precarious relationship between Hocke's Helleno-German West and Nazi ideology. The claim of the narrator to articulate, even in this episode, what Germans have in common, makes him construe the Greek spirit as order throughout the text. It is adumbrated in descriptions of architecture as 'the masterful element' (Hocke 1939: 141), as 'the elite' of a 'race' (1939: 109) and as colonization. In Hocke's descriptions of landscape, nature is dominated by art in the same way as, in his historical observations, the Volk is dominated by the elite. This spirit of domination, which is praised as masculine – repeatedly encapsulated in the expression 'Timocracy' [rule of men possessing honour] (1939: 103; 109), and associated with the name of Pythagoras (1939: 99; 104–9) – establishes a close connection between art and politics, and between Greek architecture and German fascism. This type of classicism could not be said to question in any way the central ideological tenets of Nazism, from the national community defined in terms of race, through the authoritarian 'leadership principle', to the policy of expansionism. Rather, such classicism could be seen as proposing a formal agreement between those tenets. In Hocke's words: 'It is a matter of transferring the creative idea of art, which meant so much to the Greeks, to *mankind* and to the human *community*' (1939: 105).

The applicability to politics of artistic principles which are given an authoritarian interpretation may explain why, in Hocke's travel book, the condemnation of Bari's modern architecture is followed by a politically opportunistic compromise with the fascist present, and why the significant figure of 'rebirth' (1939: 58) is seen as part of this 'reconciliation'. Hocke writes: 'We shall reconcile the Graeco-Latin heritage with the technical spirit of our own time' (1939: 212; see also 1939: 73; 78–9; 81).

It is precisely the authoritarian strain common to Hocke's conceptions of art and politics which can be heard in his wish 'to connect the politically revolutionary will of the present with the universal *anthropology* of the ancient world' (1939: 42). For protection against 'the danger of an overdeveloped, purely collectivist mechanization' (1939: 213) appears to lie in the aesthetic 'order', in the 'myth' of 'the return' of Europe 'to its original spiritual attitudes' (1939: 212) of domination, elites, racial expansion. With this application, Hocke in 1939, was again following that aestheticization of politics which had prompted Gottfried Benn's assumption of a pro-fascist stance in 1933–4. Benn's essay 'The Doric world', which had first appeared in the *Europäische Revue*, which later sang the praises of Hocke's travel, had not so much elided art and power in the images and concepts it deployed (whether these were of the column, of order, of 'anti-feminism' (Benn 1972: 17), of the military or of race) as given the autonomy of art (1972: 27) an authoritarian interpretation and applied that to politics.[2] Benn had written: 'Form [...] as enormous human power, power per se, victory over the bald facts and the state of civilization, precisely what is Western, the highest elevation, genuine spirit in a unique category of its own, the gathering and balancing of fragments' (Benn 1972: 28).[3]

Since Hocke went back to Benn's conception of the Doric, the Greek element in Italy in no sense proved to be a humanistic refuge, but rather the medium of an identification with fascism. Margret Boveri, at the end of her chapter on Italy in her book on the Mediterranean, makes the cynical remark that Italy might be able to 'reconcile' non-Italians to fascism (Boveri 1938: 207; Streim 1999).

Hocke's book on Paris of 1937 concluded by relating his definition of native and foreign to the policy of mutual understanding pursued by the fascist regime prior to Munich: 'The [...] tacit assumption that only a foreigner could and of course does commit any injustice is at least becoming rarer in France, where Germany is concerned. And this more sensible estimate of one's own and of the other's nation, which is useful for all, not just one, is at least a preliminary step to more tangible results' (Hocke 1937: 26). The menacing sound of the word 'tangible' can be read as an indication that the shared tradition which Hocke can see the modern national cultures recalling, is to form the basis of a German hegemony in Europe. Hocke discusses Paul Morand's book on France in a sympathetic way: 'Certain semitic-oriental or Balkan–Armenian, not to say [...] American influences are denounced by means of an affectionate evocation of a France of bygone days' (1939: 21). This is not to be viewed so much as a one-off concession to anti-Semitism, but more as a general trait, given Hocke's way of construing tradition.

We need to consider to what extent the racism of German fascism represented an ideology with which Europeans could, with specific reference to a certain notion of tradition and modernity, identify. Both Hitler and Rosenberg discuss, in the sections of their books concerning so-called racial doctrine, the idea which Germanists are currently rediscovering in Nazi doctrine, namely that of a 'project of 'organic' modernization' (Schütz 1995: 129) or of 'indigenous modernism' (Gräb-Könneker 1996; Emmerich/Wege 1995). The affirmation of a kind of scientific and technical modernization or civilizing modernity that in the current discussions cannot be thought of as having any connection with capitalism (Zitelmann 1991; Schildt 1994; Breuer 1995), and the negation of democracy and socialism lead, in the work of Hitler and Rosenberg, to that form of racism which draws a distinction between native and alien, healthy and diseased Modernism.

Hitler defines the 'Aryan as the founder of culture' through 'Hellenic spirit and Germanic technology' (1941: 318). He equates the Greek element with the education of rulers and the machine with 'lower individuals' (1941: 323). The paradigmatic nature of the 'Hellenic cultural ideal' (of beauty) is given a double value in *Mein Kampf*, serving as a model in both domestic and foreign policy (1941: 470). On the one hand, the national community, grounded racially in a supposedly key Aryan characteristic, the readiness to make sacrifices, is dependent on the ideal of beauty. On the other hand, the Greek ideal links the German and other Nordic races with those of southern and western Europe: 'We are halting the ever-lasting movement of Germanic peoples to the South and West of Europe, and directing our gaze to the territory in the East' (1941: 742). Hitler's justification for positing the character of the ancient world as an example to follow in deciding the course of foreign policy is as follows: 'One must not permit the greater degree of racial affinity that exists between individual peoples to be destroyed because of the differences between them. The struggle raging today concerns extremely crucial goals : a culture is fighting for its existence which contains millennia in itself, and embraces both Hellenic and Germanic worlds' (1941: 470). In terms of domestic policy, the resort to the classical tradition is a consequence of the affirmation of capitalist modernism: 'industry and technology, trade and manufacture are only able to flourish as long as an idealistically-minded national community can provide the necessary pre-conditions. However, these are not to be found in materialistic egoism, but in the spirit of sacrifice which takes joy in renunciation' (1941: 470).

That Modernism is diseased when it forgets the timeless essence of the race is the most obvious feature of Hitler's language in his speeches on cultural themes. At the party rally in 1935, he distinguished art as the expression of the 'innermost and therefore eternally healthy essence of a people' from what he called 'confusions' (Hinz 1976: 148). Referring to the Parthenon, Hitler demanded that 'the state of the German people must bear the cultural imprint of the Germanic race as an eternally valid one' (Hinz 1976: 144). In 1937 at the opening of the First Great German Art Exhibition he repudiated the term 'modern' art, because it replaces racial and national criteria with historical criteria : 'True art is and always will be eternal in its achievements [...] as an immortal revelation stemming from the deepest essence of a people' (1976: 156). Hitler certainly had his European neighbours and their common 'classical culture' in mind when he referred to the ancient world as the quintessence of eternal values. He emphasized 'the natural affinity, arising out of this, with those nations and cultures in the rest of the European family of nations which have a similar core of racial characteristics' (1976: 159). The rejection of modern art goes hand-in-hand with the demand for a 'synthesis' of the classical world with 'modern tasks' of beauty and utility (1976: 150): 'Mankind has never been closer to the ancient world than today'. (1976: 166)

While Hitler defined the relationship between the Hellenic and Teutonic by associating a timeless racist aesthetic with modern technology, Rosenberg used the typologies of intellectual history, which by their very nature tended toward synthesis, whenever he was drawing a distinction between classical stasis and modern dynamism. He wrote: 'In contrast to Greek art, German art is based "on emotional experience", but this desire to move us must not be confused with "ecstasy or straining for effect"' (Wulf 1989: 176–7). Elsewhere, he observed: 'The classical-antique spirit proves to be [...] the necessary counterbalance to the danger concealed in the Nordic-German [...], namely that of the dissolution of form through hostility to reality, and of individualistic self-destruction'. (1989: 260–1)

Before we isolate three tendencies (the Hellenistic, the reactionary-modernist (Herf 1995) and the Nordic), as Anson Rabinbach (1995: 112) has suggested, we should observe the way in which associations between such tendencies were made easy by the central position of racism in providing a justification for the national community and for foreign expansion. According to Speer's memoirs, Hitler envied Mussolini on account of the remains of classical Greek culture still visible in Italy (Damus 1981: 78–9). Speer's own architecture was underpinned by a theory of the 'heritage value' of ruins. The public buildings that he designed were planned in such a way that, even after centuries or millennia, the eternal character of the Aryan would be discernible in them. Accordingly, the building programme fitted Hitler's definition of historic action as the production of monuments : 'There is hardly a people which history deems worthy of mention which has not erected its own monument in its own cultural values' (Damus 1981: 142).

Hocke's travel book on Italy did not manage to free itself from this outlook.[4]

NOTES

1. On Castel del Monte as a model for Nazi architecture, see Hinz 1979: 217–29.
2. On this point, see Ryan (1980: 25), Dröge/Müller (1995).
3. See also Kittler (1994: 11).
4. A different interpretation, however, is given in Graf (1995: 206–86). For a critique of Graf, see Streim 1998. On Hocke's self-criticism in the early post-war years, see Peitsch 1992.

BIBLIOGRAPHY

Benn, G., 'Dorische Welt. Eine Untersuchung über die Beziehung von Kunst und Macht' (1934), in L. Rohner, ed., *Deutsche Essays. Prosa aus zwei Jahrhunderten*. München, 1972: 7–30.
Boveri, M., *Mediterranean Cross-Currents*. London, New York, Toronto, 1938.
Breuer, S., *Ästhetischer Fundamentalismus. Stefan George und der deutsche Antimodernismus*. Darmstadt, 1995.
Burdett, C., *Vincenzo Cardarelli And His Contemporaries. Fascist Politics and Literary Culture*. Oxford, 1999.
Damus, M., *Sozialistischer Realismus und Kunst im Nationalsozialismus*. Frankfurt, 1981.
Dröge, F., Müller, M., *Die Macht der Schönheit. Avantgarde und Faschismus oder Die Geburt der Massenkultur*. Hamburg, 1995.
Emmerich, W., Wege, C., eds., *Der Technikdiskurs in der Hitler-Stalin-Ära*. Stuttgart, 1995.
Farinacci, R., 'Der Faschismus und die Judenfrage', *Europäische Revue* vol.15 (1939) part 1 : 427–32.
Gärtner, M., *Kontinuität und Wandel in der neueren deutschen Literaturwissenschaft nach 1945*. Bielefeld, 1997.
Gräb-Könneker, S., *Autochthone Modernität. Eine Untersuchung der vom Nationalsozialismus geförderten Literatur*. Opladen, 1996.
Graf, J., *"Die notwendige Reise". Reisen und Reiseliteratur junger Autoren während des Nationalsozialismus*. Stuttgart, Weimar, 1995.
Grimm, G. E., Breymayer, U., Erhart, W., '"Laterna-Magica-Bilder". Italien als Ort der deutschen "Inneren Emigration"', in Grimm et al, eds., *"Ein Gefühl von freierem Leben". Deutsche Dichter in Italien*. Stuttgart, 1990.
Hausenstein, W., *Das Land der Griechen. Fahrten in Hellas*. 2nd edn. Frankfurt, 1934.
Herf, J., 'Der nationalsozialistische Technikdiskurs. Die deutschen Eigenheiten des reaktionären Modernismus' in Emmerich/Wege 1995: 72–93.
Heuss, T., 'Über Tradition', *Europäische Revue* vol. 15 (1939) part 2: 471/472.
Hinz, B., *Die Malerei im deutschen Faschismus. Kunst und Konterrevolution*. Frankfurt, Wien, Zürich, 1976.
Hinz, B., 'Das Denkmal und sein Prinzip'. *Kunst im 3. Reich. Dokumente der Unterwerfung*. Frankfurt, 1979: 217–29.
Hitler, A., *Mein Kampf. Zwei Bände in einem Band*. 7th edn. München, 1941.
Hocke, G. R., *Das geistige Paris 1937*. Leipzig, 1937.
Hocke, G. R., ed., *Der französische Geist. Die Meister des Essays von Montaigne bis Giraudoux*. Zürich, 1988 (originally Leipzig, 1938).
Hocke, G. R., *Das verschwundene Gesicht. Ein Abenteuer in Italien*. Leipzig, 1939.
Hoeges, D., 'Emphatischer Humanismus. Ernst Robert Curtius, Ernst Troeltsch und Karl Mannheim: Von "Deutscher Geist in Gefahr" zu "Europäische Literatur und lateinisches Mittelalter"', in Lange, W-D., ed., *"In ihnen begegnet sich das Abendland". Bonner Vorträge zur Erinnerung an Ernst Robert Curtius*. Bonn, 1990: 31–52.

Jesi, F., *Kultur von rechts*. Frankfurt, 1984.
Jünger, E., 'Aus der Goldenen Muschel'. In Jünger, E., *Tagebücher*. vol. 4. Stuttgart: no year.
Kittler, F., 'Benns Lapidarium', *Weimarer Beiträge* vol. 40 (1994): 5–14.
Ojetti, U., *Italienische Variationen*. Leipzig, 1942.
Peitsch, H., 'Travellers' Tales from Germany in the 1950s', in *German Writers and the Cold War*, ed. R. W. Williams. Manchester, New York, 1992: 87–114.
Rabinbach, A., 'Nationalsozialismus und Moderne. Zur Technik-Interpretation im Dritten Reich', Emmerich/Wege 1995: 94–113.
Rüdiger, H., 'Italienfahrten', *Europäische Revue* vol. 16 (1940) part 2: 768–69.
Ryan, J., 'Ezra Pound und Gottfried Benn: Avantgarde, Faschismus und ästhetische Autonomie', in *Faschismus und Avantgarde*, eds. R. Grimm, J. Hermand, Königstein, 1980: 20–34.
Schäfer, H. D., 'Kultur als Simulation. Das Dritte Reich und die Postmoderne', in G. Rüther, ed., *Literatur in der Diktatur. Schreiben im Nationalsozialismus und DDR-Sozialismus*. Paderborn, München, Wien, 1997: 215–45.
Schildt, A., 'NS-Regime, Modernisierung und Moderne. Anmerkungen zur Hochkonjunktur einer andauernden Diskussion', *Tel Aviver Jahrbuch für deutsche Geschichte* vol. 23 (1994): 3–22.
Schütz, E., 'Faszination der blaßblauen Bänder. Zur "organischen" Technik der Reichsautobahn', Emmerich/Wege 1995: 123–45.
Schwarz, F., 'Literarisches Zeitgespräch im Dritten Reich, dargestellt an der Zeitschrift 'Neue Rundschau', *Archiv für Geschichte des Buchwesens* vol. 12 (1972).
Streim, G., 'Dichtung im Dritten Reich?', *Referatedienst zur Literaturwissenschaft* vol. 30 (1998): 119–28.
———, 'Junge Völker und neue Technik. Zur Reisereportage im 'Dritten Reich', am Beispiel von Friedrich Sieburg, Heinrich Hauser und Margret Boveri', *Zeitschrift für Germanistik N.F.* vol. 9 (1999): 344–59.
Winkler, E. G., 'Trinakria', in H. Piontek, ed., *Augenblicke unterwegs. Deutsche Reiseprosa unserer Zeit*. München, 1973: 33–44.
Wulf, J., *Die bildenden Künste im Dritten Reich. Eine Dokumentation*. Frankfurt, Berlin, 1989.
Zitelmann, R., *Die totalitäre Seite der Moderne*, in M. Prinz, ed., *Nationalsozialismus und Modernisierung*. Darmstadt, 1991: 1–20.

Chapter 8

DRAMATIC ENCOUNTERS
FEDERICO GARCÍA LORCA'S TRIP TO CUBA (1930)

Sarah Wright

Federico García Lorca (1898–1936) embarked upon his journey from Spain to the Americas as a form of escape, an intermission for reflection, and to gain perspective. Emotional conflict in his personal life (a failed love affair with the sculptor Emilio Aladrén, the souring of his relationship with friend and muse Salvador Dalí) and depression following the censorship of a production of one of his plays are the main reasons cited by Gibson (1989: 228–41) for Lorca's decision to journey to the Americas: staying first in the United States, and then travelling on to Cuba.

In this chapter, I choose some of the concepts from the burgeoning field of criticism on travel writing to address writing on and from Lorca's Cuban experience. Whilst never intended to be published as travel writing *per se*, it nevertheless, like travel writing, traces 'spiralling circles between home and away' (Duncan and Gregory 1999: 1). I shall examine some of the ways in which writing produced from the period Lorca spent in Cuba is inflected by those spiralling circles between here and there, and from this point of departure, consider how far it opens up a 'space-in-between' – for transculturation (Ortiz) and landscapes of desire (Barthes). In addition, I reflect on how critical writing on Lorca's Cuban period has been concerned with mapping the travelling writer's itinerary, a project seemingly thwarted by the anonymity offered by travel, and by the unreliability of objective account. I shall use the structure of *contrapunteo* or counterpoint – a reference to Fernando Ortiz's (1940) work *Cuban Counterpoint* – to show how writing on and from Lorca's Cuban period is offset by a series of shifting articulations of dramatic encounters (contrasts and syntheses) in time and space.

García Lorca arrived in Cuba by steamer (the *Cuba*) via Tampa on 7th March 1930, at the invitation of the anthropologist and folklorist

Fernando Ortiz, to present a series of lectures and recitals of his work in various locations around the island.[1] Where he had found in New York the fragments and shards of modern mechanization – expressed in the broken images of *Poeta en Nueva York* [Poet in New York]: 'rust, fermentation, earth tremor'[2] – Cuba was, by counterpoint, balmy and soothing, 'caressing, soft, sensual' (García Lorca 1997: 686). 'If I get lost', he announced in a letter home to his parents, 'look for me in Andalusia or in Cuba', declaring of the latter, 'this island is a paradise' (García Lorca 1997: 686). Lorca's visions of Cuba were partially framed prior to departure from Spain by a colonialist aesthetic in some degree derived from the lithographs on the cigar boxes his father had sent from Havana,[3] and exacerbated by the New York experience of dehumanized urbanity. These visions became a romantic longing for a world that has been lost, what Behdad (1994) would term a sense of loss as belatedness, a sense of the loss of the non-modern world in the face of modernity: 'Havana is quintessentially Spanish, drawn from the most characteristic and profound elements of our civilization', he wrote nostalgically in a letter home (García Lorca 1997: 681). Elsewhere he described Cuba as 'America with roots' (García Lorca 1954: III, 517). While New York had brought him to a sense of alienation that was 'intensified by the blatant linguistic and cultural otherness into which he had so heedlessly plunged' (Young 1998: 2), in Cuba, by contrast, 'naturally,' he felt, he had 'come home' (García Lorca 1997: 681). Originally intending to stay just three weeks, he extended his visit to three months.

García Lorca found in Cuba a place that was at once familiar and excitingly exotic, an intoxicating contrast and synthesis between home and away. In a letter home to his family, he writes, 'It's a mixture of Málaga and Cádiz, but much more lively and soothed by the tropics [...]. I have to keep reminding myself that I am in the Caribbean, in the beautiful Antilles, and not Vélez or Motril. The sea is a prodigy of colours and light. It looks like the Mediterranean but is of a much more violent hue' (García Lorca 1997: 681). These letters home imply the sense of 'travel writing as an act of translation that constantly works to produce a space in-between' (Duncan and Gregory 1999: 4), a space of endless counterpoint. Lorca *re*-presents Cuba for his family, and in the process, enacts a double movement which Venuti (1993: 210) cites as the characteristics of translation: Lorca's writing is both a 'domesticating method', designed to bring the author back home, and a 'foreignizing method', intended to send its reader abroad. This constant blend and contrast with his homeland would continue in Lorca's descriptions of Cuba: in a lecture in 1932 he notes, 'it is the yellow of Cádiz but one shade stronger, the pink of

Seville turning to crimson, the green of Granada with a slight, fish-like phosphorescence' (García Lorca 1954: III, 517).

Lorca is struck constantly by the blend of sameness and difference that he finds in Cuba, an impression surely created in part by what Benítez Rojo (1992) has termed the specificity of the Caribbean's 'syncretic' nature. Benítez Rojo takes the example of the cult of the Virgen de la Caridad del Cobre (Patron Saint of Cuba) to show how such syncretic objects arise out of the chaotic collision and fusion of cultural expressions and signifiers (this icon in Cuba has Catholic, Taino and Yoruba religious meanings). We also might cite the example of Santa Bárbara, crudely drawn by Lorca in a letter to Martínez Nadal. Santa Bárbara the Catholic saint who Lorca would later invoke with the shooting star, symbolic of Adela's fiery rebellion in *La casa de Bernarda Alba* [The House of Bernarda Alba], is in Yoruba lore the deity Changó, god of fire and thunder. As an aside, Lorca in fact attended a *ñáñiga* ceremony with Lydia Cabrera Infante and Fernando Ortiz (1951: 394) and Afro-Cuban religion would have a strong influence on Lorca's telluric play *Yerma* (Davies 1994: 287–97). Cuba's syncretism provides Lorca with a source of endless counterpoint to his homeland: Cuba is at once reassuringly familiar after his bewildering North American experience, and yet dizzyingly exotic.

Lorca's writing *in situ* amounts to a collection of letters home to his parents, a poem, 'Son de los negros en Cuba' [Blacks Dancing to Cuban Rhythms], a series of dedications imprinted on scraps of paper or on copies of his books, drafts of his play *Yerma*, and probably a draft of the *Oda a Walt Whitman* [Ode to Walt Whitman]. García Lorca later wrote about his Cuban experience in a lecture in 1932, an example of what Wordsworth would term 'emotions recollected in tranquillity'. In Cuba Lorca also wrote the main body of his plays *Así que pasen cinco años* [Once Five Years Pass] and *El público* [The Public], both of which are influenced by the strains of the avant-garde and depart radically from the rest of his oeuvre. When viewed against the work written before and after his Cuban period, these plays appear to be closely framed by the Cuban experience. The transient iridescence of travel, its stagey impermanence, inflects his writing. *El público* is a carnivalesque, liminal riot of licentiousness, characterized by shape-shifting, gender-switching, fluidity and complexity. *El público* is also, as García Lorca (1997: 690) was later to affirm in a missive to Martínez Nadal, 'frankly homosexual in theme', a departure in his dramatic writing. Cuba was for Lorca a 'space in-between', a rite of passage, an interior as well as geographical liberatory excursion, in artistic as well as personal terms.

In addition to Lorca's writing, numerous personal testimonies by friends and acquaintances describe the period García Lorca spent in Cuba. But rather than elucidations, these are often flagrantly contradictory, such as the incompatible accounts by the Loynaz family (at whose eccentrically named 'enchanted house' Lorca spent most of every day) and that of Antonio Quevedo (the Spaniard who with his wife Maria had formed the Bach conservatory and the journal *Musicalia* where Lorca published his famous poetic 'Son'), concerning his last day on the island: both write in minute detail of spending the last hours with him before he set sail (Bianchi Ross 1980, Quevedo 1961). García Lorca's physical locality and spatial presence is thus a contested site. This notion can also be evidenced in the controversy surrounding Lorca's journey to Santiago de Cuba, foreshadowed in his poem, 'Son de los negros en Cuba', whose hypnotic backbeat choruses, 'Iré a Santiago' [I will go to Santiago]. The Loynaz family's contention that Lorca never visited Santiago de Cuba was refuted in the 1960s by a journalist, Nydia Sarabia (1965), provoking a ding-dong battle between herself and another critic, Loló de la Torriente. Leading revolutionary and intellectual Juan Marinello (1968) was credited with having proved categorically that Lorca did indeed make the trip. Lorca, it was admitted later by the Loynazs, would disappear for days on end, refusing to say where he had been upon his return. The anonymity offered by travel allows Lorca a degree of invisibility, whilst claims to objectivity are problematized by information partially buried, tantalisingly glimpsed through the filter of our temporal and spatial distance. What emerges is a tension between the critics' desire for closure and resolution in the face of gaps, as attempts are made to plot an authoritative and definitive trajectory of Lorca's visit to the island,[4] and the shadowy figure of the mythical García Lorca dancing trickster-like in the uncharted territory in and behind, like the shape-shifting elusive spirit of his play *El público*.

The desire to plot an itinerary, to map a physical presence, has consumed studies of Lorca's Cuban period. Most critics of Lorca's 'Son de los negros en Cuba' have been occupied with the fragility of testimonial account, seeing the poem's refrain, 'Iré a Santiago' [I will go to Santiago] as evidence of a frustrated or fulfilled desire. Jean Schonberg (1956: 235), however, constructs a psychoanalytical interpretation of the poem, to posit that the 'blond head of Fonseca' is the 'dry fountain' of Lorca's own sterility, a stance scorned by Marcelle Auclair (1968), who (following Marinello's [1965] description of Lorca's sources for the piece), ridicules Schonberg's 'pseudo-Freudian' reading of the poem, and announces anecdotal testimony to elucidate the images of the poem. The blond head of Fonseca is nothing more than the image on a cigar box sent to Lorca's father during his youth; Romeo and Juliet, and the 'paper sea and silver money' are likewise references to cigar boxes; the 'coach of black water', for Auclair, means that Lorca is imagining a journey to Santiago in a paddle steamer. Paul Julian Smith finds both of these stances (what he terms the allegorical obsessive and the anecdotal witness) unsatisfactory as critical positions: the former 'presses into service the most unlikely details to serve his totalizing interpretation', the latter 'cannot raise incidents to the level of ideas' (Smith 1998: 84). Schonberg, we could add, spins a psyche out of Lorca's literary excursion, whilst Auclair reduces Lorca's imaginary geography to an unimaginative travelogue.

Returning to the repetitive refrain of the poem 'Son de los negros en Cuba', I contend that Lorca's insistence on Santiago is not an attestation of the desire to make a physical journey, but rather political avowal. Lorca's 'Son de los negros' was published in 1930, contemporaneous with the publication of Nicolás Guillén's *Motivos del son* (1980). The *son* (a syncretic Cuban folkloric rhythm) derives from the famous 'son de la ma Teodora' of 1580 and was popularized in the 1920s and 30s by Eliseo Grenet and Miguel Matamoros travelling from the eastern Santiago folkloric scene (capital of Afro-Cuban culture) to the Havana tea and dancing salons. But as Kutzinski writes, 'its transformation into a literary form was quite a different matter, with unsettling political implications' (1993: 153). Guillén's *Motivos del son* lent formal emphasis to the African presence in Cuba. These poems had problematic representations of women (which are incorporated by Lorca in his images of Cuba as a *mulata*),[5] but despite these they also raised questions about social inequality in what to many middle-class blacks were loathsome vernacular voices from the 'Afro-Cuban underworld'. Guillén's poems were published in *Ideales*, the page for Afro-Antillean culture which had published Langston Hughes's poems in earlier issues that year (Hughes was leaving the island as Lorca arrived – his autobiography recounts tales of racism on the Havana beaches [Hughes 1956]). Lorca's 'Son' was published in the more colonially influenced journal, *Musicalia*.[6] Hence, whilst the representation Lorca paints is of a picturesque, folkloric Cuba, nevertheless, given the politically charged implications of the *son* at that time, Lorca's 'Son de los negros en Cuba' can be read as the creation of a space for *negrismo* within the colonialist press.[7] Kutzinski (1993: 152) makes the point that Afro-Cubanism, unlike, for example, the Harlem Renaissance, 'was not supported, financially or otherwise, by a nascent African-American middle-class surrounded by a host of wealthy white patrons'. It was the wealthy middle classes in Cuba who attended Lorca's lectures around the island. Lorca had experienced examples of racism in

Cuba, defending some blacks who were excluded from the Havana yacht club. Read against his descriptions of disgust at New York materialism (the Wall Street Crash had happened while Lorca was in New York) prior to his departure for Cuba, and alongside Guillén's 'antidote to Wall Street', the poem becomes an assertion of an ethnic, colour related identity developed in opposition to the pragmatic character of the U.S. hegemony, what Fanon would refer to as the 'radicalization of thought'. Lorca's 'Son de los negros', then, might be seen as a space for what Ortiz (1940) terms *transculturación* [transculturation]. Derived from his notion of *contrapunteo*, Ortiz goes on to explore the possibility of opening a space for the synthesis (or more precisely, the fermentation and toil that precedes synthesis) of cultures. Transculturation (which replaces *acculturation* and *deculturation*) is a transition, a process, a passage between cultures which is dialogic, composed of 'overlapping territories, intertwined histories' (Said 1993), rather than a question of domination and submission. García Lorca's 'Son' moves the reader away from the metropolis and into Cuba's regions, a movement central to transculturation. Lorca's appropriation of the *son* and his insertion of it within the colonialist press, articulates a celebration of the blending of cultures, a 'contact zone' (Pratt 1992) which is exuberantly utopian.

The poem is an ebullient evocation of Cuba's musicality, its rhythmic underbelly. The 'gotas de madera' [drops of wood], rather than the dry tears seen by Schonberg, are a reference to the claves: a Cuban instrument responsible for the main line of the *son*. Lorca sees Cuba as throbbing with musicality, a pulsating cathedral of sound, with palm trees which sing above the rooftops and 'arpas de troncos' [a harp of living tree trunks] reminiscent of Baudelaire's 'Correspondences' (1999) in which words are 'living pillars' and 'They sing. All being is a unity'. Lorca's imaginary Cuba is an harmonious riot of ecstatic musicality: 'Oh Cuba! Oh rhythm of dried seeds!' This is an utopian vision. García Lorca's imaginary panorama has been constituted as a landscape of desire. Roland Barthes (1981: 38–40), describing his own reactions to a nineteenth-century photograph of the Alhambra by Charles Clifford, remarks that it moves him to a recognition: 'I want to live *there*.' Focusing on his insistent desire to inhabit, Barthes decides that it is neither oneiric ('I do not dream of some extravagant site') nor empirical (no practical plans for buying a house) but simply fantasmatic, 'deriving from a kind of second sight that seems to bear me forward to a utopian time, or to carry me back somewhere in myself.' Examining Freud's analysis of the psychic phenomenon of the false recognition of landscapes, Barthes writes, 'looking at these landscapes of predilection, it is as if *I were certain* of having been there or of going there' (Barthes 1981: 40). Freud relates this recognition to the *heimlich* remembrance of the maternal. Lorca's insistence on 'I will go to Santiago' should be read, I suggest, like Barthes's photograph, as a desire to inhabit, a fantasy of habitation. We might describe the poem as an oneiric landscape ('as soon as the full moon rises, I'm going to Santiago'), but the desire evoked is not empirical: 'I always said I'd go to Santiago in a coach of black water' is not a statement of intent. Rather, 'I will go to Santiago' captures the writer and reader at a point of potentiality, forever 'travelling hopefully' towards their destination. The 'Son' carries within it the double movement outlined by Barthes: carrying Lorca forward to a utopian time ('paper sea and silver coins') and simultaneously back towards the familiarity and comfort of childhood, the *heimlich* (the 'blond head of Fonseca', the rose of Romeo and Juliet, the nostalgic images from the cigar boxes of his youth) and a feeling of having been there before. In the 1932 lecture, García Lorca reflected on his Cuban experience, thus: 'Havana emerges among bamboo groves and the sound of maracas, Chinese horns and marimbas. And in the harbour, who comes to greet me? The dusky Trinidad of my childhood, the one who "went walking one morning along the quayside in Havana, down the quayside in Havana one morning went walking"' (Gibson 1989: 283). Trinidad is the protagonist of one of the *habaneras* [a slow Cuban dance in double time] that Lorca had learnt as a child and from which these lines are taken (Gibson 1989: 283). Lorca projects a romanticism formed in childhood onto his surroundings. His depiction of Cuba as a blend of the familiar and the exotic is in part due to Cuba's syncretic nature: but moreover it is a way to conflate past and future, creating fantasy out of nostalgia (from the Greek *nostos* meaning 'home'), to project an utopian vision of an imaginary landscape.

If Lorca's 'Son de los negros en Cuba' is a form of souvenir, an appropriation of foreign culture to bring back home, then at the same time, Lorca's imaginary geography is kept very much alive in the writings of the intellectuals of Castro's Cuba. Lorca is credited with contributing to 'the renewal of our art and letters and above all, to the enriching of our artistic sensibility' (Santos Moray 1986: 6). Lorca (with Brecht) is the foreign playwright most often performed on the Cuban stage.[8] A recent book by César López (1999), *Arpa de troncos vivos* [Harp of Living Tree Trunks], collects the many odes and dedications to Lorca's name.[9] García Lorca has left his mark on Cuba, as the unveiling of a bust at the Gran Teatro de la Habana in July 1999 testifies.

A playful fluidity of form and movement is expressed in the 'Son': 'I'm going to Santiago, when the palm wants to be a stork/ I'm going to Santiago/ When the banana tree wants to be a sea wasp.' These lines recall the exchange of the figure of vine-leaves and the figure of bells from the play *El público* which Lorca worked on whilst in Cuba. 'If I became an apple?/ Then I would become a kiss/ If I became a breast?/ Then I would become a white sheet' is the playful, homoerotically charged exchange of these two characters. The exploration of sexual identity with a surrealist aspect in *El público* (a radical departure for Lorca in his artistic practice) has been seen elsewhere as evidence of the sexual and creative freedoms offered by the Cuba he experienced in the 1930s.[10] Despite the knock-on effects of the 1929 economic crisis, and continuing political tensions, in 1930 Cuba was billed as a 'pleasure island'. As Schwartz (1997: 15) has written, 'lush, tropical foliage, climate and location were fortunate accidents of nature, but human inventiveness, imagination and perseverance turned Havana into a naughty Paris of the Western Hemisphere' during the fat years of Cuban tourism, from 1924 to 1931. Testimonies of Lorca's time in Cuba focus on the lectures he presented at the Institución Hispano-Cubana, the social events at the Havana yacht club, the excursions he made to lush valleys (including a crocodile hunt), and the time he spent at the house of the Loynaz family, writing and composing at leisure. Brief mention is made of visits to Marinao, then Havana's entertainment playground. Rumours of fleeting homosexual liaisons abound: detailed by Gibson (for example, the Scandinavian sailor, lover of the poet Porfirio Barba Jacob, who Lorca is believed to have poached) and hinted at by the photographs of unidentified young men who appear with Lorca (Gibson 1989: 292–4). This was also a period of intense artistic reflection and creativity. Whilst most of his lectures had been very well received (in a letter home, Lorca writes with joy that in Cuba 'to be a poet is something akin to being a prince in Europe' [García Lorca 1997: 686]) nevertheless the presentations he gave of his work in Cienfuegos, for example, raised a harsh polemic concerning the merits of the avant-garde (a detail omitted in Gibson's biography although documented in press cuttings from the Cienfuegos dailies).[11] In addition, Cardoza y Aragón (1986) writes that Lorca had planned to write an *Adaptation of Genesis for Music Hall* which was to be a blend of the grotesque and the blasphemous. Above all, *El público* reflects experimentalism with new forms for the theatre. 'Frankly homosexual in theme', as he put it, despite negative reactions from members of the Loynaz family when he read excerpts in the balmy afternoons, he would later announce that, 'this is *my* theatre', but simultaneously it was, 'theatre for the future'. With *El público* Lorca writes a creative space for artistic and sexual freedoms. Seen in counterpoint to his work dating from before and after the Cuban trip it seems like an *hiatus*, a time-out from the repressive constraints of home, a bounded space of licentiousness within the hermetic parameters of both travel and the Cuban island. Read against *El público*, Lorca's Cuban period becomes a charged, erotic space, a notion exacerbated by the lack of information we have about his romantic affairs: the gaps incite desire in the critics for knowledge, but at the same time the covering over the homosexual desire makes of Lorca's Cuba a 'closet', a space where desire remains hidden.

This island is a paradise', wrote Lorca in 1930, and it is surely in part the hermeticism of the island as metaphor which created of Cuba a space (both textual and imaginary) for the playing out of artistic and personal freedoms. This bounded site has been overlaid with a spectrum of meanings (politicized, folkloric, romantic, utopian) which interact contrapuntally, contrasting and synthesizing at every turn, so that Lorca's Cuban period exists as a dialogue of shifting and often contradictory dramatic encounters in time and space.

Notes

1. In a lecture of 1932, Lorca fails to mention his long train trip from Manhattan to Miami, giving his audience to understand that he had travelled by boat, as 'doubtless it was more picturesque to leave New York as he had come, by sea' (Gibson 1989: 282).
2. All translations are my own unless otherwise indicated. 'Poeta en Nueva York' and 'Son de los negros en Cuba' are translated by G. Simon and S. F. White (Lorca 1988).
3. The lithographs contained scenes from the plantation or else 'zoological alphabets, Cuban fruits, and, most frequently, cartoon-like scenes of contemporary life that included, of course, many depictions of blacks and mulatos' (Kutzinski 1993: 45).
4. Important documentary work about the specific time and place of Lorca's visit to Cuba has been conducted by Dobos (1979 and 1980) and Eisenberg (1977). A map compiled by R. del Río charts the 'Places visited by the Spanish poet Federico García Lorca from 7 March to 12 June 1930 in the island of Cuba'. Santiago de Cuba is highlighted as part of the poet's route. My thanks to Nydia Sarabia for providing me with a copy of this map.
5. In a letter to Rafael Martínez Nadal, Lorca includes a drawing of 'La negrita Santa Bárbara' [The Little Black Saint Barbara]. The inscription reads, 'los negritos vendrán a adorar esta diosa, esta Santa Bárbara del coño tremulante' [The Blacks come to worship this goddess, Saint Barbara of the tremulous cunt] (Maurer 1985: 13).
6. *Musicalia*, vol. 11, April – May 1930, 43–4. The poem is dedicated to Don Fernando Ortiz.
7. Said (1993: 275–7) draws out the ambiguities surrounding 'the nativist phenomenon' (e.g. *négritude*) as a 'result of the colonial encounter': the paradox that adoring the Negro is as sick as abominating him (277).
8. From a private interview with Rosa Ileana Boudet, Casa de las Américas, Havana, July 1999. Lorca does not intrude heavily into tourism in Cuba (saturated by Hemingway and the iconic imagery of Che Guevara) as he has recently begun to do in Granada, Spain, where postcards and T-shirts are now sold in the Cuesta de Gomérez at the foot of the Alhambra.
9. Lebbacue (1997–8) documents Lorca's presence in Cuba from 1930 to 1997.
10. The fortunes of *El público* have been closely linked with Cuba. It was written on notepaper bearing the insignia of the Hotel Unión, Havana, where Lorca stayed during his time in Cuba. Later, he presented it to Carlos Manuel Loynaz, who is believed to have burnt it during one of his rages (Loynaz 1987). It was performed for the first time in Havana in 1997 by Carlos Díaz and his company (possibly influenced by the success of Tomás Gutiérrez Alea's 1993 film *Strawberry and Chocolate* which portrayed homosexuality with sensitivity). Díaz followed anecdotal evidence from Dulce María Loynaz (who wrote notes on the version of *El público* from which they had heard excerpts) and included a 'missing scene' which featured a Tower of Babel which went up in flames. From a private interview with Carlos Díaz, Havana, July 1999.
11. From newspapers archived at the Biblioteca Nacional, Havana. An article by Morales (1976) documents this episode.

Bibliography

Auclair, M., *Enfances et Mort de García Lorca*. Paris, 1968.
Baudelaire, C., *Baudelaire*. trans. L. Lerner., London, 1999.
Barthes, R., *Camera Lucida: Reflections on Photography*. trans. R. Howard, London, 1981.
Behdad, A., *Belated Travellers: Orientalism in the Age of Colonial Dissolution*. Durham, N.C., 1994.

Benítez Rojo, A., *The Repeating Island: The Caribbean and the Postmodern Perspective*. trans. J. Maraniss, Durham, N.C., 1992.
Bianchi Ross, C., 'Federico en Cuba', *Cuba Internacional*, vol. 9 (1980): 24–31.
——, 'Federico García Lorca: Su último día en la Habana', *Cuba Internacional*, vol. 200 (1986): 58–61.
Cardoza y Aragón, L., *El río. Novelas de caballería*, México, 1986.
Davies, C., '*María Antonia*; tragedia cubana, tanto africana como hispana', in A.D. Deyermond, A., ed. *Actas del Congreso Internacional de la Asociación de Hispanistas de Gran Bretaña e Irlanda. Quinto Centenario, Huelva, abril 1992*. Madrid, 1994: 287–97.
Dobos, E., 'El viaje de Lorca a Santiago de Cuba', *Revista de la Biblioteca Nacional*, Jan-April, 1979.
——, 'Nuevos datos sobre el viaje de Federico García Lorca por Cuba en el año 1930', *Acta Litteraria Academiae Scientarum Hungaricae*, vol. 22 (1980): 392–405.
Duncan, J., and D. Gregory. 'Introduction' to *Writes of Passage: Reading Travel Writing*. London, 1999.
Eisenberg, D., 'A Chronology of Lorca's Visit to New York and Cuba', *Kentucky Romance Quarterly*, vol. xxiv (1977): 233–50.
García Lorca, F., *Obras Completas (en tres tomos)*. ed. A. del Hoyo, Madrid, 1954.
——, *Poet in New York*. trans. G. Simon and S. F. White, ed. and intro. by C. Maurer, London, 1988.
——, *Epistolario Completo*. A. A. Anderson and C. Maurer (eds), Madrid, 1997.
Gibson, I., *Federico García Lorca: A Life*. London, 1989.
Guillén, N., *Motivos del son: Música de Amadeo Roldán, Alejandro Gracia Caturla, Eliseo Grenet, Emilio Grenet*. Edicion Especial 50 Aniversario. Havana, 1980. [Originally published 1930]
Hughes, L., *I Wonder As I Wander: An Autobiographical Journey* (1956). New York, 1984.
Kutzinski, V. M., *Sugar's Secrets: Race and the Erotics of Cuban Nationalism*. Charlottesville and London, 1993.
Leccabue, F., 'La Presenza di Federico García Lorca a Cuba dal 1930 ad Oggi', doctoral dissertation, Università degli Studi di Parma, 1998.
López, C., *Arpa de troncos: De Cuba a Federico*. Havana, 1999.
Loynaz, D.M., 'Yo no destruí el manuscrito de *El público*', *ABC*, 30 May (1987): 42.
Marinello, J., *García Lorca en Cuba*. Havana, 1965.
——, 'El poeta llegó a Santiago', *Bohemia*, May 31, (1968): 22–7.
Maurer, C., *Federico García Lorca escribe a su familia desde Nueva York y la Habana 1929–30*. Madrid, 1985.
Morales, F., 'La visita del poeta-dibujante "vanguardista" García Lorca provoca polémicas en Cienfuegos', *Signos* Jan-Aug, vol. 18 (1976): 341–63.
Ortiz, F., *Los bailes y el teatro de los negros en el folklore de Cuba*. Havana, 1951.
——, *Cuban Counterpoint: Tobacco and Sugar* (1940). trans. Harriet de Onís, New York, 1970.
Pratt, M. L., *Imperial Eyes: Travel Writing and Transculturation*. London and New York, 1992.
Quevedo, A., *El poeta en La Habana. Federico García Lorca. 1898–1936*. Havana, 1961.
Said, E. W., *Culture and Imperialism*. London, 1993.
Santos Moray, M., 'Federico García Lorca', *Trabajadores*, 17 July 1986: 1–10.
Sarabia, N., 'Cuando García Lorca e stuvo eu Santiago, *Bohemia*, La Habana, 10 Sept (1965): 58–61.
Schonberg, J-L., *Federico García Lorca: l'homme, l'oeuvre*. Paris, 1956.
Schwartz, R., *Pleasure Island: Tourism and Temptation in Cuba*. Lincoln and London, 1997.
Smith, Paul Julian, *The Theatre of García Lorca: Text, Performance, Psychoanalysis*. Cambridge, 1998.
Venuti, L., 'Translation as Cultural Politics: Regimes of Domestication in English', *Textual Practice*, vol. 7, no. 2 (1993): 208–23.

Young, H., 'Broken Images: Eliot, Lorca, Neruda and the Discontinuity of Modernism', *Exemplaria* vol. 2, no. 1 (1998): 1–14.

A research grant from the A.H.R.B. enabled me to conduct research in Cuba in July 1999. I would like to thank Alison Sinclair, Andrew A. Anderson, Patricia McDermott, Catherine Davies, Robin Blackburn and Nydia Sarabia. Roberto Fernández Retamar, Rosa Ileana Boudet, Salvador Bueno, Pablo Armando Fernández and Aracelis García-Carranza also deserve special thanks.

Chapter 9

GIDE IN EGYPT 1939

Naomi Segal

The following conversation took place in March 1950, about a year before Gide's death aged eighty-one. The account is from the memoir of his son-in-law, Jean Lambert:

> I tell him how extraordinary I find it that, in his long life, he has never had any problems with the law – he sees this as a sign of grace worth showing off to Claudel! He replies: 'This immunity of mine embarrasses and disgusts me a bit. There is a lot to be written about the question of immunity'.
>
> 'What I wonder', I say, 'is how far they would dare to pursue you now you've got the Nobel Prize'. Not at all, he thinks.
>
> 'In the big *Pléiade* edition of the Journal, did you have to destroy any pages like those we were talking about?'
>
> 'No. But I've written some in the *Carnets d'Égypte* which are just as compromising. It would be very foolish to publish them now'. (His actual word is 'hypocritical'.) His view is that in fifteen years' time all this will have changed.
>
> 'Yes,' I say, 'but not in the direction you're hoping. Look at the reactions to the Kinsey Report…'
>
> He likes the definition I give him of himself: 'the first Nobel Prize winner that can't be safely placed in everyone's hands'. (Lambert 1958: 141)

Gide was fully aware of the anomaly of his impunity as a lover of boys who had written about his desire with an explicitness found in no other French writer of his time. His discomfiture at the contrast between his fate and Wilde's is clear, for instance, in the political fantasy of martyrdom that opens the argument of *Corydon* (Gide 1924), or in his determination that if he had been in a similar position to Aragon's in 1932 he would have 'considered it a point of honour to go to prison' (Gide 1968: 495–6). As for being compromised by his publications, one side of him took a mischievous pleasure in the thought of being thrown to the lions after his death, another gave minute attention to his image (Martin du Gard 1951: 127–9) and a third insisted that most great artists 'only win their cases on appeal', and that he was writing 'not for the coming generation but for the one after next' (Gide 1996: 1160 and 1191). Indeed, while swearing that he did not believe in the posthumous, he insisted on entrusting certain papers to his friend Pierre Herbart 'because I wish you to compromise me' (Van Rysselberghe 1977: 75).[1] There is here a certain fantasy of being attacked and surviving with courage, which was, in his lifetime, never tested out.

The *Carnets d'Égypte* were written during Gide's only visit to that country, from January to March 1939. It is one of two texts composed during the trip and published after his death. The other is a memoir of his relations with his wife Madeleine, entitled *Et nunc manet in te* – I will come back to the meaning of this title later.

Egypt was a special case for Gide. He had visited French colonial Africa many times, especially the Maghreb, and had been once, for a long trip, to the equatorial states Congo and Chad. But he had never seen Egypt before and he had rarely before travelled on his own, a condition that made the experience seem strangely unreal. As he explained to his young friend Claude Mauriac just after the trip: 'in Egypt, on my own, I couldn't get anything out of the experience. I need someone to confide in. Otherwise nothing attracts or even interests me' (Mauriac 1990: 44). But a decade later, in another of his pieces of travel writing, the confessional tale 'Acquasanta', dedicated 'to my companion Jef Last' (Gide 1954: 1106), he suggests something rather different:

> And yet the few journeys I have taken on my own may well have been the most valuable. I think there is a sort of cowardice in this need for a companion, someone to follow. Now that I am older, I feel that I am picking up something of his youth, that I am feeling things through him, that it is his astonishment that makes me capable of being surprised again; I have a share in his delight, knowing as I do that, when I experience them alone, the most charming landscapes on earth, the most smiling invitations to pleasure, tend to plunge me into despair. But the memories of things I enjoyed at second hand, so to speak, slip away from me more easily, as if they had never really belonged to me, whereas everything I have been forced to take on alone, pain or pleasure, remains deeply etched in my heart.

As this more reflective analysis suggests, having no travelling companion in Egypt does not seem to have dulled Gide's responses. Rather the contrary – it seems to have made him more than usually active in two other directions: sexual curiosity and confessional writing.

Both the *Carnets d'Égypte* and *Et nunc manet in te* were published posthumously, then, and described by their author in terms of their riskiness : 'compromising', 'indiscreet', 'unpublishable' (Lambert 1956: 141; Gide 1954: 1060; Mauriac 1990: 44). Giving Claude Mauriac the manuscript of *Et nunc manet in te* to read in May 1939, Gide described it thus: ' I'm making some terrible confessions about myself, about the development of my nature... I'm revealing some frightful secrets...' (Mauriac 1990: 52). Three months and two hundred pages later, referring to an evening in August 1939, Mauriac describes the experience of watching Gide smirk and Robert Levesque grin while the latter reads aloud the diary of their trip to Greece together immediately after Gide's weeks in Egypt:

> It is an unforgettable scene. Gide listens, the fingers of his right hand pressed into his cheek, his eyes half closed, Levesque's monotonous voice does not stop at any detail, however shocking. Description after description of the pair of them (Gide and him) looking for boys and finding them. It was Holy Week, and they didn't hesitate to go into churches, even, to flush them out. 'Who cares, I'll just read everything', says Robert Levesque, between sentences. Everything? Things like this: 'To get the child, Gide pretends to be thirsty; we go inside...' Or this: 'He picks up the child and offers him to Gide'. Neither Gide nor Robert shows the slightest embarrassment. I hide my astonishment. (Mauriac 1990: 240)

Spring 1939, then, was a season of intensive sexual tourism for Gide. Exactly a year earlier, on Easter Day 1938, his wife had died. He had, as his friend Maria Van Rysselberghe put it, 'lost his counterweight, the fixed measure against which he tested his actions, his real tenderness, his greatest fidelity; in his inner dialogue, the other voice has fallen silent' (Van Rysselberghe 1975: 78). That December he decided that the time had come to tell the story of his unconsummated marriage and also to print the passages he had omitted from his published Journal while Madeleine was alive. He wrote the first nine pages in Amsterdam, the remaining twenty-nine in Luxor.

The aim of this essay is twofold. First I want to set side by side the two remarkable texts that resulted from those isolated weeks in Egypt, and look for the ways in which, for all their obvious contrasts, they gain from being considered together. Then I want to try and understand why they were produced side by side, by considering what happened to that counterweight and interlocutor once her voice was not so much reanimated as reinterred in posthumous print – how, in the course of his homage, Gide took a very precise revenge for an old injury, one which perhaps explains the exceptional garrulousness of the sexual confessions he interspersed with its production. Both these discussions will allow me to speculate about the famous split between love and desire which the two texts represent so starkly, and to suggest a different way of understanding it.

Let me supply a context. Twenty years earlier, in his autobiography *Si le grain ne meurt* ... (written 1919, published 1926), Gide describes his first visit to North Africa in 1893. In the course of discussing different modes of desire, he comments: 'there are some people who fall in love with what resembles them; others with what differs from them. I am among the latter: what is strange appeals powerfully to me, just as I am repelled by what is familiar. Let us say also, and more precisely, that I am attracted by the afterglow of sun on brown skins' (Gide 1954: 565).

He had gone to Algeria for the first time at the age of twenty-four, determined to lose his virginity at last and liberate himself from the dual tyranny of piety and masturbation. Whether he knew the direction his desire would take him is not clear; a first encounter with a boy on a beach, though joyous, was not apparently used to extrapolate a sexual destiny. It is only two years later on a second visit that, through the mediation of Oscar Wilde and his lover Alfred Douglas, Gide recognizes his sexual 'nature': 'at last I found my normality' (Gide 1954: 593). But a few months later he went back to France, his mother died and he quickly became engaged to his cousin Madeleine, whom for years he had been begging to marry him, but who had always, until then, said no.

Marrying your first cousin, whom you have known since childhood, is not the mark of an exogamous impulse. But Gide was setting up an absolute distinction: between love, which is rooted in the familiar and seeks proximity, and desire, which harks towards far-off lands gilded with orientalism. Here is how he describes that split in his coming-out book: 'I had made up my mind to dissociate pleasure from love. It even seemed better to me to split them off in this way, for it seemed to me that pleasure was purer and love more perfect if the heart and the flesh had nothing to do with each other' (Gide 1954: 551–2). Recounting his engagement in the closing lines of the text, he returns to the paradox: 'I was driven by my fate, and perhaps also by a secret need to defy my nature; for in loving Emmanuèle [Madeleine] wasn't I in love with virtue itself? It was the marriage of heaven with my insatiable hell; I had forgotten that hell for the moment: the tears of my bereavement had put out all its fires' (Gide 1954: 613).

So we have here a conscious, apparently simple, split – on the one hand desire, unnamed and unnumbered boys, the African sun on black skin; on the other chastity, piety and the pure specific love object, the sister-wife. But I would like to add a nuance: Madeleine herself had bright eyes, arched eyebrows and unusually dark skin, inherited from her mother, whom many people took for a Creole and who had indeed been born on Mauritius but brought up in Le Havre. Mathilde Pouchet, after a twenty-year marriage to Gide's maternal uncle Émile Rondeaux, left under a cloud of scandal, never explained and almost certainly much exaggerated, when her eldest child Madeleine was nineteen and Gide himself was seventeen.[2] In two places – *Si le grain* and the fictitious and more tendentious *La Porte étroite* (Gide 1909) – Gide accounts for his attachment to his cousin in terms of her traumatic knowledge of her mother's 'sins'.

As I have argued elsewhere, the portrait of the exotic Lucile Bucolin in *La Porte étroite* is coloured by a paedophilia that Lacan and, after him, such often brilliant psychocritics as Jean-Marie Jadin and Catherine Millot accept as historical – or at least psychic – truth about the relationship between André and Mathilde. I see no reason to infer this; rather, the representation of the child both fascinated and repelled by an adult's attempt at seduction seems to me to suggest how aware Gide was of the possibility of a negative and damaging response to his desire in its objects. Nowhere shown in his portrayals of man-boy love, that negative response is expressible only in his representation of the effects of the 'excessively feminine' desire of the aunt. In a familiar move, the sexual effect of women is felt to inhere in or emanate from them. In both versions of the moment of the boy's discovery that his aunt is adulterous, only the healing fluid of his cousin's tears can wash away that dangerous emanation.

The whiff of transgressive desire was thus never far away from the supposed marriage of heaven and hell, and never as unthinkable as Gide wishes to pretend in the context of the homely and familiar. Indeed, the relation between transgression and virtue is, in his system, not one of mutual exclusion but one of cause and effect. It follows from this that the absolute difference of gender set up between *desire*, whose repository is the cluster male/foreign/younger, and *love*, whose repository is the cluster female/familial/older, is never as clear-cut as it is intended to be. Those elements of the feminine cannot be hermetically enclosed in a Normandy homestead far away from the locations of desire; the latter exists also in the 'wrong' times and places – even, potentially, in the good wife.

Let us now go back to Egypt and see how this emerges in its two texts. Gide opens his 'notebooks' with a declaration that has echoes in every one of his less happy travel memoirs: 'I find myself utterly lacking in curiosity towards Cairo. In my short stroll last night after dinner, did I see a single face that it was a pleasure to lay eyes on?' (Gide 1954: 1049). And again the same evening: 'To break this boredom, one attractive face would be enough. I come back to the hotel with all my bakshishs still in my pocket and my heart full of unspent smiles'. On 3 February, he has gone to Luxor, where, despite an uncomfortable journey and the worry of the international situation, he feels unaccountably better, properly cut off from the torments of the political situation and ready to work. The next entry reads:

> No, I no longer have a real desire to fornicate, or at least it's no longer a need as it used to be in the happy days of my youth. But I need to know that I could if I wanted to – do you understand that? I mean that a place doesn't interest me unless it offers multiple opportunities to fornicate. The finest monuments in the world can't replace that – why not admit it frankly? This morning, at last, walking through the native quarter of Luxor, I found what I was looking for. There were at least ten, twelve, twenty charming faces I

caressed with my eyes. I'm sure my gaze was instantly understood; the smile I got in return was unmistakable. There are villages, whole countries, where the most lust-laden gaze picks up not a single echo; others where ... take Russia, for instance: from top to bottom, the slightest wink would return to you, like the dove, bearing its olive branch. This has nothing to do with the laws of the land (Gide 1954: 1052–3).

The use of a chatty second-person form here is unusual for Gide's diary style. Effectively, he is making the text his cruising companion, a role taken by many friends – like Levesque – in the later years, but in the early years of his marriage most often by Henri Ghéon, with whom he shared a relationship of some months in Paris in 1905 with the fifteen-year-old Maurice Schlumberger, the first boy from his own milieu to whom he was attracted. In 1905, Ghéon became sexually involved while Gide, perturbed no doubt by the challenge to his geographical love/desire split, held back; it was only twelve years later that the split broke down irrevocably, with consequences that we shall see.

In Luxor, Gide has an encounter with a boy of around fourteen, bursting with health and smiling broadly through perfect teeth. Ali walks beside Gide, picking out for him the choicest leaves of a lettuce he was taking to his family. Another boy eventually leaves them, as Ali leads the way down alleys and paths to a low door in a wall, crosses a couple of courtyards and takes the ever-curious old man into a shadowy room, where he lifts his long tunic, drops his trousers and 'offered himself to me from behind. That was enough for me and I had no desire to take the encounter any further, especially as I was carrying all my money on me and might be at serious risk, if his companion, who had no doubt followed us at a distance, decided to join us with reinforcements, as they had perhaps agreed between them' (Gide 1954: 1054). In this frank and unpublishable confession, Gide is at pains to show the way in which he desires and does not desire: curiosity is his motive, the wish to be beckoned, but not such forgetfulness of self that he ignores the practical risks of his tourism, and above all not a penetrative act.

Gide was famously intolerant of any homosexual practices that involved penetration. In a prefatory footnote to *Corydon* and in the *Journal* entry on which it is based, he distinguishes between pederasts, 'of whom I am one' (Gide 1996: 1092), sodomites and inverts, adding 'they are so different that, generally, each group feels a deep disgust for the others.' He goes on to argue that the inverts, who 'take the woman's role in the drama of love' are the only ones who deserve the reproaches and accusations commonly levelled at all homosexuals. Similarly, in a scene from *Si le grain ne meurt* ... , Gide voices his horror at the act of anal sex between his friend Daniel B. [Eugène Rouart] and the Arab boy Mohammed, concluding: 'As for me, who can only understand pleasure when it is taken face to face, reciprocally and without violence, and who often, like Whitman, gets satisfaction from the most fleeting contact, I was horrified both by Daniel's act and by seeing Mohammed accept it so obligingly' (Gide 1954: 596).

The encounter in Luxor ends without the pederastic bargain being broken. He finishes the entry: 'I'm in no doubt that there are plenty of Alis in Luxor, though no doubt not quite as handsome. I had evidence of it the same evening. [...] As a result of which I had an excellent long restful night. Tried to work this morning' (Gide 1954: 1054). He works steadily most days, including on *Et nunc manet in te*, and takes walks in the afternoons, during which he observes the charming faces of the girls, the smiling flirtatiousness of some and the obscene sign-language of other garden boys, the latter dishonourably willing to offer themselves in the invert's role. He finds Ali again, after some persistent searching. Again the relation of correct pederastic tourism between the wealthy traveller and the unperverted youth is established: 'His hideous outfit of rags does not succeed in making him ugly. He is certainly very poor but I believe not unhappy. It pleases me that he is not a scrounger' (Gide 1954: 1056). Ali will be no Mohammed so long as Gide is no Daniel – and vice versa.

It is, as we shall see later, the sight of and contact with healthy masculine youth that Gide seeks above all in the street-boys he follows;[3] but even this can prove too much. By March, apart from a few interludes, 'the excessive abundance of offers takes away my appetite' (Gide 1954: 1067), and it is almost a relief to find that in Alexandria neither begging nor prostitution is permitted. The diary ends in Delphi, in a first-person plural that marks the meeting up with Levesque and the restoration of companionate travelling.

Et nunc manet in te begins with a description of Madeleine's absent presence: 'Yesterday evening I was thinking of her, talking to her, as I often did, more easily in my imagination than when she was actually there; when suddenly I said to myself: but she's dead ...' (Gide 1954: 1123). It is clear that the presence of Madeleine during her life – despite the desperate years in which he begged her to marry him – was not something that ever demanded proximity; what it needed was permanence. It was a geographical phenomenon: Madeleine had to be there (*there*, specifically, not *here*) in order for Gide to be wherever he was. She had to be *one* thing – grounded, constant, pure, different from him, in order for him to be all the other things – vagrant, promiscuous, changeful, creative and also safe. A fascinating description of the two of them together by Roger Martin du Gard exposes the danger of this tense balance, this bargain: beneath a genuine surface of mutual courtesy and smiles, 'a base of impenetrable coldness, something like a sudden drop in temperature at the depth: the absence not only of what might resemble normal conjugal familiarity but even the intimacy you would find between two friends, two travelling companions' (Martin du Gard 1951: 62). They did sometimes travel together, but not (of course) sexually. Their marriage *was* a balance, and each seems to have understood its aim very clearly, though, as Gide repeats in this text in a constant state of wounded surprise, nothing was ever said between them. Its aim was to nurture him and his life. By dying, Madeleine left him bereft of her shadowy polar presence. But as Maria Van Rysselberghe sharply notes immediately after the observation quoted earlier: 'I believe her memory will take on a firmer shape, and who knows? she may take up more room in his life than when she was alive' (Van Rysselberghe 1975: 78).

Et nunc manet in te was written to restore her presence, at exactly the right distance again, now no longer 'in' the world, but rather 'in' him – or to be precise, in his text. The title is a quotation from Virgil, from the story of Orpheus and Eurydice. It means: 'henceforth she remains in you' – only in you, that is, not in the world. Actually, as a phrase, it represents very well what it means: the feminine pronoun swallowed up in the verb *manet* is all that remains of a lost female body. The motif of writing a dead woman into text is, of course, far from new in 1939: it is a staple of the French *récit* (from *Manon Lescaut* via *Adolphe*, *Carmen*, *Sylvie*, up to and beyond Gide's own four *récits*), in which a young man confesses how he loved, misloved, was misloved and lost. It was exploited most starkly in Gide's first publication, the turgid *Cahiers d'André Walter* (1891), written explicitly to persuade Madeleine to marry him, in which the diarist writes of his beloved Emmanuèle, who marries another man and then dies: 'she dies; *therefore* he possesses her' (Gide 1986: 119), and, a few pages later, 'Your existence now? nowhere but inside me: you live because I dream you, when and only when I dream you; that is your immortality' (Gide 1986: 153). The fantasy he nursed in 1891 of what would or should happen if she continued to refuse him is clear; what has not been much noted elsewhere is how the writing of *Et nunc manet in te*, as well as a homage, is a final enactment of that threat.

As has been well observed by Jean Schlumberger (another sometime cruising companion, but also a loyal husband and family friend based near Cuverville where Madeleine lived),[4] the text tries repeatedly to represent the true, smiling, kindhearted Madeleine but keeps returning to her severe judgments, her physical clumsiness and the wilful uglification of the girl-self whom the boy Gide had loved. She neglects her intellect, abuses her beautiful hands with housework, her eyes and voice become altered with age: one day, at a hotel, the servants take her for his mother.

Gide begins by denying that Madeleine 'is' the Alissa of his *Porte étroite* but ends up showing how, in all these ways, she became her – and this despite the fact that she *did* marry him! He knows, and honestly confesses, the reason why: she might just have had desires (for sex, for motherhood) of her own. But he does not take that line of thinking very far, for two important reasons: first, as we have seen, because the very definition of Madeleine as good and lovable depends upon her having no desire, on being utterly different both from her caricaturally sexual mother and from the libidinously insatiable Gide;[5] and second, because the overwhelming aim of this confessional text is to show us – and, in some dim sense, to show her – that, despite the unspoken reasons that she, he (and we) may have to doubt it, he really did love her.

To this end, he fulfils the aim of producing this doubly posthumous book in which he will, as survivor, recreate a past that is gone.[6] Almost half the text consists of the excerpts from his diary which he withheld from publication during her lifetime out of sensitivity to her wish for obscurity. The fascinated reader turns to them in anticipation: will we find out what she was really like? But there is almost nothing of Madeleine in these passages; instead they represent a Gide intensely but sporadically – the entries span twenty-two years, from 1916 to 1938 but, welded together here, appear like an unbroken *cri de cœur* – struggling with the fact that the unspoken bargain seems ruined, based on nothing any more. They are often very poignant, but they insist on telling only one half of the story. There is no sign anywhere in *Et nunc manet in te* that Gide thought there was anything odd about this.

Cuverville, 8 October [1919]

> (Our wedding anniversary.) I don't know which is the more terrible, not to be loved any more, or to see that the person you love, and who still loves you, no longer believes in your love. I have not been able to make myself love her less, and I remain beside her, my heart bleeding, but without any words. Oh, will I ever be able to speak to her again? (Gide 1954: 1150)

31 October 1922

> She behaves towards me the whole time as if I no longer loved her, and I behave towards her as if she still loved me ... Sometimes it is atrociously painful (Gide 1954: 1156).

What event precipitated this collapse of the relationship, that dominates the intended homage? In 1917, Gide fell properly in love for the first time, at last combining definitively in one object the polar principles of need and desire. This love-object was Marc Allégret, the seventeen-year-old son of pastor Élie Allégret, a family friend since Gide's late teens and best man at their wedding. Madeleine somehow put two and two together and, the evening before his departure for a holiday in England in 1918, she asked him straight out if he was going with Marc. He stammered a reply, she told him to say nothing more – 'Don't ever say anything to me any more. I prefer your silence to your deceptions' – and he departed after a sleepless night, leaving her a letter in which he said he 'was mouldering' at Cuverville and had to get away (Schlumberger 1956: 189).[7] After a happy three months in England he returned and found everything just as usual: a smiling welcome, the return of routine. Then in November, writing what was to become *Si le grain ne meurt ...*, he asked Madeleine for one of his old letters to her, to check a detail, and she said – one account says 'with such effort that her lips trembled' (Gide 1954: 1148), another 'coldly' (Schlumberger 1956: 191) – that she had reread and then burnt them all, one by one, the night after he left.

Gide is clearly not unaware of the anguish that caused Madeleine to destroy what she called 'the most precious thing I had in the world' (Gide 1954: 1146), but it is his own loss that he mourns long and loud, comparing it to a wife telling her husband she has killed their child, to her needing to steal the air he breathes, and most specifically, to her destroying his best writing: 'the best part of me has gone; it is no longer there to counterbalance the worst' (Gide 1954: 1145). Again we find the image of absolute opposites set in a polarity of good and evil, heaven and hell. The betrayal he describes as filicidal is not so much towards a child they might have had – though clearly he considers his now impossible textual productions to be these – as towards the child he once was. Beyond even the shocking myopia of this judgement, something else deadly is implied here: in order for Gide to be the eternally youthful body that travels and desires, Madeleine must remain a virgin, stay at home in sunless Normandy, age visibly and prematurely and ultimately disappear altogether except as text.

A week of solid weeping in November 1918 left Madeleine apparently unmoved (he seems seriously to have expected her to ask his forgiveness). This book I suggest, is the delayed revenge. Disinterring repeated avowals that 'I have only lived, since, in a more or less posthumous way, in the margins of real life' (Gide 1954: 1157), Gide turns the ghostly couple around and publicizes their marital crisis over her dead body.

We should not ignore the fact that, in Maria Van Rysselberghe's account – she kept a two-thousand-page secret diary of their daily encounters from 1918 until his death – he veered, even at the time of the crisis, between deep mourning and crowing about how delightful Marc was (Van Rysselberghe 1973: 9–14). Now, as a direct result of writing *Et nunc manet in te*, he revives not so much the good boy who loved her as the bad boy who did not. The evidence for that is the *Carnets d'Égypte*, in which, having finished his homage, the seventy-year-old indulges in another kind of time-travel, thinking back to other North African journeys:

> I sometimes wonder what I would think nowadays of those boys who seemed so charming in the past, if I could see them again exactly as they were then. Would I recognize them? Some of them, I'm sure. What I loved most of all about them was undoubtedly their youth. And that is what I find in others today, what prevents me from falling into melancholy – a little, at least, for the only youth that no springtime can bring back is my own. Let me hope that I have left a little of its warmth in my writing! Now it's the turn of other people. But I'd like the mortal remains that the grave will soon claim from me not to be too chilled. I cannot accept the wisdom that tells us to put out the last embers of desire; on the contrary, we should try to keep them glowing. Let death do its work: why should we help it along? (Gide 1954: 1062)

One last point: you might be wondering about that son-in-law. Gide had a daughter, born to Élisabeth Van Rysselberghe, Maria's daughter, in 1923 – and no, despite the encouragement of Claude Mauriac, he did not include any mention of that literal child of his flesh in *Et nunc manet in te*.[8]

Notes

NB All translations from French are my own and reference is to the original. Any quotation without a page-reference in my text is taken from the last-cited page.

1. For a fuller discussion of Gide's idea of posterity, see Lucey (2000).
2. See discussions in Segal (1998), chapter 6 and Segal (2000), chapter 18. It is, in my view, not fortuitous in relation to Gide that the French slang word for an effeminate gay man is *tante*. For the other viewpoint, see Lacan (1966), Jadin (1995) and Millot (1996).
3. In the *Journal* (1954: 1059), Gide discusses the sudden clamping down of the Dutch colonial authorities in Bali against gay sexual tourism on the grounds of corruption of minors; not the tourists themselves but 'the unworldly youth of Bali have been rounded up and interrogated: since the Balinese never know their exact age, they have simplified matters by arresting crowds of brutalized, terrified adolescents'.
4. In reaction to *Et nunc manet in te*, Schlumberger wrote a warm and angry defence of their marriage in which, however, he went further than Gide had gone in publishing extracts from Madeleine's letters and diaries which she would certainly have wanted kept hidden – but how else counteract Gide's portrait effectively? See Schlumberger (1956).
5. The most idealized image of Madeleine appears in the only text, according to Gide, that he did not write in order to persuade her to understand him, *Les Faux-monnayeurs* (1926); addressed instead to his lover Marc Allégret, it presents the image of the utterly resigned, understanding and liberal-minded Pauline, the perfect wife, mother and sister, who tolerates and even enables the sexual gratification of all her menfolk while having no share of pleasure herself. On Gide's insatiability, see Martin du Gard 1993: 232–3.
6. See Van Rysselberghe 1975: 119: 'I think, though he hasn't said it explicitly, that he'd like to write something in memory of Madeleine, using all the passages concerning her from his *Journal* which he has never before published'.
7. This is from the account told by Gide to Roger Martin du Gard and reproduced in Schlumberger (1956). In *Et nunc manet in te*, with all the skewing of issues that this implies, Gide recounts the episode of the burnt letters, but not the holiday with Marc that explains it.
8. See Mauriac 1990: 66–70. When Gide insists the issue between him and Madeleine was not Catherine but only Marc, Mauriac comments: 'I am not convinced; neither is he'.

Bibliography

Gide, A., *La porte étroite*. Paris, 1909.
_____, *Corydon*, Paris, 1924. [Originally published 1911]
_____, *Les Faux-monnayeurs*. Paris, 1926.

_____, *Si le grain ne meurt* .... Paris, 1926.
_____, *Journal 1939–1949; Souvenirs.* Paris, 1954.
_____, *André Gide – Roger Martin du Gard Correspondance 1913–1934.* Paris, 1968.
_____, *Les Cahiers et les Poésies d'André Walter.* Paris, 1986. [Originally published 1891]
_____, *Journal 1887–1925.* ed. Éric Marty, Paris, 1996.
Jadin, J-M., *André Gide et sa perversion.* Paris, 1995.
Lacan, J., 'Jeunesse de Gide ou la lettre du désir', in *Écrits.* Paris, 1966.
Lambert, J., *Gide familier.* Paris, 1958.
Lucey, M., 'Gide et la postérité: la place de la sexualité', in *Le Désir à l'œuvre: Gide à Cambridge 1918. 1998,* ed. Naomi Segal, Amsterdam, 2000.
Martin du Gard, R., *Notes sur André Gide 1913–1951.* Paris, 1951.
_____, *Journal.* vol 2. ed. Claude Sicard, Paris, 1993.
Mauriac, C., *Conversations avec André Gide* (1951). Paris, 1990.
Millot, C., *Gide Genet Mishima.* Paris, 1996.
Schlumberger, J., *Madeleine et André Gide.* Paris, 1956.
Segal, N., *André Gide: Pederasty and Pedagogy.* Oxford, 1998.
_____, *Le Désir à l'œuvre: Gide à Cambridge 1918,* 1998. Amsterdam, 2000.
Van Rysselberghe, M., *Les Cahiers de la Petite Dame.* 4 vols. Paris, 1973, 1974, 1975, 1977.

Part 4

COLONIAL ENCOUNTERS

Chapter 10

MAKING THE CASE FOR CROSS-CULTURAL EXCHANGE
ROBERT BYRON'S *THE ROAD TO OXIANA*

Howard J. Booth

Robert Byron's last travel book, *The Road to Oxiana* (1937), has been widely praised. There has, though, been little sustained contextualization or analysis. Bruce Chatwin, who was strongly influenced by Byron, noted that, 'Anyone who reads around the travel books of the thirties must, in the end, conclude that Robert Byron's *The Road to Oxiana* is the masterpiece' (Chatwin 1994: xi). Byron's text shows a remarkable responsiveness to the decade in which it was written, and thoughtfully deals with the challenges of form and language posed by a period of extremes. In work on writing of the 1930s, the impact of conflicts between nations and ideologies in Europe has received attention. Less well addressed – indeed almost totally neglected – has been the relation between the writing of the 1930s and colonialism. The journey that Byron wrote up in the book, from Italy through Palestine and Syria to Iran, and eventually to Afghanistan and down into India, between 1933 and 1934, came in the period when British interests in the Middle East had reached their maximum. The campaigns against the Turks during the First World War were followed by League of Nations mandates and increased influence throughout the region. When Jerusalem fell to Allenby in early December 1917, and the Union flag was flown over the city, the bells of Westminster Abbey were rung for the first time in the war. The main popular story of bravery from the conflict was to be that of Lawrence of Arabia, rather than anything that emerged from the Western front. The Middle East became the last area of British colonial expansion (Holland 1999: 134–5). Byron's text engages with a part of the world open to the traveller in new ways, when to be British there was particularly significant. Byron is, though, deeply responsive to a late colonial context which saw not only continued support for colonialism, but also the questioning of whether the British Empire could be sustained. Byron managed to be a remarkably incisive critic of his period – though, inevitably, some of the prejudices of his class, country and time find their way into his work. His most significant achievement was to use the travel book form to gesture towards aspects of the decade that threatened to lie beyond the resources of existing language and genres.

Accounts of the 1930s are being influenced by an increased questioning of the term 'Modernism' in English Studies, the decade being included in most, though not all,[1] efforts to establish beginning and terminating dates for the movement. Modernism is now being re-historicized and re-examined, something that has been in progress for longer in other literary periods defined by a set of unifying ideas, such as the Renaissance and Romanticism. The Modern Movement, in its own time the literature of the new and the radical, has become the past, with a period, Postmodernism, that follows it. Perhaps to our surprise we no longer have ready access to a very different society and political context. Further, the post-Second World War formation of modernist studies – what was included for analysis, the main lines of debate, the ways of making aesthetic judgements – often said as much about the attitudes and values of the postwar period as it did about the years 1900 to 1945. Feminist critics and those working on sexuality and literature were among the first to challenge the hegemony of institutional modernist literary studies. Recent efforts to look at the relation between Modernism and colonialism can be seen in a similar way, with part of the project being to analyse the resistance to giving sustained attention to the issue. Modernist studies, formed in the immediate context of the trauma of decolonization, preferred to marginalize Empire and literature from consideration, confining the issue to a few texts (really in the teaching of Modernism) and certain controversies. Even Primitivism was discussed without sustained attention to issues of race and empire.

It is in the light of such a reconsideration of the modernist period that efforts to think about colonialism and the 1930s should come. This has a particularly marked impact on the consideration of the travel book, which was often ignored in old-style modernist studies, for all the popularity of the form in the period. The danger of not being sufficiently questioning about the broader terms of debate is shown in the most widely disseminated account of Byron's work, a chapter in Paul Fussell's *Abroad*. He argued that, 'perhaps it may not be going too far to say that what *Ulysses* is to the novel between the wars and what *The Waste Land* is to poetry, *The Road to Oxiana* is to the travel book' (Fussell 1980: 95). Fussell wants to elevate the status of the text, but the only way he feels able to do so is by associating it with Eliot and Joyce and suggesting that if it is good it must be formally modernist. Despite using short sections and a range of styles and voices, the book does not really qualify when tested against the postwar definition of Modernism. However, *The Road to Oxiana* is still an important text – it is just that the case has to be made more carefully than Fussell allows.

The 'mix' in the period of different kinds of texts can be extended to include the simultaneity of other kinds of opposites. Particularly important here was the coexistence of attitudes that both supported and condemned colonialism. The travel book is particularly well suited to capturing different, perhaps indeed contradictory, attitudes in suspension. In literary studies there is perhaps an assumption that support for colonialism rapidly ebbed away after the Victorian and Edwardian periods. E.M. Forster's *A Passage to India* (1924) would be an example text of the liberal questioning of Empire. Historical studies see things rather differently. In the first half of the twentieth century, historians such as Nicholas Owen (1999) find little evidence of thoroughgoing anti-imperialism. The popular reach of colonial discourses was increased by the BBC, which had special programming on Empire Day (instituted in 1904, and held on the late Queen's birthday) and at Christmas. Though the high-water mark of colonial events was reached with the Wembley exhibitions in 1924 and 1925, the Imperial Institute in South Kensington in London (where Imperial College now stands) had over one million visitors a year in the early 1930s (Mackenzie 1999). However, only a few, mainly Leninists, were wholly against empire, but there were those who advocated reform of one kind or another. Historical studies find it difficult to register both the continuing deployment of colonial discourses *and* the weakening of the imperial project. The key underlying changes were the erosion of the economic advantages of Empire, and of the United Kingdom's relative economic power. The decline of military and diplomatic strength followed. The forces and discourses that had driven colonial expansion were beginning to ebb. This occurred in a context of independence movements in the colonies gaining strength. Overall, though, the late colonial period needs to be seen as 'mixed', with imperialism and its critique coexisting in a relationship that awaits full analysis.

The tendency to demand a single narrative of the period – either colonialism was strongly sustained or collapsing – can be seen in the limited work there is in cultural theory on the relationship between Modernism and empire, and whether the writing of the period questioned or supported colonialism. Michael Bell sees a move towards cultural plurality captured in modernist form and language (Bell 1997: 149), and it is also possible to imagine an argument that *avant garde* art could disturb the colonialist centre in society. However, this position does not respond to the challenge of thinking together anti-colonial questioning and the simultaneous deployment of discourses that sought to perpetuate empire. Also one-voiced, though forceful, is the argument of Ashcroft, Griffiths and Tiffin (1989) who claim that the awareness of other cultures, and the exhibition of colonial loot, initially made Modernism possible. However, this awareness was not unsettling and oppositional for long as Modernism came to register and make its own art from fragments from other cultures. It took to itself the world's cultures, which it then used, ordered and judged. The West's discourse of Modernism was a way of appropriating what was multiple and subversive and making it into its own high culture. Thus tamed and controlled, the supposedly new and radical developments in the arts were offered up for export and imitation to the colonies through the education system. Modernism is therefore perceived as cultural imperialism.

The major theoretical piece in the area is similarly limited in its failure to account for complexity and the coexistence of difference in the period. Fredric Jameson's article 'Modernism and Imperialism' is important because it sees colonialism as registering on writing of the modernist period not only at the level of theme but also in terms of form and language. For Jameson, after the Congress of Berlin, the 'First World' subject felt her- or himself to be part of an economic and social system that was now global. Troubled by the silence where the voice of the other and different should be, Western representation's figuration of space was affected. The argument is, however, undermined by its didactic and simplifying framework and by Jameson's disturbing 'First World' confidence that he can rapidly sum up the relationship between Modernism and empire. He distinguishes Modernism from a literature '*of empire*' – he mentions Kipling, Rider Haggard, Verne and Wells (Jameson 1988: 5) – which he sees largely as a late nineteenth-century phenomenon. He totally ignores the existence of writing *from the empire*. He does not adequately address the 'Voyage-In' that staffed Anglo-American Modernism. This not only consisted of exiles and emigrés but also of colonial subjects who brought with them their cultural backgrounds and concerns: one thinks of Mansfield and Rhys here. Non-metropolitan Modernisms are excluded by Jameson. Unaddressed too is the insight of Deleuze and Guattari that when the world map was coloured in by European empires an 'interior colony' was mapped by psychoanalysis, with Oedipus becoming 'our most intimate colonial relation' (Deleuze and Guattari 1983: 170). Jameson also fails to address the key discourse that Modernism and colonialism shared: degeneration theory. Writing often maintained simultaneously and despite the contradiction that, firstly, Europe was about to be overrun by a tide of disease and decay from the geographical margins, while declaring, secondly, that given the exhaustion and decline of the West, the 'other' alone provided a way towards rebirth and cultural reinvigoration (Edmond 2000).

The travel book has always been, as Steve Clark has recently noted, 'a mixed and middlebrow form throughout its history' (Clark 1999: 1). In Jonathan Raban's words it, 'accommodates the private diary, the essay, the short story, the prose poem, the rough note and polished table talk with indiscriminate hospitality' (Raban 1987: 253). Unashamedly commercial, it has nevertheless played a role in the birth of high cultural forms, such as the novel. Perhaps what post-colonial studies most needs to say about the travel book at present is that it can challenge and disturb. This is the main thrust of Clark's introduction to his edited volume *Travel Writing and Empire: Postcolonial Theory in Transit* (1999). His observations come in a general context in post-colonial studies of a turn towards the complexities of particular situations and away from the totalising theories of the 'big name' pioneers in the field. He argues that the travel book has been said to have only one form of relationship with empire. The powerful case has been made that in its narratives of cross-cultural contact, the Western form of the travel book continually sees otherness as inferiority. The form is particularly useful because, says Clark summarizing this position, of 'its relative explicitness in demonstrating the workings of colonial power', indeed that 'the traveller cannot do other than reproduce [colonialism's] fundamental structures of oppression with varying degrees of blatancy' (1999: 3, 8). Clark associates this position with Said, producing a rather reductive account of his book *Orientalism* (Said 1978). It is difficult to follow Clark in his rather heated attack on travelling post-colonial critics or in his claim that a more 'generous' view of imperial textuality is needed – whatever, precisely, that word means here (1999: 4). However, Clark is right to call attention to how the traveller could unsettle readers back home by not fulfilling their expectations of different cultures, and by disrupting their world views.

This is certainly important for *The Road to Oxiana*, which is very much a questioning text. However, it seems to resist other general conclusions Clark reaches. He argues that, 'Travel reference is to do with world-coherence: the book projects a world, and it is the ethics of inhabiting that alternative domain that are primarily at stake' (Clark 1999: 2). Byron's text is certainly concerned with ethics but, because the decade in which it was written saw overly-firm and insistent world views, its deliberate use of ambivalence forces the reader to engage with difficulties of interpretation. That said, the book does have an overall trajectory. Byron's aim was to question the dominance and univocal deployment of

Western and colonialist narratives. Such a view of Byron's text is different from that of other writers. I do not see his last travel book in terms of the final achievement of a fully realized prose style (Sykes 1946), as the height of the British interwar travel book (Fussell 1980), or as uncannily prophetic about the future of Iran and Afghanistan (Chatwin 1994). In the limited space that remains, I intend to pursue this examination of Byron through a discussion of his life and career, and by looking at the issues raised by the ambivalence of tone in *The Road to Oxiana*.

Robert Byron's travel writing has often been seen in biographical terms. It is perhaps the very lack of materials that makes such a reading attractive. Indeed, the absence of scholarly attention, which would not be the case had he been an important poet or novelist rather than a cultural critic and travel writer, extends to the lack of a comprehensive bibliography. The picture of Byron that emerges from existing writing is of an 'establishment rebel'. Coming from an eccentric family that shared its name, coat of arms and motto with the poet (though the precise relationship between the two family lines has never been satisfactorily traced) he was close to his parents and siblings, and especially to his mother. Though the family was not that wealthy, and indeed getting poorer in the first decades of the twentieth century, he was nevertheless sent to Eton and Oxford, where he came at the tail-end of the Acton generation. Early detestations, expressed with vigour, included Americans, Roman Catholicism, the influence of classical attitudes on the culture of West, Winston Churchill, Rembrandt and Shakespeare. During his lifetime all of these were moderated or reversed – except, it seems, for the last two. In accounts of his work the juicy barbed comments he made have been repeated, but the general conclusion towards which these tend, that he was drawn towards a general questioning of what was asserted by the West, has not been drawn.

Byron's first travel book, published when he was twenty-one, recorded a motor journey to Greece. *Europe in the Looking Glass: Reflections of a Motor Drive from Grimsby to Athens* (1926) shows Byron's attention to the crossing of borders, to the liminal, and also the cultural impact of modernization, here in the form of the motor car and speed, on culture and forms of perception. It also begins to show his special responsiveness, among all the arts, for architecture; for the buildings of the past, and what their survival says about the presence of the past in the present. Visiting Greece again in 1926 and 1927 the resultant travel book, *The Station: Athos, Treasures and Men* (1928), focussed on Byron's time in the Greek Orthodox monasteries there. The volume was welcomed, with some reservations around the use of humour and a certain obvious artifice and constructedness in the style, by the greatest British travel writer of the preceding generation, D.H. Lawrence (Lawrence 1936: 383–4). Byron's identification with Byzantium at first only fuelled his fury at Catholicism and its impact on the West. This anti-Catholicism has been suggested as a reason for his estrangement from his sometime close friend, Evelyn Waugh. Byron noted how the depiction of Byzantium as decadent had become deeply ingrained in histories in the West – he particularly deplored the role of Gibbon's *The History of the Decline and Fall of the Roman Empire*. Correcting the perceived distortion of the historical record was the project of his book *The Byzantine Achievement* (1929) and, over-reaching himself somewhat, of the co-written *The Birth of Western Painting* (1930), where he insisted on European art's too-little acknowledged debt to the East.

The questioning of the Western cultural narrative of Europe's past, and the attack on those who held it with an easy, prejudiced confidence, is present in Byron's interest in colonial India and Soviet Russia. Byron flew to India with a ticket bought by Lord Beaverbrook (in return for writing a number of newspaper articles). Byron was surprised at how the Indian situation began to preoccupy him, and he published the volume *An Essay on India* in 1931. He was disturbed at the implications for the colonial project in India of the small-mindedness, racism and bigotry of the English colonial rulers. In large measure he put this down to their lack of travel and sustained engagement with other cultures before they went to India. This text may seem to be wholly separate from Byron's travel writing, but the concern with cross-cultural contacts, where the Western subject has to admit that she or he should open their assumptions to questioning, is central to all his work. Byron acknowledged that his precursor in making such a critique of British rule in India was E.M. Forster, and the novel *A Passage to India* (1924).

Byron travelled within the emerging national powers – including Russia, America and China – that were to supplant global British influence. His response to the first of these he recorded in his travel book *First Russia, Then Tibet* (1933). There he embarked on sustained questioning of Soviet Russia, with strong evidence of personal engagement with the issues. In fact, as the 1930s progressed, Byron became close to a number of British Marxists (much to the horror of his Roman Catholic friend Christopher Sykes, the 'Christopher' of *The Road to Oxiana*). Byron had become increasingly opposed to Nazism and by the end of the decade was calling himself a 'warmonger'. He commented on the irony of his becoming a political bedfellow of Churchill. But there was, as always in Byron, a deeper underlying question about cultural narratives, and a perception that the West was in crisis. He felt that he was embarked on a 'quest', a modern European traveller in search of meaning. He put this with great force in the opening chapter of *First Russia, Then Tibet*:

> I have travelled, I must confess, in search of both instruction and improvement. As [a] member of a community, and heir to a culture, whose joint worth is now in dispute, I would discover what ideas, if those of the West be inadequate, can with greater advantage be found to guide the world. And to this end I would also know, in the language of my own senses, in whom and what the world consists. (Byron 1985: 9)

The sense of a response to a culture in crisis is clear, yet the passage is couched in the language of an appeal to the Western empirical tradition, with its reliance on knowledge gained through the senses and its assumption of a Cartesian subject. The aim appears to be a form of expression that is somehow uncontaminated by the social sphere.

As well as Byron's questioning project, his position in-between cultures, shown in his views on nation, empire and culture, one further area needs to be addressed: Byron's sexuality. Beyond a few stories there is little that survives of Byron's attitude to his homosexuality, though its traces in the writing can be discerned. There is a concern with male beauty, and the world described in Byron's writing is very masculine. References to European women are courtly and distanced. His homosexuality may have been the reason for Evelyn Waugh's increasing distance from him. Other reasons can be given, as well as Byron's anti-Catholicism, for Waugh's attitude. Harold Acton felt that his relations with Waugh had cooled because he had known Waugh's first wife. Byron had been at the wedding, and the marriage had ended badly (Carpenter 1989: 229–30). Most likely of all, though, is jealousy on Waugh's part at Byron's talent as a travel writer. Byron's sexuality adds to ways in which he represents a combination of social marginality as well as privilege.

In his comments on *The Road to Oxiana* Christopher Sykes remembered that Byron had kept a journal during their trip. This was carefully rewritten later, though the journal style, and the impression that it was written at speed on the journey, were retained. Sykes regretted the 'dramatic pruning operations' involved in the process of revision (1946: 157). He felt that while Byron was intent on curbing the excesses of his prose style – in which he succeeded – the book had been left with what Sykes calls 'a fault of tempo':

> It is written in the style of casual jottings during a journey from Venice to the East, the same style in which the original notes for the book were made. So conscientiously is it disguised as a book of hurried entries into a diary that a reader may easily and pardonably read it too quickly, mistaking it for an amusing record of an amusing trip and no more. It needs to be read slowly. (Sykes 1946: 129)

Sykes's argument helps establish that much careful reworking was done by Byron – though more was involved than paring down the original travel notes. His argument about the book needing to be read slowly, though the text suggests that as it was written quickly and could therefore be read at speed, may be a valid point. It perhaps accounts, as Sykes contends, for the fact that many of the first reviewers missed the importance of the book: Waugh's ungenerous response probably had other origins (Waugh 1983: 198). Readers expected little that was challenging from the travel book, and failed to move past the surface of the text – something that raises issues about the status of the genre in the period and its reception. As carefully rewritten, *The Road to Oxiana* in fact offered a response to the 'other' that differed from the intolerant and extreme right-wing views which were common in Europe and from British attitudes to the colonized. The book celebrated the possibilities for cultural renaissance and personal growth that could result from cross-cultural encounters.

The main theme of the book was described by Sykes as 'a quest for the origins of Islamic art' (Sykes 1946: 129). Sykes and Chatwin note that Byron has a specific thesis. The great artistic achievements of Persia and Afghanistan were influenced not by the West, or from the past of the region, but by cross-fertilization with the cultures of the nomadic peoples from the north-east (Chatwin 1994: xvi). More than a historical argument is being mounted by Byron. He is showing that migration and engagements between different peoples are positives: a point that needed to be made in the 1930s (and one, sadly, that still has to be restated in contemporary Europe). Byron points up the parallel with events in the Europe of his time by noting the evidence of forced Jewish migration in his text. At the start of the book he describes Jewish people leaving Europe, and at the Eastern geographical extreme he sees them being expelled from Afghanistan, having previously left Russia (Byron 1992: 119, 294–5). A narrative of the past about the cultural wealth of non-Western tradition and the importance to it of the other and different is set off against contemporary 1930s intolerance. As so often in the text, there are ambivalences here, the tone is difficult to judge in ways that parallel the challenge of reading the late colonial context and 1930s Europe.

Byron's opposition to what was wrong with British imperialism in Palestine and Cyprus – even if it does not lead to a full scale attack on colonialism itself – does not mean that Britain is the only world power that Byron responds to in *The Road to Oxiana*. The Southern borders of the Soviet Union are brought into the text. Byron also registers growing American strength, not only through the American tourists that he clearly detests, but also through his treatment of technology. There is much attention given to means of transport; the British are associated with the failed charcoal burning cars that were to have taken Byron and Sykes to

Afghanistan. The car that takes them down into India without a single problem is, tellingly, a Chevrolet – a symbol of how American modernization is going to give the United States ever increasing economic and cultural strength.

For all the journal entry style, then, the narrative and argument of *The Road to Oxiana* are carefully made so as to act as a commentary on the developments in the decade. However, one also has to look closely at the level of style, and here the picture becomes more complex. The difficulty is in judging the tone and what to do with the text's ambivalence. This style allows Byron to gesture towards a pervading sense of menace, not representable by conventional means. To take a few examples from the text to pursue these points, *The Road to Oxiana* begins as if at the start of a new volume of a diary. We can still understand the meaning without the implied earlier entries, but the appearance is created of reading an ongoing journal. The style is of a young upper-middle class educated person's speech rather than of prose:

> Venice August 20th, 1933. – Here as a joy-hog; a pleasant change after that pension on the Giudecca two years ago. We went to the Lido this morning, and the Doge's Palace looked more beautiful from a speed boat than it ever did from a gondola. The bathing, on a calm day, must be the worst in Europe: water like hot saliva, cigar-ends floating into one's mouth, and shoals of jelly-fish.
>
> Lifar came to dinner. Bertie mentioned that all whales have syphilis. (Byron 1992: 3)

It is not a holiday but a 'joy-hog' and it is assumed that we know about the experiences in the Giudecca pension. Only half-obscured by the playful tone here is an attack on the tourist facilities of Venice. The Doge's Palace, which was for Ruskin 'a model of all perfection' (Ruskin 1995: 188), is seen not from a gondola – of course Ruskin first approached Venice from the water (Ruskin 1989: 267) – but by motor boat. Byron introduces the use of speed, and so modernization and those aspects of Modernism – one thinks, in particular, of Italian Futurism – that welcomed it. A few pages on he notes, 'Give me Venice as Ruskin first saw it – without a railway; or give me a speed-boat and the international rich' (1992: 5). Byron's travels hardly show him to be besotted by the pleasures of cosmopolitan Europe, however. What is happening here is the overturning of what had been the dominant narrative of Venice since it was 'rediscovered' by North Europeans in the mid-nineteenth century, where the decline of Venice was linked by artists to an aesthetic that celebrated decay (Pemble 1995).

In the accounts of European buildings in and around Venice, Byron questions the dominant narratives of his time, but he also shows his ambivalence towards them. This architecture also exercises a strong attraction. He says of a drive to the Palladio – designed Malcontenta:

> I stood with Diane on the lawn below the portico, as the glow before dusk defined for one moment more clearly every stage of the design. Europe could have bid me no fonder farewell than this triumphant affirmation of the European intellect. 'It's a mistake to leave civilization,' said Diane, knowing she proved the point by existing. I was lost in gloom. (1992: 4)

Though the appeal of travel is celebrated throughout the book, and Byron criticizes the West sharply, he is European himself and the West is here celebrated as *the* civilization. It is done with a rare appeal in this text to female beauty, though through a rather mannered compliment, which has the effect of distancing him from the suggestion of any sexual attraction.

There is much in *The Road to Oxiana* that is incisive, but many demands are made of the reader. It is as if a direct statement of the European and colonial situation is impossible, and indeed an undesirable project to pursue. An example is the description of the departure from Venice:

> The departure of this boat from Trieste was attended by scenes first performed in the Old Testament. Jewish refugees from Germany were leaving for Palestine. On the one hand was a venerable wonder-rabbi, whose orthodox ringlets and round beaver hat set the fashion for his disciples down to the age of eight; on the other a flashy group of boys and girls in beach clothes, who stifled their emotions by singing. A crowd had assembled to see them off. As the boat unloosed, each one's personal concerns, the lost valise, the misappropriated corner, were forgotten. The wonder-rabbi and his attendant patriarchs broke into nerveless, uncontrollable waving; the boys and girls struck up a solemn hymn, in which the word Jerusalem was repeated on a note of triumph. The crowd on shore joined in, following the quay to its brink, where they stood till the ship was on the horizon. At that moment Ralph Stockley A.D.C. to the High Commissioner in Palestine, also arrived on the quay, to find he had missed the boat. His agitation, and subsequent pursuit in a launch relieved the tension. (1992: 5)

How does one judge the tone here? It could be said that Byron establishes a highly questionable level of comic distance between himself and the emigrating Jews, making light of a painful farewell to Europe. The description of Stockley's failure to catch the boat – though with his privileges he manages to get on board eventually – rounds off what on one level appears to be a comic scene. However, Stockley's late arrival is said in the last word of the paragraph to relieve the 'tension'. Until this point Byron has acknowledged no such feeling. Byron thus reveals that he has been describing comically something too painful to be approached in other ways, and the reader is now forced to reconsider the passage.

When Byron resumes his journey, going from Cyprus to Palestine, there are nine hundred aboard his ship:

> Christopher took me on a tour of the third-class quarters. Had their occupants been animals, a good Englishman would have informed the R.S.P.C.A. But the fares are cheap; and being Jews, one knows they could all pay more if they wanted. (1992: 13)

At first sight this appears to be baldly anti-Semitic on Byron's part, however the tone is surely ironic. The suggestion is that while the English would not treat an animal in this way, their anti-Semitism would see them raise no objections to the accommodation afforded to these Jewish travellers. In Palestine itself Byron's pro-Jewish approach comes to the fore, and he praises their contribution to economic growth in the Mandate (1992: 26). This support goes, though, with prejudice against Arabs – he refers confidently to their 'ill manners'. For all the barbed comments against the way the British do things his remains a characteristically 'mixed' late colonial world view. The Jews are better off with the British there – the Empire itself is not to be overthrown, colonialism should just be done better. He observes with disdain 'an extreme party that want to be rid of the English and set up a Jewish state. I don't know how long they think the Arabs would suffer a single Jew to exist once the English went' (1992: 23). Byron does not reach a position wholly beyond the prejudices and imbalances of his time.

Alongside Byron's confident questioning of British ruling class attitudes in Cyprus and Palestine is the easy assurance of his class and connections; he always seems able to gain access to the most significant and 'best' people. However, the response to this world is unsettling, as seen in the account of dinner with the High Commissioner in Jerusalem:

> We dined with the High Commissioner, most pleasantly. There were none of those official formalities which are very well at large parties, but embarrass small ones. In fact, but for the Arab servants, we might have been dining in an English country-house. Did Pontius Pilate remind his guests of an Italian squire? (1992: 25)

The pleasures of the small party and informality are praised, while Byron shows familiarity with large formal functions and country house life. The final sentence though alters the tone, introducing a temporal dislocation that draws attention to the geographical continuity, the British Empire being linked to Imperial Rome and to the events of the Passion.

The demands *The Road to Oxiana* makes on the reader, then, are considerable. The text condemns right-wing politics and colonial injustices, though Byron's own privileged position, anti-Arab prejudices and commitment to a reformed Empire are evident. It embeds at the level of its narrative an opposition to 1930s intolerance and nationalism, praising cross-fertilization with other cultures and the achievements of non-Western art. At the level of style, an ambivalence of tone is deployed to reflect the challenge of reading the 1930s. Byron suggests that the reader should learn to work and acknowledge difficulty, and so not accept any of the single-line explanatory models offered by extreme ideologies. If 1930s intolerance is accepted as a cause of the Second World War, then Byron himself was a victim of the decade's attitudes. He died on a torpedoed ship in 1941, while seeking to return to the Middle East, four days short of completing his thirty-sixth year.

Note

1. For example, two texts from the 1970s give 1930 as a terminating point, Faulkner (1977) and the influential Bradbury and McFarlane (1976).

Bibliography

Ashcroft, B., Griffiths, G. and Tiffin, H., *The Empire Writes Back: Theory and Practice in Post-Colonial Literatures*. London, 1989.
Bell, M., *Literature, Modernism and Myth: Belief and Responsibility in the Twentieth Century*. Cambridge, 1997.
Bradbury, M., and McFarlane, J., eds. *Modernism: A Guide to European Literature 1890–1930*. London, 1976.
Byron, R., *The Byzantine Achievement*. London, 1929.
———, *An Essay on India*. London, 1931.
———, *Europe in the Looking Glass: Reflections of a Motor Drive from Grimsby to Athens*. London, 1926.
———, *First Russia, Then Tibet*. London, 1985. [Originally published 1933].
———, *The Road to Oxiana*. London, 1992. [Originally published 1937].
———, *The Station: Athos, Treasures and Men*. London, 1928.
Byron, R., and Talbot Rice, D., *The Birth of Western Painting*. London, 1930.
Carpenter, H., *The Brideshead Generation: Evelyn Waugh and his Friends*. London, 1989.
Chatwin, B., Introduction (1981) in R. Byron, *The Road to Oxiana*. London, 1994.
Clark, S., ed. *Travel Writing and Empire: Postcolonial Theory in Transit*. London, 1999.
Deleuze, G. and Guattari, F., *Anti-Oedipus: Capitalism and Schizophrenia*. Trans. R. Hurley, M. Seem and H. R. Lane. London, 1983.
Edmond, R., 'Home and Away, Degeneration in Modernist and Imperialist Discourse' in H. J. Booth and N. Rigby, eds. *Modernism and Empire*. Manchester, 2000: 39–63.
Faulkner, P., *Modernism*. London, 1977.
Forster, E. M., *A Passage to India*. London, 1924.
Fussell, P., *Abroad: British Literary Traveling Between the Wars*. New York, 1980.
Holland, R., 'The British Empire and the Great War 1914–18' in *The Oxford History of the British Empire: Volume 4, The Twentieth Century*. Eds. J. M. Brown and Wm. Roger Louis. Oxford: 1999.
Jameson, F., 'Modernism and Imperialism', *Nationalism, Colonialism and Literature*. Derry, 1988.
Lawrence, D.H., *Phoenix: The Posthumous Papers of D.H. Lawrence*. Ed. E. D. McDonald. London, 1936.
Mackenzie, J. M., 'The Popular Culture of Empire in Britain' in *The Oxford History of the British Empire: Volume 4, The Twentieth Century*. Eds. J. M. Brown and Wm. Roger Louis, Oxford: 1999: 212–261.
Owen, N., 'Critics of Empire in Britain' in *The Oxford History of the British Empire: Volume 4, The Twentieth Century*. Eds. J. M. Brown and Wm. Roger Louis, Oxford, 1999: 188–211.
Pemble, J. *Venice Rediscovered*. Oxford, 1995.
Raban, J., *For Love and Money: Writing, Reading, Travelling*. London, 1987.
Ruskin, J., *Praeterita*. Oxford, 1989.
——— *Selected Writings*. Ed P. Davis. London, 1995.

Said, E. W., *Orientalism*. London, 1978.
Sykes, C., 'Robert Byron' in *Four Studies in Loyalty*. London, 1946: 80–179.
Waugh, E., *The Essays, Articles and Reviews of Evelyn Waugh*. Ed. Donat Gallagher. London, 1983.

Chapter 11

INVESTIGATING INDOCHINA
TRAVEL JOURNALISM AND FRANCE'S CIVILIZING MISSION[1]

Nicola Cooper

France had been established formally in Indochina since 1887, when the Union indochinoise was created regrouping Cambodia, Laos and Vietnam under French tutelage. By the first decades of the century, France seemed to have settled into a comfortable relationship with Indochina. The violence of conquest and pacification had become a distant memory: the memoirs and diaries of France's 'heroic age' of imperialism in Indochina were consigned to the bookshelves, and a new literature emerged which shunned exploration and dashing tales of military bravery in favour of themes of government and administration. Travel writing gave way to fiction, intrepid explorers gave way to settlers. Indochina, it seemed, had been domesticated.

The nation's colonial attitude was presented as reformist and cooperative. France had eschewed the older rhetoric of domination and force and had embraced a politics of association and partnership. The fundamentally violent impulse of conquest had been contained and harnessed within a legal framework: the paradigm of 'the right of the strongest' (*le droit du plus fort*) was replaced by 'the right of the strongest to help the weak' (*le droit du plus fort à aider le faible*) (Sarraut 1931: 106). Imperial legitimacy was to be measured by the nation's benevolence, generosity and humanitarianism abroad. The figure of *le colon bâtisseur* (constructive settler), popularized both through fiction and official propaganda, demonstrated that the virile energy of conquest had been channelled instead into new projects: building, construction, improvement and development.

Within the greater imperial structure of *la plus grande France*, Indochina had become something of a showcase for France's benevolent *doctrine coloniale* – Indochina was 'the pearl of the French empire', a more culturally sophisticated raw material for France to mould and develop than the perceived blank cultural, political and technological slate which French Africa, for example, represented. Indochina was a rival to Britain's jewel in the crown, it was France's trump card in the international game of imperial one-upmanship.

By the 1920s and 1930s then, the French press tended only to cover major events or diplomatic visits to Indochina. A certain complacency had developed with regard to French colonialism in Indochina. Few critical views of French rule in Indochina emerged, and those which expressed reservations concerning certain aspects of the Franco-Indochinese relationship remained convinced that it was within the capabilities of the French Republic to remedy these minor wrongs and to implement the necessary improvements.[2]

Between the turn of the century and the early 1920s, a steady trickle of largely positive reports confirmed the view that French rule in Indochina was successful and that the Indochinese populations were peaceable and appreciative subjects. Paul Claudel, for example, visiting Indochina in 1921 as part of his duties as French Ambassador to Japan,[3] was full of praise for the colony, seeing only 'perfect tranquillity' (1952: 333), and signs 'of regular growth, and peaceful development'(1952: 334).[4] For Claudel, Indochina of the 1920s appeared as a model of Franco-indigenous collaboration and harmony: 'Collaboration between Europeans and natives in Indochina has never been more intimate or more peaceful' (1952: 337–79).

His perception of the involvement of the Indochinese in the colonial relationship demonstrates the view which had come to be accepted of the indigenous populations as peacefully and gratefully collaborating with their French rulers. It was a vision also to be propagated by the colonial exhibition some years later, where the Indochinese participants were displayed as a compliant, industrious people: peaceful peasant populations, and eager francophiles.

In 1930, however, as the mainland was gearing up to staging its greatest colonial extravaganza the following year, the *Exposition coloniale de Vincennes* – which was to be an international *mise en scène* of France's great colonial oeuvre – it was Indochina, France's showcase colony, which threatened to overturn the apple-cart and reveal an altogether different face of French colonialism.

Economic hardship and recession had gradually led to growing discontent and dissatisfaction amongst the indigenous populations of Indochina, which found expression in a series of revolts and rebellions. Nationalist movements in Indochina, it seemed, were becoming more organized; and the growing elite of French-educated Indochinese appeared to be turning the Republic's own legacy of revolutionary principles against France itself. Suddenly it seemed, a vision of unruly natives had begun to provide a counterpoint to the positive images disseminated by 'official' France.

These worrying developments in Indochina did not however prepare opinion in the mainland for what was the most serious rebellion in Franco-Indochinese history: the Yen Bay uprising of 1930. While the mainland was celebrating its colonial *génie* [genius] at the 1931 colonial exhibition in Vincennes, Indochina was still suffering the after-shock of the Yen Bay uprising. While partisans of French colonialism were congratulating themselves on the generous, humanitarian and benevolent doctrine which metropolitan France had developed vis-à-vis its colonized peoples, the Indochinese were being submitted to probably the most severe repression the territory had yet seen under French rule.[5]

The texts upon which I will focus here were written to a great extent in response to the Yen Bay uprising of 9–10 February 1930. Louis Roubaud, having worked for some time as the colonial correspondent for *Le Petit Parisien*, travelled to Indochina in the wake of the uprising in order to assess the extent of nationalist sentiment in Vietnam and to interview some of the movement's leaders: to discover whether these nascent movements had come under the influence of communism (as was being suggested in press reporting in the mainland). His *Vietnam: la tragédie indochinoise* was published in 1930. Andrée Viollis visited Indochina in the last three months of 1931 as a journalist attached to Paul Reynaud's entourage. On her return in December 1933, extracts from her travel diaries were published in the left-leaning journal *Esprit* and were subsequently collected in a single volume entitled *SOS Indochine* (1935).

The uprising itself occurred when the Vietnamese nationalist movement (VNQDD – Viet Nam Quoc Dan Dang) attacked the French garrison post at Yen Bay. Joined by a significant number of indigenous troops stationed there, they seized the arms depot and killed a number of French officers.[6] Although the uprising was part of a series of rebellions, demonstrations, attacks and protests, the fact that French officers were killed in number called for a show of strength on the part of the colonial authorities. Eighty-three indigenous 'rebels' were sentenced to death, thirteen of whom were guillotined in June 1930 after a distinctly undemocratic trial.[7] The French airforce pursued sympathizers into the surrounding country, indiscriminately bombing assembled crowds and 'suspect' villages.

Reports of the uprising and the manner of its repression had shocked a significant proportion of the metropolitan French public. As Roubaud noted in the introduction to *Vietnam: la tragédie indochinoise*: 'What was going on? Nothing, absolutely nothing, could have prepared public opinion for events such as these' (1931: 9). This vision of French colonialism, which pitted disaffected natives against merciless European masters, was not easily reconciled to the notions of duty, responsibility and fraternal solidarity which were being expounded by all French colonialism's major apologists. Reports of the repressive action of the French colonial administration in Indochina undermined accepted notions of French colonialism as enlightened, benevolent and humanitarian, gratefully embraced by a loyal, subject people.

Dismay over events following Yen Bay prompted Félicien Challaye, a travel writer and journalist who had visited Indochina in 1901, to republish his travel diaries, now containing a reassessment of his views of French colonialism. His opening paragraph reveals the extent to which the 'official' rhetoric of French colonialism was the dominant and most widely accepted version of France's colonial history:

> I naively believed what I had been taught in the Republic's schools. I believed that colonialism was a humanitarian enterprise intended to help inferior races to progress through contact with white civilization. I believed that backward people sought the help of whites, and were grateful for this devoted aid. I believed that France was the most benevolent of all the colonial powers and that the loyalty of her subjects was proof of their gratitude. (1935: 3–4)

Reports from Yen Bay effectively shattered the comforting views of the Indochinese as a docile and compliant native population.

Moreover, news of the repression in Indochina had acted as a catalyst for protest on the part of Indochinese students in Paris. Indochina's problems, it seemed, were being played out in France, much to the consternation of a puzzled public (see Charles Forsdick's comments, Chapter 2). Inaugurating the *Maison de l'Indochine* at the *Cité universitaire*, Gaston Doumergue (then President of the Republic) was heckled with cries of 'Liberate the Yen Bay prisoners!' Applications for places were retracted by the students, and tracts distributed:

> Don't let yourselves be taken in by the sumptuousness of the *Maison indochinoise*. Be wary of this colonial philanthropy. Accept nothing from those who exploit us...Denounce all hypocritical gestures of friendship...Fight all attempts at corruption. Boycott the *Maison indochinoise*. (Roubaud 1931: 11)

While the image of the Yen Bay mutineers, although shocking, had seemed distant and perhaps largely unconnected with France, here those Indochinese who had most benefited from France's cultural 'generosity' were displaying an unprecedented lack of gratitude. What did this emerging elite find to support in the nationalist protests?

At this juncture the travel writer turned investigative journalist with the objective of exploring the disjunction between official images of Indochina, and the seeming reality of growing nationalism in Indochina.

The travel journalism of the 1930s, unlike the traditionally 'exotic', pseudo-anthropological mappings of the late nineteenth century, or the largely military narratives of heroism and bravery, set out its stall as political journalism. This is reflected in the seemingly radical and contestatory titles of both Viollis' and Roubaud's work. There emerged, in response to indigenous testing of the colonial system, a form of politicized metropolitan travel writing.

Although initially reluctant to believe that the repressive and inhumane reaction of the French colonial authorities to the Yen Bay uprising was anything more than a singular aberration, the writers who travelled to Indochina in the early 1930s were steadily bombarded with indications and attestations to the contrary. A large proportion of Viollis' and Roubaud's work is taken up with 'revelations' of colonial abuses: the torture of political prisoners, the failures of the French rice distribution networks, press censorship etc. The very fact of these revelations has prompted many historians and critics to view these texts as examples of a burgeoning anti-colonialism in France. It is my contention, however, that on the contrary, these writers draw conclusions from their respective travels in Indochina which more often than not underwrite and reinforce the colonial rhetoric, ambitions and principles of the period. I will therefore argue that Viollis and Roubaud helped to perpetuate the strong belief in France's civilizing mission.

They did this firstly by positing the notion that France's colonial ideals had been betrayed. Thus although at times critical of colonial policy in Indochina these documents cannot be viewed as political tracts against colonization. For the most part, the critical views of French colonial policy in Indochina expressed in these texts remain circumscribed by the cultural assumption that the legacy of French civilization was of intrinsic value, but that its colonial heirs had betrayed it. Not only were Roubaud and Viollis reluctant to shed the 'official' version of French colonialism as benevolent, but when provided with proof to the contrary they sought not to denounce the principle of colonialism but to point to the corruption and debasement of that perfect ideal.

The discovery that colonial rule in Indochina was not always managed according to the principles of human solidarity, paternal protection and nurturing enlightenment was mitigated by the adoption of a view which asserted that in the past, French colonial policy had been exemplary. Disappointment was thus transformed into nostalgia for a lost, glorious past: a golden age of complicity between colonized and colonizer premised on the benevolence of France's *doctrine coloniale*.

Former relations between France and Indochina, which in these texts are never more specifically dated than 'autrefois', or 'avant' (previously, before) thus take on a paradigmatic status. This vague and utopian notion of the past was held up as an archetype of 'good' colonialism, which had to be recuperated. Viollis draws up an inventory of positive examples of French action in Indochina (the Pasteur Institute, road and dam building etc.) which reveals a specific ideal of French colonialism that was admired, and which she hoped to see re-established in Indochina. 'Good' colonialism according to Viollis, encompassed the same themes which dominated the propaganda of the contemporaneous Colonial Exhibition: economic and moral progress, the channelling of colonial 'energy' into visibly successful projects which would be objects of national pride, and symbols of French prestige. Viollis' vision was one of benevolent pastoralism: she envisaged an ideal of domestic order and tranquillity which had been brought about by the thoughtful application of European technology to an impoverished people.

Capitalist principles are also viewed as having degraded the colonial enterprise. The Pasteur Institute in Indochina, which was cited as a prime example of 'good' colonialism, found its 'admirable travail' was thwarted by colonial administrators who viewed the Institute's work in terms of manufacturing profit and loss. Viollis thus quotes a businessman's response to the Pasteur Institute's hope of sending a mission into an area particularly stricken by malaria: 'Why bother...there aren't any factories or plantations there' (1935: 37). Viollis articulates the clash between the supposed economic reality of colonialism and her own ideological faith through a 'them' and 'us' opposition (the authorities, and business are pitched against 'us' on the side of the Pasteur Institute), which attributes the nefarious effects of colonialism to the capitalist and individualist forces of the modern era. The old 'human' relationship between colonizer and colonized has, for Viollis, been debased by materialism. She resolves the evident conflict through the myth of 'autrefois': visiting a small French enclave in Southern India, Viollis notes that, 'the natives are really friendly towards us ... proof that our former colonial method of cooperation was not so bad'. (1935: 6)

Thus this golden age of edifying action and pre-capitalist economy is accompanied by the vision of an equally golden age of colonized/colonizer relations. Throughout these texts, former relationships between colonized and colonizer are viewed as exemplifying 'harmony', 'cooperation' and 'understanding'. Viollis uses the words of a former *résidant* of Laos to elaborate a romanticized portrait of that perceived harmony which previously existed between the French and the Indochinese:

> In the past we used to travel by horseback along the tracks in the bush: we were received by the village notables in the evenings and learnt to understand and value each other.

Since the advent of the motor car, colonial officers hurtle along the main roads past villagers bowing down in respect. They know nothing of what is going on in their districts. We were pioneers, explorers even. They are just bureaucrats. (1935: 124)

Former colonial administrations are here viewed as having sustained solidarity and complicity between colonized and colonizer, thus allowing a harmonious order to prevail. The past compliance of the colonized (in contrast with their present rebelliousness) is presented as affirming a familial bond between France and Indochina, whilst it is implied that the current troubles have been provoked by the disintegration of the familial order. This portrayal of 'autrefois' recalls a heroic age in which the settler was an explorer, as if the administrative responsibilities and consequent domestication of the colony have brought about the debasement of an idealized (and masculinized) community.

Viollis thus reproduces a romantic narrative which plays upon a myth of social integrity and harmony, and regrets the destruction of a seemingly proto-social community. She contrasts a pastoral simplicity with urban bureaucracy through the emblematization of the modes of transport preferred in each era. Although, ideologically, France was expounding ideas of progress, writers such as Viollis seemed to advocate a return to a pre-modern era, in which the power structures are more reminiscent of a feudal model. The myth of *autrefois* would thus appear to represent French Indochina as the last outpost in which aristocratic values survived. The *colon*, innately superior by birth, nationality and class, commanded immediate respect from his underlings through his very bearing and demeanour.

It begins to become clear that if this 'golden age' of French colonialism has disappeared, then it is the new settler community who are to blame for its disappearance. Portrayals of an undesirable 'new style' of colonial administrator are taken up with alacrity in the texts under discussion. Viollis, for example, quotes the *Chef de la Sûreté* in Annam:

All these problems in Annam, he said, are due to the incredible negligence, the stupidity of the civil service personnel. Instead of sending out to these troubled places talented and experienced men, who have proved themselves in the services where they were in contact with the natives – customs officers, civil engineers, doctors, etc – we have employed young people, straight out of the *Ecole Coloniale*. They are vain, smug in their theoretical knowledge, solely interested in their own comforts: servants, ice, ventilators. They rarely do the rounds of their district and neglect their duties to such an extent that some villages go fifteen, twenty years, without seeing a single Frenchman. These administrators can't even speak Annamite. (1935: 129–9)

Once again, activity is contrasted with passivity; theory with practice; a consumerist, egotistical and feminized society with a pioneering, selfless and masculinized one. It praises the warrior-like qualities of an elite male order ('des hommes de valeur et d'expérience, qui ont fait leurs armes et leurs preuves'), contrasting this mythical, almost chivalric, fraternal community with a feminized bureaucracy.

These perceptions of a lost age point up the confusion inherent in the gendered roles taken up by imperial nation and enacted upon the colonized territories. A confusion embodied not only in France's oxymoronic self-identification as *la mère patrie*, but also replicated in France's perception of its own role in Indochina: *la plus grande France* functioned as both protective and nurturing mother, and constructive and edifying father to its colonial offspring. France in Indochina perceived the need for the dissuasive power of a forceful masculine presence, but hoped that the indigenous peoples would simply accept and comply with this situation rather than testing French authority.

At a time when the value of Western 'civilization' was being called into question, and the Indochinese nationalists were testing the authority and strength of French rule, it became doubly important to emphasize the superiority of French morals, culture and technology. If the superior qualities of the metropolitan French settler in Indochina were not asserted, if the boundaries and limits of difference were not upheld, then the risk of collapsing boundaries would further threaten the French position in Indochina and the integrity of the *Union indochinoise*.

In Laos, Viollis comes across yet more administrators who fail to meet the exacting standards of *autrefois*:

> We stopped at the residences of several colonial officers. I was stupefied by their conversations over dinner, their selfishness, their childishness. They only think about promotions, allowances, returning to France, spreading malicious gossip. Can it be possible? Are these people blind? Have they no concern for their duty, nor any idea of the problems here? (1935: 124)

In both quotations a distinction is made between the maturity of the old style colonial administrator and the puerility or immaturity of their younger counterparts. Given the tendency to imagine the colonial relationship as a gendered and familial configuration, it appears that Viollis and her interviewees are lamenting the disappearance of the hierarchy which distinguished the 'parent' imperial nation from the 'child' colony. French and Indochinese had appeared to cooperate because the distance between the two communities was clearly demarcated, and hierarchy was immediate. The immaturity of the colonial officials now in office in Indochina had allowed the indigenous population to shorten the distance separating colonized and colonizer; the superiority of the French, which justified their continued presence in Indochina, was no longer immediately apparent.

Further descriptions of members of the newer settler community highlight an anxiety that distance and hierarchy between colonizer and colonized were not being maintained. Roubaud, for example, regretted that the colony had become a sort of 'dumping-ground', receiving unwanted elements of the metropolitan community:[8] 'The European employee is often a young dunce whose family shipped him out here having failed to find him a job in the mainland' (1931: 246).

The qualities of former settlers ensured that French power and authority were immediately recognisable. Their aristocratic social position, their breeding, stature and class, demanded and obtained respect. This community of nobles, it was implied, had been polluted and thus degraded by the influx of the masses. French cultural and moral superiority, which Sarraut had cited as imperative to the maintenance of colonial rule in Indochina, had been undermined by the arrival of sections of the metropolitan population who demonstrated moral standards which were little better (if not worse) than those of the indigenous populations they were intended to dominate.

In these texts it appears that the arrival of European women settlers had been the main catalyst in the degradation of the colonized/colonizer relationship. The beginnings of the corruption of the idealized period of harmony, order and respect of the colonizer is posited with the arrival *en masse* of metropolitan French women to Indochina in the 1920s. Roubaud notes of the female settlers in Indochina:

> Those sort of women, whose numbers have increased far too much over the last ten years, who, having left their little flat in the fifth arrondissement where they stingily eked out their hours of domestic help, suddenly found themselves in a large mansion, in charge of a whole cohort of servants ... So, in the space of the twenty eight days it takes to arrive here, these lower middle-class women acquired the status of colonial nobility, and have imported here scorn for the native irrespective of his class or education. (1931: 243–4)

He emphasizes the artificiality of their newly acquired bourgeois lifestyle, regretting that class superiority is no longer inherent in the French community, but has to be proved through ostentation and overt displays of power.

The unproductiveness and passivity of the women settlers is implicitly contrasted with the desired values of the masculinized community of *autrefois*: activity, creative energy, virility. Viollis and Roubaud contrast a passive, narcissistic attitude with the rough, pioneering outlook of the past. Women appear in these texts as a debased substitute for the motherland. Viollis describes the women settlers she meets in the following terms:

> I was horrified at the emptiness of their minds, their souls, their lives. There wasn't a single one who seemed aware of her responsibilities, the terrible problems over there; not one who saw in the Annamites anything other than inferiors to be exploited. None of them protested against the monstrous abuses which should have revolted them. In the

towns they were astonished when I asked if they had any dealings with the women of Annamite society; in the countryside they were stunned when I asked whether they took an interest in the health and well-being of the peasant families and their children. It has to be said, French women in Indochina are not up to the task which could be so rewarding to them. (1935: 35)

She regrets that the female settlers are unable to offer the nurturing, protection and education which the motherland should confer upon the indigenous populations. She implicitly calls for a form of patriarchal feminism, in which the French women in Indochina would undertake to perform the role of moral tutors to the 'uncivilized' natives; and a return to the former relationship of *entente* (harmony), and (ostensible) mutual respect, in which there was contact between colonizer and colonized of a similar social class.

It appears that, for these authors, the arrival of women and the consequent feminization of the settler community in Indochina marks the beginnings of an artificial, consumerist society which spelled the ruin of the earlier, more authentic and creative masculine society. The idyllic era of the aristocratic and heroic *broussard* (bushman) was thus corrupted, polluted and undermined by the combination of materialism, inferior colonial personnel, the sheer number of metropolitan immigrants from an 'undesirable' social class, and women who were unwilling or incapable of performing the duties required of a benevolent French colonialism. The fears over this erosion of masculine control manifested themselves in a nostalgia for a lost paternalism and a reassertion of a patriarchal colonialism.

The assessment that these writers presented of the situation in Indochina in the 1930s was one which viewed the civil disobedience of the indigenous populations as a response to colonial mismanagement rather than a legitimate protest against French presence. Their criticism of certain aspects of French colonial policy in Indochina was not, therefore, formulated as an attack on the fundamental justice of the entire system, but as a springboard for future action. By pinpointing the various, and numerous instances of colonial mismanagement and abuse, Viollis and Roubaud provided a challenge to the authorities to right these problems. Heirs to the humanitarian view of French colonialism, and concerned for the suffering of the Indochinese, they thus envisaged remedying the unrest with reformist measures. Roubaud stated, 'We must not give in to these rebellions, and once peace has been re-established, we must remember our promises and fulfil them gradually.' (1931: 285)

Furthermore, the reformist agenda present in these texts underwrote the view that Indochina continued to remain a field for French action, an area for development. The impulse to reform and to remedy suffering can thus be viewed as a renewal of the French colonial mission: Viollis and

Roubaud were not appealing for the right of the Indochinese to govern themselves, but for a reinforcement of French 'civilizing' action in Indochina. The preoccupation with these moral and humanitarian duties indicates not simply a desire that French colonial rule be perpetuated, but that France's civilizing mission be intensified. Roubaud noted: 'France has not completed her task in Indochina. Through his kind deeds, the benefactor creates duties for himself. The ingratitude of some and the selfishness of others must not prevent France from accomplishing her generous work'. (1931: 284) The vilification of the newer members of the settler community enabled Roubaud and Viollis to envisage the redemptive return of the aristocratic *colon*, whose authority and stature would ensure that the lines of difference between colonized and colonizer were redrawn and reinstated. Their texts can therefore be read as reaffirmations of the hierarchies and disequilibrium of traditional French colonial ideology.

CONCLUSIONS

Roubaud's conclusion, having travelled extensively throughout Indochina and having interviewed scores of Indochinese, was that certain 'selfish and clumsy French' (1931: 275) had simply created a 'misunderstanding' (284) between France and Indochina. 'It is logical to suppose', he stated, 'that the Annamites have been repelled and disgusted by a handful of ungenerous French who masked the true face of France.' (1931: 273)

The ideal of colonialism, what Roubaud terms France's 'true face', and the repressive or abusive face it had presented to these writers in the wake of the Yen Bay uprising were reconciled through the myth of *autrefois* and the vilification of the settler community. There were striking similarities between the 'official rhetoric' of colonialism and the future (redeemed) situation of Indochina envisaged by these writers. Both parties remained convinced of the enlightening potential of France's *mission civilisatrice*, and emphasized that this philanthropic work had yet to be completed; both were implicitly insistent that distance and hierarchy between colonizer and colonized should be reasserted in order that French authority be maintained. The revalorization of the *colon* in official texts, was mirrored in Viollis' and Roubaud's nostalgia for the heroic and aristocratic *broussard*, and their repudiation of the contemporary settler community.

The travel journalism in 1930s Indochina thus not only presented a case for the perpetuation of French colonial presence in South East Asia, it did so by adopting the rhetoric and ideology which underwrote official versions of France's *doctrine coloniale*. Far from legitimizing the Indochinese nationalists' demands through their portrayals of colonial abuse, and thus introducing an anti-colonial perspective to the Indochinese debate after Yen Bay, these writers remained firmly convinced that the legacy of French civilization was of value to overseas populations, and that the slippage from this ideal was temporary and simply attributable to the incompetence or inferiority of the incumbent administrations. Thus rather than constituting a counter-narrative to French colonialism, this ostensibly radical and contestatory journalism did little more than shore up the strong residual belief in Empire.

Notes

1. This chapter forms part of a broader study of French responses to and representations of colonial Indochina (see Cooper 2001).
2. See the work of Durtain (1930), Monet (1930), and Dorgelès (1994), which expresses a growing unease with the situation in Indochina, whilst remaining convinced that these minor problems could be remedied within the framework of a humanist colonialism.
3. Claudel was first Ambassador to China (1895–1909), then to Japan (1921–27). He visited Indochina on a number of occasions, making six short trips, and three longer visits in 1903, 1921 and 1925. It was his 1921 trip which gave rise to written reflections on the colony, which appear as a combination of the *récit de voyage* with a *rapport de mission*. These first appeared in May 1922 in *La Revue du Pacifique*.
4. All the ensuing English translations are my own.
5. For an account of indigenous rebellion and French repression in Indochina, see Van (1995).
6. This was intended as part of a more widespread rebellion to include the fledgling Indochinese Communist Party (founded 1930), but communications failed, and the Yen Bay 'mutineers' found themselves isolated.
7. See Viollis' (1935) appendices transcribing the trial.
8. Albert Sarraut uses the same metaphor, referring to certain elements of the settler community as 'déchets' (1931: 210).

Bibliography

Challaye, F., *Souvenirs sur la colonization*. Paris, 1935.
Claudel, P., *Oeuvres complètes de Paul Claudel: Tome 4, Extrême-Orient*. Paris, 1952.
Cooper, N., *France in Indochina: Colonial Encounters*. Oxford, 2001.
Dorgelès, R., *Sur la route mandarine* (1925). Paris, 1994.
Durtain, L., *Dieux blancs, hommes jaunes*. Paris, 1930.
Monet, P., *Les Jauniers, histoire vraie*. Paris, 1930.
Roubaud, L., *Vietnam: la tragédie indochinoise*. Paris, 1931.
Sarraut, A., *La mise en valeur des colonies françaises*. Paris, 1923.
_____, *Grandeur et servitude coloniales*. Paris, 1931.
Van, N., *Viet-nam 1920–1945: révolution et contre-révolution sous la domination coloniale*. Paris, 1995.
Viollis, A., *SOS Indochine*. Paris, 1935.

Chapter 12

ARISTOCRATS, GEOGRAPHERS, REPORTERS ...
Travelling through 'Italian Africa' in the 1930s

Loredana Polezzi

The title of this article contains some suspension marks. This is not a fashionable elision, but rather the acknowledgement of the complex and elusive nature of travel as a practice and of travellers' accounts as texts. It is common for scholars of travel and travel writing to refer to their objects as hybrid, and to underline the marginal and yet all the more significant position which they occupy in cultural and literary systems.[1] Questions of identity, (inter)cultural representation, textual authority and discursive power have been variously mapped onto travel and its many texts, yet the definition and the taxonomy of travel and travel writing remain largely problematic. It is this theoretical context which provides the framework for the analysis of texts and personalities (or personas) which will follow. The focus will be on two main issues: periodization and genre affiliation.

As far as periodization is concerned, the 1930s are often associated with the idea of 'the end of travel'. The assertion that 'real' travel and travel writing came to an end with the closing of that decade is often associated with Claude Lévi-Strauss and the famous opening chapter of his *Tristes Tropiques* (1955). The chapter is explicitly devoted to the 'end of travel', and is full of caustic remarks on post-Second World War travel books, their mystifications, and their credulous readers.[2] Lévi-Strauss's negative views were reiterated, in 1980, by Paul Fussell, according to whom British travel writing declined after the trauma of the Second World War and the spread of worldwide mass tourism. For Fussell, in fact, 'travel is hardly possible anymore', and neither is travel writing (1980: 37). What Lévi-Strauss and Fussell have in common, is the vision of a still recent past when travel was synonymous with exploration and travellers retained their heroic aura; they both seem to look back with envy to nineteenth-century models of travel, contrasting them with a contemporary world where there is no more space, or at least no unmarked, untrodden space; no space which is not already commodified and reified; no space for travel, discovery and adventure, that is, for travellers, discoverers, adventurers – and their accounts. Yet this kind of linear periodization may be called into question, as I hope to show, especially when applied to a genre as complex and as implicated in the multiple stratifications of historical and ideological representation as travel writing.

The second problem I intend to take issue with is precisely the thorny question of genre. In the same volume in which he so openly subscribes to the theory of the 'end of travel', Paul Fussell also describes travel books as a 'double-barrelled' genre, commenting that, 'perhaps it is when we cannot satisfactorily designate a kind of work with a single word [...] but we must invoke two [...] that we sense we're entering complicated territory' (1980: 202).[3] The 'double' nature of travel writing is also underlined from a different critical perspective by Mary Louise Pratt, in an article entitled 'Fieldwork in Common Places' (1984) in which she traces the parallels between travel narrative and ethnography. Pratt notices that the two are never completely autonomous: it is customary for ethnographers to at least include a personal, autobiographical sketch at the beginning of their scientific monographs, and very often the same experience will also be the subject of separate narratives which tend to take the form of travelogues; hardly any travel book, on the other hand, is completely devoid of passages devoted to the 'objective' and 'learned' exposition of the history, geography, art or, indeed, anthropology of the places and people encountered.[4] According to Pratt, although formal ethnographic description posits its textual authority on claims to objective scientific status, it seems to be unable to renounce the 'anchoring' in 'intense and authority-giving personal experience' which is the basis of travel accounts; and, vice versa, the travel account seems to be bound to invoke scientific objectivity as well as experiential 'anchoring' (1984: 32). What both Fussell and Pratt are pointing out is the hybrid nature of travel writing (and, at least in the case of Pratt, also its different but complementary uses), held together by the voice and persona of the travel writer, his or her different kinds of authority, stemming from his or her position as at once the protagonist, the narrator and the author of the travel account.[5] In both Pratt's and Fussell's description of the genre, then, the eye of the traveller, his or her unified subjectivity, his or her experience and expertise, sustain his or her call for textual authority and for readers' attention.[6]

These two claims – the impossibility of 'real' travel and travel writing after the 1930s, and the hybrid but 'subjectively unified' nature of the travel writer's narrative – provide the context for the case-studies in the following sections which focus on a short series of miniature sketches of Italian travellers in Africa. The analysis takes issue with both claims, proposing an increasingly fragmented view of travel writing as a genre, of its uses, of its voices, and of any chronology we may attempt to impose upon it. At the same time, the case-studies provide a (partial) picture of the way in which travel writing acted as a central site for the development and the involution of colonial discourses during and after the Italian attempt at building an African empire.

Italy entered the 'scramble for Africa' at a very late stage (in the 1880s), and this resulted in what has often been described as an atypical or even anomalous form of colonialism. The myth of an Italian 'place in the sun' was constructed on the dubious foundations provided by Italian explorers and adventurers such as Giovanni Miani, Orazio Antinori or Romolo Gessi, who functioned as heroic models for the Italian penetration of Africa and at the same time legitimized the national presence by rooting it firmly in the middle of the nineteenth century. Yet this heroic, historicized model, made popular by publications such as the magazines *Rivista delle Colonie* and *L'Azione Coloniale* (Tomasello 1984; Burdett 2000), was undermined from the beginning by a strong sense of belatedness (Behdad 1994) which, even at the apex of the imperial propaganda, marked Italian colonial representations of Africa with nostalgia and an aestheticizing vein of exoticism. There were clear attempts to build a genealogy for the Italian presence on the continent (Traversi 1935; Truffi 1936), based to a great extent on the 'great tradition' of Italian explorers already adopted by the young Italian state as a sign of national glory (Branca 1873); yet a sense of anxiety, of coming after and too late, was never far from the surface of Italian colonialism.

The travellers and travel writers I am going to discuss were invariably – though differently – caught in this fundamental contradiction between the collective need for the legitimization of the nationalist spirit of colonialism and the deep yearning for an 'unspoilt' (i.e. primitive and pristine) Africa, already sensed as an unattainable object of desire. It is precisely the dynamics of belatedness and desire which made the heroic model of travel, as well as the linear chronology of travel writing, impracticable for the protagonists of the three sketches that follow. The alternatives they tried to find led them to the discourses of exoticism, narcissistic voyeurism and unrestrained nostalgia.

1 THE INSPIRED REPORTER

The first book under examination is very much the hybrid product of a unified and unifying subjectivity, and poses no apparent problems to the application of a linear chronology. Angelo Piccioli's *La porta magica del Sahara: Itinerario Tripoli Gadames* [The Magic Gate of the Sahara] was published in the early 1930s and re-printed in the middle of the decade, at a time when Africa meant a variety of things to Fascist Italy and its people: it was the fabled 'fourth shore', the site of the (re)building of the Roman Empire, the mythical land for emigrants (now defined as colonizers) to travel to, the site of a 'better kind of colonialism' which was meant to take civilization back to Africa after centuries of absence.[7]

It is in this climate that Angelo Piccioli's *La porta magica del Sahara*, the account of a trip through Italian occupied territories in Northern Africa, appeared. The book was published first in Tripoli, by Editrice Minerva, in 1931, in a luxury numbered edition illustrated with works by a number of Italian artists, and then reprinted in Italy in 1934 in a popular edition which included no full-size illustrations, but was decorated by orientalizing graphic motifs of Arab inspiration. An English version translated by Angus Davidson – later to become well known as the main English translator of Alberto Moravia's work – appeared soon afterwards as *The Magic Gate of the Sahara* (1935).

The volume won the acclaim of the Italian establishment, from Mussolini himself to Pietro Badoglio (then Governor of the Italian colonies of Tripolitania and Cirenaica); Pavolini and other *Accademici d'Italia*; travellers and orientalists such as the renowned 'Tibetologist' Tucci; journalists and critics writing in Italian, European and colonial papers.[8] The book won the Gold Medal for the 'Best Book of the Year 1931', a prize awarded by a jury nominated by the Fascist Federation of Authors and Writers of Latium for its 'great moral and literary value, inspired by the laudable aim of furthering the national and colonial cause'. In the newspaper *Giornale d'Italia* the reviewer, Osea Felici, remarked that, 'when this kind of literature about a colony starts to appear, it means that the colony has become an integral part of national life, and there is a solid link, at once ideal and moral, between the Nation and the Colony'. Another newspaper, *Il Tevere*, even suggested that extracts from Piccioli's book should be included in school anthologies 'so that the new generations may perceive the beauty of Africa and feel, from their early years, profound love for the Colonies'. Such remarks become particularly significant once we consider that the Abyssinian campaign was fought in 1935–36 and that the fascist regime orchestrated a massive propaganda campaign in favour of that war and of the imperial enterprise as a whole.

Angelo Piccioli (born in 1886), had been for some time 'Director of Education in Tripolitania' (Piccioli 1934: 343) as well as serving as director of the aptly named 'Research and Propaganda Office' of the same area. He also contributed a chapter, 'The Re-birth of Tripolitania', to the first full-size tourist guide to the colonies, published by the Touring Club Italiano in 1929 and described as an integral part of the Touring Club's project of a complete guide to Italy, as originally planned in 1912.[9]

When *La porta magica del Sahara* appeared, Piccioli was widely praised for his patriotism and colonial spirit, exemplified by chapters such as the ones devoted to Italian soldiers in Tripolitania ('The Creators of the "Pax Italica"'), or to the colonists ('Our "Boys" in the Sahara').[10] The following passage, taken from the chapter 'Sowers of Good Seed', is a perfect example of this kind of writing:

> Before the advent of fascism, Libya was in a state of disorder, disaffection and treachery. Now, after a few years, order, peace and confidence – the law of Italy – have been everywhere restored. The foundations of the colony's renascence, both civil, economic and political, have been firmly laid. The great Latin emblem of the Lictors' *fasces* has given this land a new baptism of life, consecrating it afresh for European civilization, according to the will of the man who controls the new destinies of Italy. (1935: 86)

Here Piccioli is perfectly in tune with the official propaganda of the period, which claimed a classical genealogy for the civilising mission of Fascist Italy, while also praising the (supposedly) immense economic potential of the colonial enterprise, promoted in Italy as the long awaited solution to the social problems which had lead to mass emigration between the end of the nineteenth century and the 1930s. Thus in Piccioli's passage the 'renascence' of Libya mirrors the nation-building myth of the Risorgimento, of which it becomes a 'natural extension', just as the actions of the Italian colonizers become, by implication, an extension of the heroic efforts of the fathers of the nation (and of Mussolini as their self-appointed heir).

Piccioli was also praised, however, for the deeply poetic qualities of his volume, and the book was described as 'a pilgrimage of love', devoted to '"mysterious" Africa, the one which takes the hand of the writer and turns him into a poet'; 'a work of art which reconciles us with the terrible and the boundless, that is to say with the imponderable elements of the mystery of Africa'; a book which could capture 'the soul of a country [...] incomprehensible and yet real, elusive and yet complex, fascinating though alien and distant'.[11] 'Mystery' and 'mysterious' are words which recur obsessively in the reviews, often coupled with adjectives which further underline this 'elusive' quality of Africa. The sentences quoted above, for instance, contain a sequence of adjectives denoting magnitude and yet also absence or deprivation of precise dimensions, while also suggesting the combination of this absence, this void, with highly subjective emotional responses (the pilgrimage of love, the writer turning poet and capturing the soul of the country ...).

In the book itself, the 'poetic' passages become increasingly prevalent as we advance through the desert and through the narrative, which is strewn with religious imagery and lyrical hyperbole, 'mystic' moments and elegiac portraits. The following example, taken from the chapter entitled 'Dawn over the Desert', is a case in point:

> The soul turns pure, just as we are returned to purity by the wave of peace which at time lingers in the spirit after a heartfelt prayer. And the human creature believes it can still hear – just as it could when it was naked, simple and alone in front of creation – the secret voices of the universe, the mysterious words which were given to it, on the threshold of life, facing infinity. (1934: 206)

Piccioli's prose strives for effect, using rhetorical strategies such as repetition and assonance, as well as some affected lexical choices, which combine with the religious images to create what Piccioli (and many of his reviewers) must have perceived as the rendition of an epiphanic experience in an appropriately sublime tone.

It is significant that, while this and many similar paragraphs were cut in the English translation, Italian critics used precisely these 'poetic' qualities of *La porta magica del Sahara* to come to terms with the fact that this was, after all, just a travel book. One reviewer compared Piccioli to the famous journalist and reporter Luigi Barzini, 'who was the first to produce this kind of artistic journalism', then distanced the book from 'mere' journalism thanks to the poetic qualities of the author, who 'possesses the great gift of lyrical and yet at the same time pathetic tones [...]: the whole of the wild and poetic Orient is reflected in these colours, with sensual intensity'. Another commentator went as far as to compare *La porta magica del Sahara* to Heine's *Reisebilder*, where he found 'the same impulse and an equal breadth of poetic inspiration'.[12]

Italian reviewers seemed desperate to establish literary credentials for Piccioli's book, which could otherwise risk being 'confused' with journalism given the absence of a specific slot for travel writing in the Italian literary canon.[13] In fact, this need to establish the literary status of travel books may offer a clue to the contradiction noted by Tomasello (1984:15–21) between the fascist regime's demand for a colonial literature whose main goals should be educational and political on the one hand, and the continuing production and success of works marked by 'colour' and 'lyricism', as well as heavy rhetorical embellishment, on the other. In a period when Italian literary life was dominated by an aesthetic school of criticism and by phenomena such as the 'prosa d'arte' (Russo 1967), the request for a literature dominated by facts and action rather than by romantic lyricism and formal perfectionism was something of a contradiction in terms – all the more so, paradoxically, for a marginal genre such as travel writing.

Yet something more seems to be at stake in the comments made by reviewers about Piccioli's prose: while ingredients such as heroism, colonial ethos, or the eroticization of the African landscape were all well known and acceptable traits of an international tradition of African travel which was still alive in the 1930s, the poetic and even mystic slant imposed by Piccioli on the trope of the 'magic of Africa' seems more specific to the Italian context (and in fact, as already noted, passages such as the one quoted above were often cut in the English translation). Piccioli's 'poetic reportage' unmakes Africa as a historical location, transforming it into the backdrop for heroic action on the one hand, and poetic inspiration on the other: this is the landscape, the blank space inhabited only by primitive or mythical beings, where Italy – and 'civilized' Italians such as Piccioli – could make their mark, while also going back to their own mythologized origins, literally back to the day of creation, liberating themselves from the constraints of history. Stressing the subjective response of the traveller (the lyrical element) and the mythical components of the landscape (often introduced via learned references) instantly projects this Africa into a new dimension: out of history, that is, where, amongst other things, the 'normal' laws of society do not apply, and where the belatedness of Piccioli's travels (and of Italy's empire) can be, at least temporarily, forgotten.[14]

2 The Scientist as Voyeur

Angelo Piccioli's *La porta magica del Sahara* appears to be perfectly contained within the chronology and typology of 'European Travel Writing in the 1930s', yet its analysis has already called into question definitions of genre, highlighting, for instance, the existence of discrepancies between the English and the Italian definition (and reception) of 'travel writing'. The book which is the object of this second section, on the other hand, poses radical problems for the use of simple chronological labels, while presenting an interesting case-study for the critical analysis of forms of textual authority and of the role of a 'unified subjectivity' in travel writing. *Un medico in Africa* [A doctor in Africa] was in fact not written in the 1930s, but is based on memories of that period. Its author, Alberto Denti duca di Pirajno, premises his claim to the readers' attention on two kinds of authority: he pledges his reliability, directly, on his identity as a scientist and, vicariously, on having been a loyal participant in a 'heroic enterprise' whose main protagonists (and greatest sources of authority) were other people.

First published in 1952, *Un medico in Africa* had at least two Italian editions in the 1990s, was translated into English in 1955 and reprinted in 1956, and a further English edition appeared as late as 1985.[15] The author was an aristocrat, a doctor and a colonial official, who introduces himself at the beginning of the book (that is, he establishes his credentials) by claiming a close link to the Duca d'Aosta, one of the 'heroes' of the Italian African enterprise, and (together with his uncle, Duca degli Abruzzi) a model explorer and 'good colonialist';[16] yet, Denti di Pirajno hurries to stress, the duke was a misunderstood, forgotten, unsung hero, like so many others – including, the reader is left to deduce, the author himself (1956: 9–10). Nostalgia and vicarious (as well as personal) heroism are, from the very beginning, central elements in Denti di Pirajno's book – and it is worth noting that, although the book presents him as the personal doctor of the Duca d'Aosta,[17] biographies of the duke make no mention of his name. At various points in the narrative, the author also openly complains about the corruption and inadequacies of the Italian colonial administration in Rome. This has the effect of increasing the nostalgic quality of the book, its elegiac view of 'good colonialism' and its commendation of the ethos which fired the men involved in it, at the expense of politicians and bureaucrats in Rome, who had no right to either of the two kinds of authority Denti di Pirajno is claiming for himself: scientific objectivity and direct autobiographical experience.

Denti di Pirajno had a moderately successful career as a writer in the second part of his life,[18] and, significantly, the 1994 edition of *Un medico in Africa* stresses his 'writerly' credentials, giving pride of place on the back cover to a portrait of the author with Karen Blixen. Yet it is of the colonial and medical qualifications of the author that the book makes the most: the colonial duties provide the context for the narrative, while it is the physician's role, already foregrounded in the title, which grants Denti di Pirajno both unlimited access and unquestioned authority, justifying his rampant and unrepentant voyeurism, coating even the most dismissive judgements in an aura of humanitarianism and selfless dedication, and crediting even the most extravagant tall stories with the truthfulness of rational scientific observation. Denti di Pirajno can expand on his familiarity with prostitutes (and on the most intimate details of their bodies), enter harems and Bedouin tents, become familiar with chieftains and princesses, report the blazing career of an inveterate young liar whose adventures would be perfectly at home in the *Thousand and One Nights*, and still maintain the persona of the faithful and impassive observer. Occasionally, however, he decides (for the sake of witnessing 'the whole reality' of the places and people he encounters) to become involved in the shenanigans of the Arabs and 'Negroes' who are milling around him in a perpetual show which seems to be especially organized for his own (and his readers') benefit.

If irony and caricature are the dominant notes when Denti di Pirajno is dealing with the male part of the African population, voyeurism is rampant every time women are involved, from the morbid portraits of the early decay of African women's bodies, to the invasive gynaecological observations prevalent throughout the book. One of the most striking examples of Denti di Pirajno's voyeurism comes in the first chapter, when he describes the 'spectacle' of Fusúda, the enchantress of scorpions. The woman first arrives wrapped in a huge *barracano* [barracan] which only discloses one of her eyes, but she gradually undresses revealing 'a young negress with thick, purplish lips' (1956: 41). The scene reaches its climax when, after first introducing the scorpion into her mouth and then cocooning it between her armpit and her breast, Fusúda completes her morbid strip-tease:

> Then with a swift movement she unfastened her shoulder buckle and let fall her surîja so that she was naked to the thighs. She thrust the scorpion between her legs, leaving only the tail, obscenely protruding. (1956: 42)

Space is similarly eroticized: the African landscape, as well as African villages, are full of secret hiding places from which to spy on the life of the land; and the desert is littered with Bedouin tents within whose shadowy recesses women, in particular, practice their magic and elusive arts. Voyeurism and scientific observation are never as close as in the episode in which Denti di Pirajno crouches down in a disused storeroom, peeping through the cracks of the wooden walls, to observe a ceremony which is meant to cure 'a girl suffering from what I suppose we could call extreme melancholia' but is locally believed to be 'caused by some dark and evil spirit' possessing her (1956: 45).

Africa, its land, its people, are reduced by Denti di Pirajno to a constant spectacle, in what Francesco Surdich (1995: 20) has recently described as the common tendency to reduce African humanity, as well as its geography, to 'a stereotypical collection of the most bizarre and extravagant types and situations'. The resulting mixture no longer distinguishes between reality and imagination, reason and 'magic' — Western rationality and 'the magic of black Africa'. Yet despite, or perhaps because of, this, both direct experience and scientific authority are invoked throughout Denti di Pirajno's narrative in order to demand the reader's unconditional trust for the author, and to engineer a 'realistic' reception for the book. This justifies Pirajno's voyeurism, and even allows the scientist, author and authority of the text to abandon the world of Western rational science for that of African magic. In one episode, for instance, the traveller triumphs over the physician, and the rational, Western man renounces his science to transform himself into a charlatan and perform a fake operation on a superstitious patient, convinced that all his problems are caused by a snake dwelling in his stomach rather than by his own deep hypochondria.[19]

In *Un medico in Africa*, then, memory and fantasy hijack the narration, transforming a realistic, factual, autobiographic, even scientific travel account into a testimony (at least in part vicarious, or collective) of the Italian imagination's nostalgia for the African Empire, of its *mal d'Africa* [African sickness], as it is often called. The ambiguous play of desire, narcissistic mirroring and anxiety created by the historical impossibility of a renewed possession of Africa (its land, its bodies) is displaced into voyeuristic spectacle, masked by the strategic interventions of memory and by claims of scientific objectivity. Protected by the stratagems of realist, autobiographical narrative, Denti di Pirajno's all-powerful subjective gaze still holds together the different kinds of textual authority exploited by the text – but chronological boundaries become blurred as this 1950s book retells the story of the 1930s, hardly mentioning what happened next, and thus turning *Un medico in Africa* into an emblematic text of Italy's forgetfulness, of the taboos which still envelop its colonial past, and of the unresolved anxieties and desires that go hand in hand with them. The narrative closure of the book is in fact provided by the English occupation of Tripoli, a city of which Denti di Pirajno had become the last Italian governor. In the final few pages, we see him handing the city over to Montgomery in 1943, then vanishing over the horizon, on a British jeep heading towards a prison camp. The last word is left to the doctor, to whom the closing of a gate sounds like 'the metal shutters closing on my African dispensary for the last time' (1956: 264).

3 Heroes Don't Write – But Geographers Do

This third and final sketch is devoted to a figure and a series of texts which further unhinge notions of periodization, and also undermine the idea of a unified and unifying subjectivity posited as the pivotal centre of the travel book. Here decades become highly interchangeable, genres and authors multiply and proliferate, and yet claims are made to various kinds of textual authority.

In 1935 a volume entitled *I grandi viaggiatori: Avventure di terra e di mare* [Great Travellers: Adventures over Land and at Sea] was published by UTET in its series *La scala d'oro* [The Golden Stair], a popular series aimed at children and teenagers.[20] The volume opens with Marco Polo, and, after a number of portraits of famous travellers such as Christopher Columbus and Walter Raleigh, it ends with a series of nineteenth and twentieth-century Italian explorers of Africa. The closing portrait is reserved for Luigi Amedeo di Savoia Aosta, Duca degli Abruzzi, the hero of many expeditions which took him from Africa to the Himalayas. At one point he was the holder of the record for the highest altitude ever reached by man, as well as the one for the northernmost latitude. At the end of his life, we read in *I grandi viaggiatori*, the hero turned peasant, he devoted himself to the colonization of Somalia, and created a model village on the Uebi Scebeli river, where he behaved like a benevolent father to the locals who adored him:

> But he is tired, too tired.
> And, as he feels death approaching, he asks to be buried there, far away in his tropical village.
> There he sleeps, our vanguard sentry, in the furthermost corner of Italy.
>
> (Brigante Colonna 1944: 113)

Within two years of his death, the Duca degli Abruzzi, who had died in Somalia in 1933, had thus been crowned as the last great traveller and the ultimate Italian 'good colonialist'.

Luigi Amedeo certainly had all the makings of the classic hero: born in 1873 within the cadet branch of the Italian royal family, he had no aspiration to the throne and was soon bitten by the travel bug. Living at a time when 'simple' geographic discoveries were becoming increasingly rare and the ideal image of the explorer was increasingly combined with that of the record breaking sportsman, he channelled his thirst for heroic adventure towards mountaineering, and soon learnt to identify suitably extreme goals. From his twenties onwards he led expeditions, usually accompanied by alpine guides and fellow officers of the Italian Royal Navy. Daring and attractive, he soon became popular with the press – to the point of being hounded by journalists during his love affair with an American heiress. The royal family also soon discovered the potential for publicity associated with the duke and his adventures, and responded by welcoming, and financing, his plans.[21] Yet the most frequent adjectives used by the biographers of the duke are 'reserved' and 'silent', two labels which seem to return obsessively, and are used to explain all of his choices: his preference for the mountains and for men of the mountains, such as his beloved alpine guides; his retreat to Africa after the First World War; and, last but not least, the fact that he did not produce full accounts of his enterprises.

This hero, in fact, unlike many who preceded or followed him, did not write. All he ever produced were a few official reports for his sponsors (usually the Italian Royal Navy), notes for the public talks he held to raise funds or satisfy the royal family's need for publicity, and some introductions to accounts of his expeditions written by others.[22] Many people, however, from the geographer and anthropologist Filippo de Filippi (1909) to the novelist Emilio Salgari (1901), wrote about the duke and his achievements. From the very beginning of his career as an explorer, the contrast between Luigi Amedeo's silence and the noise made by his chroniclers emphasizes the growing distinction between the public and the private dimension of his travels: while the construction of a popular hero figure might well exploit the duke's shy and modest attitudes, national interests required the popularization of Italian enterprises and conquests (geographic, rather than political, in this case).

By the 1930s, the Duca degli Abruzzi and his travels (which had effectively ended in 1909 with his Himalayan expedition and the failed attempt to reach the summit of the K2)[23] had become an integral part of the propaganda of the fascist regime and of its plans for an Italian Empire. In this historical context, while the duke's heroic adventures and exploits in the Arctic or in Asia could be presented as a model of Italian achievement, it was his African explorations, and his African death, which best signalled suitable collective goals for the Italian nation as a whole. So paradoxically, even though for him the age of travel had effectively ended with the First World War and he had actually left Italy before the advent of fascism, the duke became a symbol of travel and conquest for the Italy of the 1930s.

This appropriation of the figure and memory of Luigi Amedeo is another sign of the contradictions which characterized travel and travel writing in Fascist Italy.

The propaganda of the regime needed to keep alive older models of travel and exploration: an increasingly anachronistic colonial enterprise was best served by a kind of travel writing which, in classic nineteenth-century style, was based on the factual, linear narrative of heroic adventures (even though the underlying anxiety of belatedness had to be exorcized in one way or another). Luigi Amedeo's silence, then, may well have been a sign of his uneasiness with the conflicting requirements of the genre, but the absence of full first person accounts of his travels certainly made it easier for the fascist regime to adopt his figure, at the height of the imperial propaganda, as the perfect model of the heroic qualities and expansionist aspirations which all Italians ought to embody.

This close (though involuntary) association with the 1930s, their ideals and their events is probably also at the origin of a further appropriation of the duke, which was to take place decades later. In 1967 UTET (the same publishing house which had produced the volume on *I grandi viaggiatori*) published a book entitled *Il Duca degli Abruzzi: Le imprese dell'ultimo grande esploratore italiano* [The Duke of the Abruzzi: The Exploits of the Last Great Italian Explorer]. The author was Giotto Dainelli, a geographer, geologist and inveterate traveller, as well as wholehearted supporter of the fascist regime and of its imperial enterprise.

Born in Florence in 1878, Giotto Dainelli repeatedly travelled to Africa as well as to the East, and wrote books such as *La conquista scientifica dell'Impero* [The Scientific Conquest of the Empire] (1936), as well as a monograph on Marco Polo (1941) which is a model of national mythologizing.

During the final days of the regime, Dainelli became the last fascist *podestà* [mayor] of Florence, and eventually fled to the Repubblica di Salò (Sestini 1969). He continued to publish numerous books, mostly with UTET, until his death in 1968, including the two volumes of *Gli esploratori italiani in Africa* [Italian Explorers in Africa] (1960), which is possibly the fullest (though by then totally anachronistic) attempt ever made at justifying the Italian presence in Africa through the construction of an uninterrupted genealogical line leading straight back to classical Rome.

The monograph on the Duca degli Abruzzi was Dainelli's last published work, and it is in many senses an appropriation of the duke's figure and of his adventures. In fact the book concentrates so much on the travels of its protagonist that its structure is much more similar to that of a travel account than a biography, and the best way to describe it is perhaps by calling it a vicarious travelogue.

Dainelli, who had never even travelled with the duke, evoked his figure six decades after the end of Luigi Amedeo's travels, and thirty years after the end of his own, producing what is in effect a form of unsolicited and unassisted 'ghost writing', and also a memorial and a nostalgic apology for Dainelli's own unforgotten 1930s: the decade in which his career and the duke's myth were at their respective apex. The identification of Dainelli with the duke becomes overpoweringly clear in the epilogue of the book, when the 'old geographer' evokes his memories of a visit (he calls it a pilgrimage) to the tomb of the duke in Somalia. Dainelli describes how the people accompanying him, sensing the strength of his feelings, left him alone on the lawn where a simple granite pillar marked the resting place of his hero, the man who had been a model to him and to the whole country. What follows is Dainelli's description of his own reactions:

> Alone, the little wandering geographer, faced by such greatness, standing to attention, then, and in total silence, his eyes staring at that pillar of bare stone, which nevertheless said so much, his right arm extended in the Roman salute, the only one worthy of him. (1967:331)

The overwhelming strength of Dainelli's feelings is conveyed through the a-grammatical quality of this unfinished sentence, where the final 'him' entirely conflates Dainelli with his hero.

Conclusions

The texts discussed in the previous sections are extremely different from each other, and so are the personalities they portray; yet all of them are in many ways integral to the history of travel and the genre of travel writing. Travelling in Italian Africa in the 1930s encompassed the whole range: from Piccioli's mixture of 'poetic' mysticism and imperial propaganda to Denti di

Pirajno's nostalgic memories and voyeuristic explorations; from the popularization of (silent) heroic travellers in children's books to the mixture of vicarious glorification and very personal bitterness in Dainelli's travelling biography of the Duca degli Abruzzi.

If there is a conclusion we can draw from acknowledging this variety, it is that even the partial distinctions between periods and genres proposed by Lévi-Strauss, Fussell, Pratt, and many others do not hold, at least in the case of the complex tissue of representations created by Italian travellers to Africa during and after the period of the colonial enterprise. Instead of clear boundaries, what we find is a series of cases of multiple identity and displacement, whose flashbacks are still with us, not only in Dainelli's late 1960s evocation of the memories of a forgotten old geographer, but also much later and in much more 'central' locations. In the 1970s they were to be found in Moravia's nostalgic, voyeurisitic gaze, directed at a history-less Africa still mysteriously wrapped in the mist of pre-civilization and resulting in the kind of prose that Pratt (1992: 216–221) has called 'the white man's lament'.[24] Similar traits can also be recognized, well into the 1990s, in Erminia dell'Oro's semi-fictional memories of Asmara, with their nostalgia for 'the great plains of Africa', and for a time when individual destinies, however tragic, seemed easily justified by the great hand of (European) history and by a way of life still regulated by close social networks, strict gender roles and clear moral rules. Dell'Oro's Africa, often seen through the eyes of children as in *Asmara addio* (1988) or in *La gola del diavolo* (1999), is still a continent without history, or at least only endowed with a different, magic, mythical kind of history, upon which European events and lives are superimposed – or within which they are lost.

It is this perception of a space without history that allows, to a great extent, the displacement of Italian (European) issues onto the black/blank continent of Africa. As Tim Youngs (1994:7) has pointed out, Western travel narratives about Africa may well tell us more about Europe than they do about their declared object, given that in them 'by projection and displacement, profoundly troublesome questions of national identity and self-identity were addressed obliquely, sometimes even unconsciously, as questions of authority and order, of purpose and direction, were mapped on to another landscape'. This is a tendency which, at least as far as Italian travel writing is concerned, has gone well beyond the nineteenth-century texts discussed by Youngs – in fact it has gone well beyond the 1930s. And perhaps it is precisely these displacements which have allowed Italian travel writing about Africa, with its nostalgic vein and its dehistoricizing gaze, to evade continually the anxiety of its own belatedness and to survive long after the fall of the ill-fated Italian Empire.

Notes

1. On hybridity and travel writing see for instance Thubron (1986), Raban (1987), Kowalewski (1992); on the marginal status of the genre see Cachey (1996), Polezzi (1998).
2. According to Lévi-Strauss (English trans. *Tristes Tropiques* 1976: 16), the era of great travel and great travel writing is over: 'Nevertheless this kind of narrative enjoys a vogue which I, for my part, find incomprehensible'.
3. For a detailed discussion of Fussell's definition of travel writing see for instance Cocker (1992).
4. On the subject see also Dennis Porter's observations on Malinowski and Lévi-Strauss, in *Haunted Journeys* (1991: 246–84).
5. On this superimposition of roles see Pasquali (1996).
6. On subjectivity and travel writing see also Thubron (1986); Campbell (1988); Porter (1991); Cocker (1992).
7. For ample testimony of these attitudes to colonialism see De Blasi (1942). Relevant analyses of Italian colonialism can be found in Surdich (1995); Del Boca (1976–1984; 1986–1988; 1991; 1992); Larebo (1994); Gentile (1997); Palma (1999).
8. All details and quotations relating to the reception of Piccioli's book are taken from the selection of reviews published in the 1934 edition, pp. 337–43. All translations are mine, except where otherwise stated.
9. On Piccioli's contribution see pp. 5–6 and pp. 250–69. A smaller guide in two separate volumes, *Tripolitania* and *Cirenaica*, had been published by the Touring Club Italiano in 1923 but had soon become obsolete.
10. Both chapters are omitted in the English translation.
11. The quotations (all from the 1934 edition, pp. 337–43), are attributed, respectively, to: Ettore Cozzani; *La Tribuna*; *Roma*; *Giornale della Scuola Media*.
12. Yet another reviewer (Carlo Basilici, writing in the periodical *Cirenaica Illustrata*) could single out Piccioli's book because it revealed: 'The hidden meaning, the watchful and secret soul of things [...] that soul is constantly invoked, with never-ending moulding power, to interpret the forms and aptitudes of nature and of men' (1934:340).
13. For a discussion of this absence see Polezzi (1998).
14. A look at some of the chapter headings shows all of these mechanisms at work: 'The Meeting of West with East'; 'Primitive Dwellings'; 'Wild Eagles on the Crag'; 'The Falcon's Nest'; 'A Silent City of the Dead'; 'The City of Shade'; 'Sons of the Sun'; or '"Luce fatale dalle pietre assorta [...]"'. This last title (which Davidson does not attempt to translate but substitutes with 'Monuments and Museums'), is taken directly from d'Annunzio's 'La canzone d'oltremare' (line 102), a 1912 ode to Italy's colonial conquests. Piccioli's chapter also starts with a quotation from the same poem (lines 106–113). D'Annunzio's conception of timeless heroic action is thus invoked by Piccioli as one of the models for his own work (on d'Annunzio's influence on Italian representations of Africa see Tomasello 1984). Similar ideals are easily traced in many works on the subject of Africa produced in Italy during this

period. See for instance Giuseppe Bottai's *Quaderno Africano* (1939).
15. The English translation, by Kathleen Naylor, was published with the more exotic title of *A Cure for Serpents: A Doctor in Africa*. In the following pages, all quotations are from the 1956 English edition.
16. On Amedeo di Savoia, Duca d'Aosta, and his popular image see Tosti (1952); Curcio (1953); Scaglione (1953); Speroni (1998). Amedeo was the son of Elena d'Orléans, herself a traveller and a writer; see Hélène de France (1921).
17. See the blurb on the inner cover of the 1994 edition.
18. He wrote travel books as well as novels, contributed to a number of magazines and journals in Italy and elsewhere, had a surprise best-seller in 1950 with *Il gastronomo educato* [The Educated Gastronome] and was much appreciated by the writers Mario Luzi and Romano Bilenchi, as well as by Vanni Scheiwiller (1966).
19. Significantly, this is the episode which gives the book its English title.
20. The series, created in 1932 continued to grow well after 1946 and was still active in 1960; the volume on travellers was reprinted as late as 1958; all quotations are from the 1944 edition.
21. Details of the life of Luigi Amedeo di Savoia Aosta can be found in Dainelli (1967); Audisio and Garimboldi (1984); Speroni (1991).
22. A search for works by Luigi Amedeo di Savoia does produce some results; but a closer look soon shows that the duke's contribution did not go much further than an introduction. See for instance Savoia (1908–1910).
23. After moving to Somalia in 1920, the duke did undertake a final trip to find the sources of the Uebi Scebeli river in 1928, but both the mode and the motivation of this expedition differed substantially from previous enterprises (Dainelli 1967:291–322; Speroni 1991:193–94).
24. Pratt, incidentally, was reading an English edition of Moravia's *A quale tribù appartieni?* (1972) *Which Tribe Do You Belong to?* (1974) translated by that same Angus Davidson who had produced the English version of Piccioli's *La porta magica del Sahara*.

BIBLIOGRAPHY

Audisio, A., and Garimboldi G. eds. *Dal Polo al K2: Sulle orme del Duca degli Abruzzi 1899–1954*. Turin, 1984.
Behdad, A., *Belated Travelers: Orientalism in the Age of Colonial Dissolution*. Cork, 1994.
Bottai, G., *Quaderno Africano* (1939). Florence, 1995.
Branca, G., *Storia dei viaggiatori italiani*. Rome, 1873.
Brigante Colonna, G., *I grandi viaggiatori: Avventure di terra e di mare*. Turin, 1944. [Originally published 1935].
Burdett, C., 'Journeys to Italian East Africa 1936–1941: Narratives of Settlement', *Journal of Modern Italian Studies* vol. 5 no. 2 (2000): 207–226.
Cachey, T. J., 'An Italian Literary History of Travel', in *Annali d'italianistica* 14 (1996): 53–63.
Campbell, M. B., *The Witness and the Other World: Exotic European Travel Writing, 400–1600*. Ithaca and London, 1988.

Cocker, M., *Loneliness and Time: British Travel Writing in the Twentieth Century*. London, 1992.
Curcio, C., *Amedeo d'Aosta l'africanista*. Rome, 1953.
d'Annunzio, G., 'La canzone d'oltremare', in *Merope*, Milan, 1912.
Dainelli, G., *La conquista scientifica dell'Impero*. Rome, 1936.
———, *Marco Polo*. Turin, 1941.
———, *Gli esploratori italiani in Africa*. 2 vols, Turin, 1960.
———, *Il Duca degli Abruzzi*. Turin, 1967.
De Blasi, J., ed. *Italiani nel mondo*. Florence, 1942.
de Filippi, F., *Ruwenzori: An Account of the Expedition of H.R.H. Prince Luigi Amdeo of Savoy, Duke of the Abruzzi; with a preface by the Duke of the Abruzzi*. trans. C. de Filippi, London, 1909.
Del Boca, A., *Gli italiani in Africa Orientale*. 4 vols, Rome-Bari, 1976–84.
———, *Gli italiani in Libia*. 2 vols, Rome-Bari, 1986–88.
———, ed. *Le guerre coloniali del fascismo*. Rome-Bari, 1991.
———, *L'Africa nella coscienza degli italiani: Miti, memorie, errori, sconfitte*. Rome-Bari, 1992.
dell'Oro, E., *Asmara addio*. Pordenone, 1988.
———, *La gola del diavolo*. Milan, 1999.
Denti di Pirajno, A., *Il gastronomo educato*. Venice, 1950.
———, *Un medico in Africa*. Venice, 1952; Vicenza, 1994; Milan 1997;
———, *A Cure for Serpents: A Doctor in Africa*. trans. K. Naylor, London, 1955; 1956; 1977; 1985.
France, H. de., *Vie errante, sensations d'Afrique*. Ivrea, 1921.
Fussell, P., *Abroad: British Literary Traveling Between the Wars*. New York, 1980.
Gentile, E., *La grande Italia: Ascesa e declino del mito della nazione nel ventesimo secolo*. Milan, 1997.
Kowalewski, M., 'Introduction', in *Temperamental Journeys: Essays on the Modern Literature of Travel*. ed. Kowalewski, M., Athens and London, 1992: 1–16.
Larebo, H. M., *The Building of an Empire: Italian Land Policy and Practice in Ethiopia 1935–1941*. Oxford, 1994.
Lévi-Strauss, C., *Tristes Tropiques*. Paris, 1955.
———, *Tristes Tropiques*. trans. J. and D. Weightman, Harmondsworth, 1976.
Moravia, A., *A quale tribù appartieni?* Milan, 1972.
———, *What Tribe Do You Belong To?* trans. A. Davidson, London, 1974.
Palma, S., *L'Italia coloniale*. Rome, 1999.
Pasquali, A., 'Récit de voyage et autobiographie', in *Annali d'italianistica* 14 (1996) : 71–88.
Piccioli, *La Porta magica del Sahara* Tripoli, 1931; n.p. 1934..
———, *The Magic Gate of the Sahara*. trans. A. Davidson, London, 1935.
Polezzi, L., 'Different Journeys along the River: Claudio Magris's *Danubio* and its Translation', *MLR* vol. 93 no. 3 (1998): 678–94.
Porter, D., *Haunted Journeys: Desire and Transgression in European Travel Writing*. Princeton, 1991.
Pratt, M. L., 'Fieldwork in common places', in *Writing Culture: The Poetics and Politics of Ethnography*. Clifford J. and Marcus, G.E., eds. Berkeley, 1984: 27–50.
———, *Imperial Eyes: Travel Writing and Transculturation*. London, 1992.
Raban, J., 'The Journey and the Book' in *For Love and Money: Writing, Reading, Travelling 1969–1987*. London, 1987: 253–60.
Russo, L., *La critica letteraria contemporanea*. Florence, 1967.
Salgari, E., *La Stella Polare e il suo viaggio avventuroso*. Genoa, 1901.
Savoia, L. A., *Il Ruwenzori*, 3 vols, Milan, 1908–10.

Scaglione, F. A., *Amedeo d'Aosta il colonizzatore*. Rome, 1953.
Scheiwiller, V., *Antologia impopolare*. Milan, 1966.
Sestini, A., 'L'opera geografica di Giotto Dainelli', *Rivista geografica italiana* vol. 76 no. 2 (1969): 201–06.
Speroni, G., *Il Duca degli Abruzzi*. Milan, 1991.
———, *Amedeo d'Aosta: L'eroe dell'Amba Alagi*. Milan, 1998.
Surdich F., 'Introduzione', in C. Cavalli, *Più neri di prima: Colonizzazione e schiavitù in Congo nel diario di viaggio di un italiano afli inizi del Novecento*. ed. F. Surdich, Reggio Emilia, 1995: 13–42.
Thubron, C., 'Travel Writing Today: Its Rise and Its Dilemma', in *Essays by Divers Hands*. ed. A. N. Wilson, *Transactions of the Royal Society of Literature*, n.s. 44 (1986): 167–81.
Tomasello, G., *La letteratura coloniale italiana dalle avanguardie al fascismo*. Palermo, 1984.
Tosti, A., *Vita eroica di Amedeo d'Aosta*. Milan, 1952.
Touring Club Italiano, *Cirenaica*. Milan 1923a.
———, *Tripolitania*. Milan, 1923b.
———, *Guida d'Italia: Possedimenti e colonie*. Milan, 1929.
Traversi, L., *L'Italia e l'Etiopia. Da Assab a Ual Ual*. Bologna, 1935.
Truffi, R., *Precursori dell'impero africano*. Rome, 1936.
Youngs, T., *Travellers in Africa: British Travelogues, 1850–1900*. Manchester, 1994.

Index

A
ABC, 67, 75, 81, 83
Accame Bobbio, Aurelia, 53–54
Acevedo, Isidoro, 68, 72, 74
Acropolis, 7, 114
Acton, Harold, 164, 166
Adolphe (Constant), 150
Afghanistan, 159, 164, 167, 168
Africa, 12–14, 16, 18–20, 23, 187–202
Aladrén, Emilio, 131
Alberti, Rafael, 73
Alcalá Galiano, Alvaro 75
Alexandria, 149
Alhambra, 136, 140n. 8
Ali [*Carnets d'Égypte*], 148–49
Alissa [*La Porte étroite*], 151
Allégret, Élie, 151
Allégret, Marc, 151–52
Alvarez del Vayo, Julio, 68
Amado Blanco, Luis, 75, 81
American Colonization Society, 12
anarchism, 85–6, 88–90
Andalusia, 132
anti-colonialism, 177, 182–84
Antilles, 132
anti-Semitism, 169–170
Aragon, 88, 89
Aragon, Louis, 143
Araquistáin, Luis, 67
Archaeology, 109, 110
Arendt, Hannah 87, 91
Auclair, Marcelle, 134–35
Australia, 88
Austria, 88

autobiography, 51–61, 131–39, 143–53, 193–96

B
Ballario, Pina, 109, 111–12
Barba Jacob, Porfirio, 138
Barcelona, 86, 88, 91, 92–94, 96, 97–99, 100
Bari, 124, 125
Barthes, Roland, 110, 131, 136–37
Baudelaire, Charles, 94, 136
Bauhaus, 88, 93
Behdad, Ali, 132
Benítez Rojo, Antonio, 133
Benjamin, Walter, 87–8, 89, 90–93, 94–95, 100, 101
Benn, Gottfried, 126
Benzoni, Maria, 108, 110, 111, 114, 115–16, 118n. 8
Berlin, 88
Bianchi Ross, Ciro, 134
Bianchi, Icilio, 116–17
Blas i Vallespinosa, F., 76
Bolshevik party, 67, 72, 75
  Revolution, 65–68, 71, 75
  Spanish reactions to, 66–68
Bona, Emma, 108, 109, 112, 113, 114
Bongie, Chris, 31, 62n. 3
Bosetti, Gilbert, 54
Bosworth, Richard, 118n. 1
Boudet, Rosa Ileana, 140n. 8
Boveri, Margret, 122, 126
Brecht, Bertolt, 137
British Empire, 161, 165
  and Middle East 159–60, 167, 170
Burdett, Charles, 50, 62n. 2

Byron, Robert, 159–72
  The Birth of Western Painting (with D. Talbot Rice), 165
  The Byzantine Achievement, 165
  Europe in the Looking Glass: Reflections of a Motor Drive from Grimsby to Athens, 164
  First Russia, Then Tibet, 165–66
  The Road to Oxiana, 159–72
  The Station: Athos, Treasures and Men, 164
Byron, Lord, 164

C

Cabrera Infante, Lydia, 133
Cairo, 147
Calleja, Rafael, 81
Cambodia, 173
Capa, Robert, 89
capitalism, 68, 72
Cardoza y Aragón, Luis, 138
Carmen (Mérimée), 150
Cartier-Bresson, Henri, 89
Casanova, Sofía, 81
Castel del Monte, 125
Castro, Fidel, 137
Catholicism, 133
  prejudice against, 164, 165
Cecchi, Emilio, 108, 110, 111, 112
Céline, Louis-Ferdinand, 37–38
Césaire, Aimé, 32
Challaye, Félicien, 176
Chatwin, Bruce, 159, 164, 167
Churchill, Winston, 164, 165
Ciarlantini, Franco, 118n. 7
Cienfuegos, 138
Cipolla, Arnaldo, 107, 113, 115, 116
Clark, Steve, 163
Claudel, Paul, 174, 185n. 3
Claudel, Pierre, 143

Clifford, Charles, 136
Clifford, James, 31
CNT (Confederación Nacional de Trabajadores, Spanish anarchist trade union), 67, 100
colon bâtisseur (constructive settler), 173
colonial exhibitions, 30, 33–34, 39–41, 161
  literature, 32–33, 132, 135, 140n. 7, 162–63, 165, 190–93
  mismanagement, 165, 167, 177–82
  repression, 175–6
  French colonialism and class, 179–83
  and education, 174–5, 176
  and gender, 180–83
  as familial relationship, 179–80
colonized/ colonizer relationship, 178–81
Comisso, Giovanni, 49–63
  Avventure terrene, 56
  Cina-Giappone, 54, 55, 58
  Gioco d'infanzia, 58, 60
  L'Italiano errante per l'Italia, 55, 57–59
communism, 67, 72, 75, 90, 99
Communist International (Third International), 68, 72, 73
Communist Party of Spain (PCE), 66, 67, 72, 74, 78, 80
Conrad, Joseph, 20, 26
Corriere della sera, 54, 55, 107
counterpoint, 38, 42, 131, 136, 138
Craik, Jennifer, 118n. 2
Croisière Jaune, 35
Cuba, 131–141
Culler, Jonathon, 109, 111
Curtius, Ernst Robert, 123–24
Cyprus, 167, 170

D

d'Annunzio, Gabriele, 54, 58, 110, 201n. 14

Dainelli, Giotto, 198–200
Dalí, Salvador, 131
Daniel B. [*Si le grain ne meurt ...*], 148–9
Davies, Catherine, 133
De Certeau, Michel, 12, 21–25
  on maps and tours, 12, 22–25
  on space and place, 12, 21–25
Deleuze, Gilles, 88
dell'Oro, Erminia, 200
democracy, 2, 66–67, 71–72, 78, 80
Denti di Pirajno, Alberto, 193–96, 200
Derrida, Jacques, 11, 27
Díaz, Carlos, 140n. 10
Díaz-Reitg, Enrique, 71, 72
Diel, Louise, 4
Dobos, Erszebet, 140n. 4
Douglas, Lord Alfred, 146
Duncan, James, 25, 61
Durruti, Buenaventura, 85–6, 91, 100
E
Eisenberg, Daniel, 140n. 4
El Comunista, 67
El Debate, 67
El Socialista, 67, 71, 82
Eliot, T.S., The Waste Land, 160–1
Esposito, Rossana, 53
ethnography, 41
Eulogio Díes, Antonio, 73
exoticism, 29–42, 189
exoticization of Europe, 39–41
Exposition coloniale de Vincennes, 174, 175, 178
Exposition coloniale, see Colonial exhibitions
Egypt, 107–119
F
FAI (Federación Anarquista Ibérica), 100
Falasca Zamponi, Simonetta, 114
Fanon, Frantz, 32, 136

Farinacci, Roberto, 122
fascism (Italian), 2, 3, 88, 99, 112–17, 189–204; *see also* Nazism
  and antiquity, 113, 114
  and censorship, 56, 61
  and imperial propaganda, 191–92, 198, 200
February Revolution (Russia), 67, 72
Foro Mussolini, 113–14
Forster, E. M., *A Passage to India*, 161, 165
Foucault, Michel: on heterotopias, 24, 62n. 2
France, 3, 31–35, 39–42, 101, 173, 174, 175, 180, 183
Freud, Sigmund, 7, 16, 19, 20, 87, 134, 136–37
Fussell, Paul, 15, 26, 107, 160–61, 164, 187–88, 200
Futurism, 6, 121, 124
G
GATEPAC (Barcelona architectural group), 88, 92
Gentile, Emilio, 115
Ghéon, Henri [Vangeon], 148
Gibson, Ian, 131, 137–38, 140n. 1
Gide, André, 39, 143–55
  'Aquasanta', 144
  Carnets d'Égypte, 143, 144–45, 147–49, 152–53
  Corydon, 143, 148
  Et nunc manet in te, 144, 149–51, 154nn. 4, 7
  Journal, 148, 151, 154nn. 3, 6
  love/desire split, 145, 146, 147, 148, 151
  La Porte étroite, 146, 147
  Les Cahiers d'André Walter, 150
  Les Faux-monnayeurs, 154n. 5
  relationship with his wife, 146, 149–53, 154nn. 4, 5

Si le grain ne meurt ..., 145, 146, 148, 152
Gide, Catherine [Van Rysselberghe, AG's daughter], 153, 154n. 8
Gide, Juliette [Rondeaux, AG's mother], 146
Gide, Madeleine [Rondeaux, AG's wife & cousin], 144, 145, 146, 149–53
Gilmore, Leigh, 57
Girardet, Raoul, 30, 34
globalization, 31, 37
Goethe, Johann Wolfgang, 123
Goldman, Emma, 88
Gorkín, Julián, 81
Granada, 133, 140n. 8
Gratico, Sergio, 116
Greece, 107–119, 164–5
Greene, Barbara, 12, 26
Greene, Graham, 11–26
  Journey Without Maps, 11–26
  on maps, 17–18
  on psychoanalysis, 19–20
Gregory, Derek, 25, 61, 108
Grenet, Eliseo, 135
Griffin, Roger, 118n. 6
Guattari, Félix, 88
Guevara, Ernesto 'Che', 140n. 8
Guillén, Nicolás, 135–36
Gutiérrez Alea, Tomás, 140n. 10

H

Haggard, Rider, 26
Harlem Renaissance, 135
Harley, J. B., 11, 13, 16
Havana, 132, 135–38, 140n. 10, 11
Hemingway, Ernest, 140n. 8
Herbart, Pierre, 144
Herf, Jeffrey, 128
Hernández, Miguel, 73, 80
Heuss, Theodor, 122
Hidalgo, Diego, 75

Hitler, Adolf, 127–28, 128–29
Hocke, Gustav Rene, 121–130
homosexuality, 54–61, 133, 138–39, 140n. 10, 166
Horna, Kati, 85–103
Hoyos Gascón, Luis, 75
Hughes, Langston, 135
Hungary, 88
Huysman, Camilo, 67
Huysmans, Joris-Karl, 34–35

I

imperial conflict, 173, 174
India, 159, 165
Indochina, 173–184
Indochinese nationalism, 174, 175, 176
informe-relatos, 68, 71, 73
Institución Hispano-Cubana de Cultura, 138
Iran, 159, 164, 167
Irún, 101
Islamic Art, 167
Italian colonialism, 3, 107, 189–204
Italy, 52, 54–61, 113–14, 159, 168, 190–191, 198

J

Jadin, Jean-Marie, 147, 154n. 2
Jameson, Fredric, 12, 16, 162–3
Jewish migration, 167, 169
Joyce, James, *Ulysses*, 160–61
Jünger, Ernst, 122–23

K

Keller, Guido, 54, 56, 58
Kostof, Spiro, 118n. 3
Kowalewski, Michael, 110
Kutzinski, Vera, 135, 140n. 3

L

La Antorcha, 67
La Plus Grande France, 173, 180
Lacan, Jacques, 147, 154n. 2
Lambert, Jean, 143, 144

Laos, 173
Last, Jef, 144
Lawrence, D. H., 16–17, 165
Lawrence, T. E., 159
Le vie del mondo, 107, 108, 115
League of Nations, 12
Lebel, Roland, 32
Leccabue, Fabrizia, 140n. 9
Lefebvre, Henri, 24, 26
Leiris, Michel, 41–42
Levesque, Robert, 145, 148, 149
Lévi-Strauss, Claude, 17, 32, 187, 200, 201n. 2
Liberia, 12–26
Libya, 191
Llopis, Rodolfo, 69, 71, 78
López, César, 137
García Lorca, Federico, 131–141
    El público, 133, 134, 138–39
    La casa de Bernarda Alba, 133
    Oda a Walt Whitman, 133
    Poeta en Nueva York, 132
    'Son de los negros en Cuba', 134–140
    Yerma, 133
Loynaz family, 134, 138
Loynaz, Carlos Manuel, 140n. 10
Loynaz, Dulce María, 140n. 10
Lucey, Michael, 154n. 2
Lucile Bucolin [*La Porte étroite*], 147
Luxor, 145, 148–49
Lynch, Kevin, 16

M

Mackinder, Halford, 26
Madrid, 91, 100
Magnum (photographic agency), 89
Málaga, 132
Manon Lescaut (Prévost), 150
maps and cartography, 11–26
Marinello, Juan, 134, 141

Martin du Gard, Roger, 144, 149, 150, 154nn. 5, 7
Martínez Nadal, Rafael, 133, 140n. 5
Massey, Doreen, 24
Matamoros, Miguel, 135
Maurer, Christopher, 140n. 5
Mauriac, Claude, 144, 145, 153, 154n. 8
mechanization of travel, 35
Messianism, 90–1
Mexico, 89
Michaelis, Margaret, 85–103
Michaux, Henri 38–39
Millot, Catherine, 147, 154n. 2
Mills, Sara, 52, 53
Miró, Joan, 88
Mission Dakar-Djibouti, 41
Modernism, 5, 6, 121–130
    and empire, 160, 161–3
modernization, 127
Mohammed [*Si le grain ne meurt ...*], 148–9
Montero, Eloy, 75, 82
Monzó, Josep Vicent, 89
Morales, F, 140n. 11
Morand, Paul, 35, 36, 126
Moravia, Alberto, 49, 190, 200, 202n. 24
Motril, 132
Mundo Obrero, 73, 74
Mussolini, Benito, 113, 115, 116, 118 n. 3

N

Nazism, 88, 91, 121, 125, 127; see also fascism
negrismo, 135, 140n. 7
New York, 132, 136
Norindr, Panivong, 33
nostalgia, 75, 189, 194, 196, 199, 200

O

O'Brien, Kate, 85, 101–2
October Revolution (Russia), 67, 71, 72
Ojetti, Ugo, 122

Ortiz, Fernando, 131–33, 136, 140n. 6
Orwell, George, 91
P
Palestine, 159, 167, 170
Paquets, Alfonso, 81
Pauline Molinier [*Les Faux-monnayeurs*], 154n. 5
Pérez, Vicente (Combina), 73
Pestaña, Angel, 68, 72, 73
photography, 6, 85–103, 107, 110, 136–38
Piccioli, Angelo, 190–93, 200
Popular Front, 3, 36
Porter, Dennis, 16, 20, 26
posters, 90
postcolonialism, 29–30
Prague, 88
Pratt, Mary Louise, 51, 136, 141, 188, 200, 202n. 24
Praz, Mario, 108
proletarian travellers to the Soviet Union, 72–75
psychoanalysis, 19–20, 27
Q
Quevedo, Antonio, 134
R
Rabinbach, Anson, 128
Rato, Ramón de., 75, 76
Rimbaud, Arthur, 20
Ríos, Fernando de los., 66, 68, 70, 71, 72, 75
Rochat, Giorgio, 116
Rojek, Chris, 108, 111
Roman Empire, 115–117
Rondeaux, Émile [AG's uncle], 146
Rondeaux, Mathilde [Pouchet, AG's aunt], 146, 147
Ros, Félix, 75, 76
Rosenberg, Alfred, 127, 128
Rouart, Eugène, 148
Roubaud, Louis, 175–84

Ruskin, John, 168
Russia, 65–83
S
Said, Edward W., *Orientalism*, 38, 110, 136, 140n. 7, 163
Saint-Pol-Roux, 36
Saldaña, Quintiliano, 81
Santander, 101
Santiago de Compostela, 101
Santiago de Cuba, 134, 135, 137, 140n. 4
Santos Moray, Mercedes, 137
Sarabia, Nydia, 134, 140n. 4
Sarfatti, Margherita, 107, 108
Sarraut, Albert, 173, 181, 185n. 8
Sartre, Jean-Paul, 35, 38
Savoia, Amedeo di, Duca d'Aosta, 194
Savoia, Luigi Amedeo di, Duca degli Abruzzi, 196–200, 202nn. 22, 23
Schlumberger, Jean, 150, 152, 154nn. 5, 7
Schlumberger, Maurice, 148
Schonberg, Jean-Louis, 134–36
Schwartz, Rosalie, 138
Schwartz, Vanessa, 35
Segado, Pedro, 75, 76
Segal, Naomi, 154n. 2
Segalen, Victor, 31
Segesta, 122, 123
Sender, Ramón J., 66, 73
Sert, Josep, 88
Settler community, 179–82
Seville, 133
Sharpe, Sir Alfred, 12, 18
Sierra Leone, 16
Simenon, Georges, 37
Simon, Lady Kathleen, 13
slavery, 12–13
Smith, Paul Julian, 135
Socé, Ousmane, 34, 39–41
Socialist Party of Spain (PSOE), 67, 68, 70

Solidaridad Obrera, 67
Somalia, 197
Soviet Union, 2, 65–83, 165, 167
Spain, 65–83, 85–103
Spanish Civil War, 65, 68, 79, 80, 85–103
Spanish Republic, 68, 70, 75, 80, 85–103
speed, 6, 5–36
Spurr, David, 51
Stone, Marla, 118n. 5
Sykes, Christopher, 164, 166–7
Sylvie (Nerval), 150
T
Taino, 133
Tapia Bolívar, Daniel, 75
Teatro de la Habana, 137
Terrasa, J., 75, 76
Tomasello, Giovanna, 192
Torriente, Loló de la, 134
Touring Club Italiano, 107, 191
tourism, 6, 36–37, 68, 75–76, 107–117, 140n. 8
transculturation, 131, 136
Trotskyism, 91
Tumiati, Domenico, 108, 110, 111, 114, 115
U
Unión General de Trabajadores (UGT), 93
United States, 164, 165, 167–8
Urry, John, 111
Utopia, 65, 67, 71, 72, 74, 75, 79

V
Vallejo, César, 73, 81
Valls i Taberner, Ferrán., 75
Van Rysselberghe, Élisabeth, 153
Van Rysselberghe, Maria, 144, 145, 150, 152, 154n. 6
Venice, 168
Venuti, Lawrence, 132
Vietnam, 173
Villanúa, León, 78, 82
Viollis, Andrée, 175–84
Virgil, 150
Virilio, Paul, 36
Vivanti, Annie, 109
Vizconde de Eza, 75, 82
voyeurism, 189, 193–95, 200
W
Wasserman, Renata, 30
Waugh, Evelyn, 3, 165, 166, 167
Whitman, Walt, 148–49
Wilde, Oscar, 143, 146
Williams, Raymond, 31
Winkler, Eugen Gottlob, 122
World Exhibition, Paris 1937, 121, 126
Y
Yen Bay Uprising, 175–77, 185n. 6
Yoruba, 133
Young, Howard, 132
Youngs, Tim, 200
Z
Zugazagoitia, Julián, 71